PEDAGOGICAL PARTNERSHIPS

**Center for Engaged Learning
Open Access Book Series**

Series editors, Jessie L. Moore and Peter Felten

The Center for Engaged Learning (CEL) Open Access Book Series features concise, peer-reviewed books (both authored books and edited collections) for a multi-disciplinary, international, higher education audience interested in research-informed engaged learning practices.

The CEL Open Access Book Series offers an alternate publishing option for high-quality engaged learning books that align with the Center's mission, goals, and initiatives, and that experiment with genre or medium in ways that take advantage of an online and open access format.

CEL is committed to making these publications freely available to a global audience.

Forthcoming books in the series

The Power of Partnership: Students, Staff, and Faculty Revolutionizing Higher Education
Edited by Lucy Mercer-Mapstone and Sophia Abbot
January 2020

Writing about Learning and Teaching in Higher Education
Mick Healey, Kelly E. Matthews, and Alison Cook-Sather
Summer 2020

Pedagogical Partnerships

A HOW-TO GUIDE
for Faculty, Students, and Academic Developers
in Higher Education

Alison Cook-Sather, Melanie Bahti, and Anita Ntem

Elon University Center for Engaged Learning
Elon, North Carolina
www.CenterforEngagedLearning.org

©2019 by Alison Cook-Sather, Melanie Bahti, and Anita Ntem. This work is made available under a Creative Commons Attribution-NonCommercial-NoDerivatives 4.0 International license.

Excerpts from *Engaging Students as Partners* by Alison Cook-Sather, Cathy Bovill, and Peter Felten (2014) used with permission from John Wiley & Sons, Inc. Quoted material may not be reproduced without permission of the publisher.

Series editors: Jessie L. Moore and Peter Felten
Copyeditor and designer: Jennie Goforth

Cataloging-in-Publication Data
Names: Cook-Sather, Alison | Bahti, Melanie | Ntem, Anita
Title: Pedagogical partnerships: a how-to guide for faculty, students, and academic developers in higher education / Alison Cook-Sather, Melanie Bahti, and Anita Ntem
Description: Elon, North Carolina : Elon University Center for Engaged Learning, [2019] | Series: Center for engaged learning open access book series | Includes bibliographical references and index.
Identifiers: LCCN 2019954150 | ISBN 978-1-951414-00-9 (PDF) | ISBN 978-1-951414-01-6 (pbk.) | DOI https://doi.org/10.36284/celelon.oa1
Subjects: LCSH: Professional learning communities | Teacher-student relationships | College teaching

ACKNOWLEDGMENTS

We are grateful to our wonderful student, faculty, staff, and program director colleagues who so generously offered input and feedback at various stages of this book's production. These include Sophia Abbot, Dorothe Bach, Roseanna Bourke, Floyd Cheung, Raquel Corona, Natasha Daviduke, Alise de Bie, Jerusha Detweiler-Bedell, Irina Elgort, Eimear Enright, Miciah Foster, Anne Ellen Geller, Meredith Goldsmith, Tina Iemma, Chawne Kimber, Lauren LaMagna, Isabella Lenihan-Ikin, Beth Marquis, Sasha Mathrani, Kelly E. Matthews, Cathy Oleson, Brad Olsen, Leslie Ortquist-Ahrens, Virginia Pitts, Srikripa Krishna Prasad, Bill Reynolds, Mia Rybeck, Khadijah Seay, Diane Skorina, Kathryn Sutherland, Susanna Throop, Steve Volk, and Cherie Woolmer. We are also grateful to the editors of the Center for Engaged Learning Open Access Book Series, Jessie Moore and Peter Felten, for their enthusiasm, support, and guidance as we shaped this resource into a format appropriate for an online forum, and to Jennie Goforth for her excellent copyediting.

CONTENTS

Foreword · xi

Introduction · 1

1. Why might you develop a pedagogical partnership program and what might get in the way? · 15

2. How do you know what kind of partnership program is right for your context, and why might faculty and students want to participate? · 37

3. How can you situate and structure the program, how do you get started, and how might you plan for sustainability? · 59

4. What are the shared responsibilities of facilitating pedagogical partnerships? · 93

5. What approaches might program directors take to plan for and support pedagogical partnerships? · 121

6. What approaches might student and faculty partners use in classroom-focused partnerships? · 157

7. What approaches might student and faculty partners take to curriculum-focused partnerships? · 181

8. How might you manage the challenges of partnership? · 217

9. How might you assess pedagogical partnership work? · 253

Conclusion · 273

Afterword · 279

References · 282

About the Authors · 307

Index · 309

LIST OF ONLINE RESOURCES

Find these resources at:
https://www.CenterForEngagedLearning.org/books/pedagogical-partnerships.

Advertising Student Partner Positions

Checklist for Developing a Pedagogical Partnership Program

Choosing Names for Partnership Programs and Participants

Creating Post-Bac Fellow Positions to Support the Development of Pedagogical Partnership Programs

Five Stories of Developing Pedagogical Partnership Programs

Gathering Feedback

General Guiding Principles for Weekly Reflective Meetings of Student Partners

Guidelines for Student and Faculty Partners in Classroom-focused Pedagogical Partnerships

History and Structure of the SaLT Program

How the SaLT Program Got Started

Inviting Faculty and Students to Participate in Pedagogical Partnership

Mapping Classroom Interactions

Options for Incoming Faculty to Work in Partnership through the SaLT Program

Outcomes of Pedagogical Partnership Work

Partial List of Themed Issues of *Teaching and Learning Together in Higher Education*

Plans to Orient New Faculty and Student Partners

Questions that Facilitate Productive Talking and Listening

Representing What Student and Faculty Partners Have Explored

SaLT Program Student Consultant Application Form

Sample Message to Student Partners from the SALT Program Director

Sample Outline of Topics for Weekly Meetings of Student Partners

Sample Outlines for Student Partner Orientations

Sample Student Partners Course Syllabus

Selected Reading Lists

Steps in Launching Pedagogical Partnership Programs

Student Partners' Particular Contributions to Pedagogical Partnership

Summer Institute for Faculty Participants in Pedagogical Partnership

Templates and Activities to Explore Hopes, Concerns, and Strategies for Developing Pedagogical Partnership Programs

Three Stages of Backward Design for Creating Post-Baccalaureate Pathways to Educational Development

Threshold Concepts in Pedagogical Partnership

Visiting Faculty Partners' Classrooms and Taking Observation Notes

Ways of Conceptualizing Feedback

Ways of Thinking about Listening

Working toward Programmatic Sustainability

FOREWORD

Jessie L. Moore and Peter Felten

We are delighted to share *Pedagogical Partnerships: A How-To Guide for Faculty, Students, and Academic Developers in Higher Education* as the inaugural publication in the Center for Engaged Learning Open Access Book Series. Alison Cook-Sather, Melanie Bahti, and Anita Ntem present research-informed practices for establishing and sustaining pedagogical partnerships focused on classrooms and curricula. This integration of theory, research, and practice will continue to be a hallmark of the series, which provides an alternate publishing option for high-quality engaged learning books that align with the Center's mission, goals, and initiatives, and that experiment with genre or medium in ways that take advantage of an online and open access format.

Internationally, higher education discussions about pedagogical partnership, also known as students-as-partners or student-faculty/student-staff partnership, have steadily increased over the past decade. Pedagogical partnership is examined in dedicated journals and in other scholarly teaching and scholarship of teaching and learning publications. With this book, though, Cook-Sather, Bahti, and Ntem offer the unique contribution of a how-to guide that addresses how to enact pedagogical partnership in systematic and equitable ways. At the same time, they acknowledge the challenges of this often countercultural work and share practically focused strategies for building pedagogical partnership programs.

Pedagogical Partnerships explicitly speaks to faculty, students, program directors, and academic developers, among others, and it draws examples from diverse institutions across the globe. With this rich array of examples and careful consideration for readers' own institutional contexts, the authors avoid being prescriptive in their strategies for partnership. As a result, readers will be able to adapt the authors' strategies for a range of institution types and budgets.

The how-to guide also models partnership; two of the three authors are recently graduated students. Throughout the book, the authors share glimpses into their own partnerships.

Notably, *Pedagogical Partnerships* is not merely a stand-alone, open access book. The authors also created nearly three dozen supplemental resources that are referenced in the book (and linked in the online version) and shared on the book's website. These resources extend the descriptive nature of this how-to guide, illustrating many of the strategies the authors describe or offering additional opportunities for readers to reflect on how these pedagogical partnerships could be enacted in their own contexts.

We are grateful to Alison, Melanie, and Anita for authoring such a dynamic book to initiate the Center for Engaged Learning Open Access Book Series, and we are confident that you will find many helpful takeaways in this accessible how-to guide. We encourage you to bookmark the *Pedagogical Partnerships* website for quick reference as you (re)design your own classroom and curricular partnerships and to share this book and its resources widely.

INTRODUCTION

> If we all engaged in partnerships through which we . . . discuss how teaching and learning experiences can include and value everyone, our campuses would become places of belonging. (Ana Colón García 2017, 5)

As if to realize the vision that former student partner Ana Colón García describes in the quote above, the last decade has seen a proliferation of student-faculty partnerships in teaching, learning, research, and reform. Institutions of higher education and individuals around the world have developed programs and projects through which students, faculty, and staff participate in various forms of co-creation: of teaching and learning approaches; of scholarly analysis, presentations, and publications; and of individual, programmatic, and institutional transformation. These programs and projects not only link student engagement and faculty development through partnership's capacity to foster belonging (Cook-Sather and Felten 2017b), they invite an understanding of student engagement *as* partnership (Matthews 2016) and a reimagining of the place of students in academic development (Felten et al. 2019). The three of us have learned through our own partnership experiences and have seen at a wide range of institutions—from small, liberal arts colleges like our own to large, public universities and from across the world in Aotearoa New Zealand, Australia, Canada, England, Israel, Italy, Malaysia, Scotland, Sweden, and the United States—that partnership work has great potential to make our campuses places of belonging in which a diversity of learners and teachers can thrive. Participating in pedagogical partnership can enhance disciplinary and process learning for students, inform faculty learning about teaching and about students, and shape conversations about and approaches to developing institutions of higher education, particularly—and pressingly—in relation to fostering more equitable and inclusive teaching and learning environments.

We focus in this book on sharing our experiences of and advice for developing pedagogical partnerships in the classroom and in the curriculum. While every institution will have its own hopes, constraints, and goals and, consequently, need to develop its own approach to designing and supporting its pedagogical partnership program, we suggest that there are some basic questions to consider across contexts for those planning to support pedagogical partnerships focused on classroom teaching and on curriculum design and redesign. This how-to guide offers our responses to those questions not as prescriptions but rather as recommendations informed by over ten years of experience and by research on a variety of programs in a range of contexts. We hope our recommendations can, in turn, inform the ongoing process of dialogue and revision necessary for starting and sustaining such pedagogical partnership work in all kinds of higher education institutions.

As we explain in detail in the section below called "How is this how-to guide organized?" we offer this main text with overarching questions and our basic responses, and we include a set of thirty-four resources that you can access separately if you want to dig into greater detail. We refer you to those resources by name (e.g., Steps in Launching Pedagogical Partnership Programs) at relevant points throughout this main text.

What does pedagogical partnership have to offer?

Research across institutional and national contexts (Cook-Sather, Bovill, and Felten 2014; Healey, Flint, and Harrington 2014) and systematic reviews of the growing body of literature on partnership work (e.g., Mercer-Mapstone et al. 2017) have argued that pedagogical partnership can achieve a wide range of benefits.

In chapter 1 we argue that, for us, the most persuasive reason to develop a pedagogical partnership program is the potential of participation in such programs to affirm and empower all those involved and to support their development into versions of the selves they want to be. In particular, pedagogical partnership can foster in students a sense of belonging, support faculty in generative reflection, and contribute to the evolution of an institution into a place where members of the community feel a meaningful connection. What is the range of what pedagogical partnership has to offer in relation to these overall benefits? Below we provide a list of benefits—to faculty partners, student partners, academic developers, and the institutions at which they work—that we have experienced ourselves or heard about from people in other institutions. These are not exhaustive lists, and we invite you to think about what else you might add, either as benefits you have experienced or know about or as possibilities you could imagine.

Participating in pedagogical partnership can support faculty in:
- Acclimating more quickly to campus culture and unfamiliar students
- Developing confidence and clarity about their pedagogical commitments
- Finding the courage to follow through on their pedagogical convictions and responsibilities
- Gaining a perspective that they cannot achieve on their own
- Receiving formative feedback on teaching
- Recognizing good pedagogical practices and making them intentional
- Sharing power—and responsibility—with students
- Turning pedagogical learnings into publishing opportunities
- Developing greater empathy, understanding, and appreciation for students
- Building resilience through navigating difficult and ambiguous institutional situations

Participating in pedagogical partnership can support students in:
- Gaining confidence in and capacity to articulate their perspectives
- Developing deeper understanding of learning and themselves as learners
- Developing deeper understanding of teaching

- Developing greater empathy for faculty and other students
- Sharing power—and responsibility—with faculty
- Experiencing more agency and taking more leadership
- Feeling stronger connections to departments and institutions
- Getting to "take" as well as observe a course they otherwise might never experience
- Turning pedagogical learnings into opportunities to host workshops, lead panels, publish, and more
- Developing creative and innovative ways to troubleshoot pedagogical challenges
- Building resilience through navigating difficult and ambiguous institutional situations

Facilitating pedagogical partnership can support program directors in:
- Expanding and deepening their own pedagogical explorations
- Shifting focus from their own to others' pedagogical explorations
- Connecting with students
- Addressing larger campus issues
- Clarifying what counts as meaningful work
- Building meaningful relationships with faculty and staff
- Developing creative and innovative ways to troubleshoot pedagogical challenges
- Addressing cultural and institutional assumptions about students and faculty

Supporting pedagogical partnership programs can help institutions in:
- Nurturing faculty who are more settled, satisfied, and engaged
- Nurturing students who are more confident, engaged, and connected to their departments and institution
- Fostering belonging and retention of students and faculty

- Supporting distribution/rhizomatic spread of understanding of teaching and learning
- Contributing to individual empowerment, which in turn leads to new projects/initiatives that enhance the whole institution
- Distinguishing themselves to prospective students and faculty and in the wider world of higher education

These benefits are not achieved automatically or easily. To support program directors, faculty, and students in achieving them, we offer in this how-to guide responses to questions about:
- the reasons for developing pedagogical partnership programs and what might get in the way;
- the main problematic assumptions people make about this work;
- how to situate and structure a pedagogical partnership program, including how the program might fit into the larger institution, what relationship the program might have to other programs, and how to develop a plan for getting started and for sustainability;
- what the shared and respective responsibilities of facilitating pedagogical partnerships might be;
- the particular responsibilities of participants;
- approaches that student and faculty partners might use;
- how to manage the challenges of partnership; and
- approaches to evaluating partnership work.

We bookend these how-to discussions with reference to what research has shown to be the benefits of pedagogical partnership in chapter 1 and glimpses into the range of positive and negative outcomes of pedagogical partnership, as articulated by faculty, student, and program directors, in the "Outcomes of Pedagogical Partnership Work" resource. Throughout the book we refer to other sources of insight and examples of experience for digging deeper into the questions raised and the literature published on this work.

Is this how-to guide for you?

This guide is written for all those who aim to develop pedagogical partnership programs focused on classroom teaching and on curriculum construction and revision or who plan to include those forms among a range of partnership program options. It addresses directly the three main constituencies who have typically been involved in such pedagogical partnerships—student partners, faculty partners, and program directors—but librarians, instructional technologists, directors of offices on campus such as access services, and deans can adapt the guidelines for their purposes, as colleagues at our own and other institutions have done. So, while their titles are not listed in the title of the book, please invite colleagues in a wide range of institutional roles to think with you about how they too could be part of developing pedagogical partnership projects and programs.

We acknowledge that each of the constituencies we address is in a different institutional position, but the roles and responsibilities of pedagogical partnership do not fall so neatly within the parameters of these positions. Indeed, that's one of the premises of pedagogical partnership: that traditional roles blur, and all participants share some of the same as well as some different responsibilities. So, while some guidelines are role specific, and chapters designate those responsibilities as such, all guidelines might be of interest and use to people across roles and positions. We offer a few words of advice to each of the main constituencies we aim to address:

> **Tips for undergraduate student readers:**
> As you read, consider how your experiences as a student and the intersections of the various dimensions of your identity give you a unique perspective on what it means to be a learner at your institution. How do you see your experiences as a student reflected in the perspectives shared in this text? What experiences and skills might you draw on if you participated in partnership work?
>
> Who among the students, faculty, staff, and institutional leaders that you know might be interested in this kind of work, and how can you invite them into conversation about it?

Tips for faculty and staff readers:
As you read, think about where in your practice you already engage in work that might be considered—but not, perhaps, named—"partnership" with students. How might you use this guide to build on those existing relationships?

Where on your campus is this work already being done, or where could it be undertaken? Might you invite colleagues in other departments or offices on campus to consider how to integrate such partnership work into their approaches?

Tips for program directors:
Many of the institutional and structural responsibilities for partnership work will fall within your realm, so as you read, consider how to use and perhaps revise the questions offered to most effectively frame, introduce, and pilot partnership work on your campus. Are there particular campus norms to which you should attend or respond?

Faculty, students, and staff on different campuses have varied reactions to lived experiences and research evidence. What might be the most effective use in your context of the stories of experience and the research evidence we present here?

Who are we as authors?

In keeping with the cross-role collaboration that defines pedagogical partnership work, this how-to guide is co-authored by three differently positioned participants in pedagogical partnership with extensive input from other program directors, student partners, and faculty partners.

Alison is a professor of education at Bryn Mawr College and director of Students as Learners and Teachers (SaLT), the signature program of the Teaching and Learning Institute (TLI) at Bryn Mawr and Haverford Colleges. She co-created SaLT with students and other colleagues in 2006 and has facilitated the program since then. In addition, she has designed and taught courses in collaboration with students and has served as a consultant at institutions across the United States and around the world as others develop pedagogical partnership programs. Finally, Alison has engaged in extensive research on pedagogical partnership (cited throughout this book), and she is founding editor and founding co-editor, respectively, of two journals focused on pedagogical partnership: *Teaching and Learning Together in Higher Education* and *International Journal for Students as Partners*.

Melanie is a former student partner in SaLT, and she graduated from Bryn Mawr College in 2016 with a degree in linguistics. As an undergraduate she worked in partnership with faculty members in two different departments. In addition to co-authoring an article on partnership with Alison and another former student partner (Cook-Sather, Des-Ogugua, and Bahti 2018), she has presented at conferences and consulted on partnership, and she serves as a reviewer for *International Journal for Students as Partners*. After she graduated from Bryn Mawr, she worked for two years as a staff member in the Library & Information Technology Services Department at Bryn Mawr College, where she put her partnership skills into practice daily. In this role she also spent two semesters as an observer and co-researcher of SaLT program forums. She recently completed a master's degree in higher education at the University of Pennsylvania and now works in the Center for Teaching & Learning at Thomas Jefferson University.

Anita graduated from Bryn Mawr College in 2018 with a degree in psychology. As an undergraduate student partner in SaLT she worked in partnership with faculty in four different departments, and she served as the convener of weekly student partner meetings when Alison was on sabbatical. In addition to her experience as a student partner, she has engaged in research, both as a fellow of the Teaching and Learning Institute in the summer of 2017 and during the academic year. Anita has presented her work on partnership at conferences (Ntem 2017), co-authored articles on pedagogical partnership (Cook-Sather, Ntem, and Felten in preparation; Ntem and Cook-Sather 2018), served as a facilitator of the International Summer Institute on Students as Partners at McMaster University in Canada, and is co-editor for *International Journal for Students as Partners*.

The three of us drafted pieces of the book separately and also met regularly to help one another dig into the details of what we have come to take for granted about partnership work in the SaLT program. Sitting together around a round table, naming principles and practices, complicating and deepening one another's thinking, and arranging and rearranging structures, sections, and chapters of this book to create the most useful organization for others, we enacted another form of partnership. Honoring and drawing on one another's perspectives, insights, and commitments, we worked together to decide how best to share those with others.

This guide is also informed by the perspectives of numerous other academic developers, faculty, staff, and student colleagues who have developed, facilitated, and participated in pedagogical partnerships at a range of colleges and universities around the world. These colleagues are quoted throughout the text both in acknowledgement of their experiences and expertise and to offer readers additional resources for developing and supporting pedagogical partnerships.

What approaches to pedagogical partnership does this guide focus on?

As the idea of pedagogical partnership spreads around the world, an increasing variety of approaches to enacting this idea has emerged (see Healey, Flint, and Harrington 2014, for one mapping of this variety). This guide focuses on the approach we have developed through the SaLT program, which invites undergraduate students to take up the paid position of pedagogical consultant to faculty who teach at Bryn Mawr or Haverford College. We offer in the "History and Structure of the SaLT Program" resource a narrative of how the program came into being, but here we offer just a quick overview of the two particular forms of pedagogical partnership the program supports:

Classroom-Focused Pedagogical Partnership
- Faculty and student pairs work together in long-term (typically semester-long or sometimes yearlong) partnerships to analyze,

affirm, and, where appropriate, revise pedagogical approaches as the faculty member teaches the focal course.
- Student partners do some or all of the following:
    » convene for weekly one-hour meetings with the program director and other student partners to brainstorm, exchange, and troubleshoot ideas to inform their partnership work;
    » conduct weekly visits to their faculty partners' classrooms and take detailed observation notes focused on pedagogical issues their faculty partners—and subsequently both partners—identify;
    » expand upon and deliver their observation notes to their partners each week;
    » meet weekly with their faculty partners to discuss the observation notes, what is working well and why in their faculty partners' teaching, and what might be revised in relation to classroom practice, assignments, and assessment;
    » conduct mid-semester or other forms of feedback;
    » research pedagogical approaches in the faculty partners' disciplines to inform current or future teaching; and
    » work with their faculty partners to apply all of what they have explored during their partnerships to future pedagogical practice.

Curriculum-Focused Pedagogical Partnership
- Faculty members work with individual students or teams of students to design or redesign a course.
- Faculty partners invite students—either those who may be interested in taking the course and have an important perspective or those who have recently completed the course—to work with them to conceptualize, reconceptualize, or otherwise develop or revise the course.
- Student and faculty partners
    » decide on the approach they will take, what dimensions of the course they want to focus on, and how they will divide up the work;

» identify needs to be addressed (e.g., how to engage students in answering questions at the interface of chemistry and biology that do not simply have a "right" and "wrong" answer; how to make courses in STEM fields, which are traditionally unwelcoming to underrepresented students, more welcoming to a diversity of students);
» identify actions to address the needs (e.g., create a set of qualitative open-ended "key concept" questions that can be included in the weekly problem set assignments; redesign assignments and activities to value and affirm a wider range of learning approaches);
» meet weekly or biweekly to discuss progress; and
» generate plans for new courses or revisions of components of existing courses.

The particular approach the SaLT program enacts has been developed and expanded at other institutions. We offer in the "Five Stories of Developing Pedagogical Partnership Programs" resource descriptions of five other partnership programs or initiatives: the Student Partners Program at McMaster University in Canada; Co-create UVA at the University of Virginia in the United States; a nationally funded Learning and Teaching Fellowship in Australia; a partnership program at Kaye Academic College of Education, Be'er Sheva, Israel; and a program focused on curriculum co-creation at Victoria University of Wellington in Aotearoa New Zealand.

How is this how-to guide organized?

We have organized this guide around the kinds of questions program director, faculty, and student colleagues pose regarding how to develop classroom-focused and curriculum-focused pedagogical partnerships and around the key insights we have gained through our years of engaging in and supporting pedagogical partnership work. These include:

- Why might you develop a pedagogical partnership program and what might get in the way? (Chapter 1)

- How do you know what kind of partnership program is right for your context, and why might faculty and students want to participate? (Chapter 2)
- How can you situate and structure the program, how do you get started, and how might you plan for sustainability? (Chapter 3)
- What are the shared responsibilities of facilitating pedagogical partnerships? (Chapter 4)
- What approaches might program directors take to plan for and support pedagogical partnerships? (Chapter 5)
- What approaches might student and faculty partners use in classroom-focused partnerships? (Chapter 6)
- What approaches might student and faculty partners take to curriculum-focused partnerships? (Chapter 7)
- How might you manage the challenges of partnership? (Chapter 8)
- How might you assess pedagogical partnership work? (Chapter 9)

We offer both a core text (in pdf format) with basic responses to these questions and a set of resources (posted online at https://www.CenterForEngagedLearning.org/books/pedagogical-partnerships) that offer much greater detail. The online resources are linked throughout the pdf chapters and are signaled by name (e.g., the "Templates and Activities to Explore Hopes, Concerns, and Strategies for Developing Pedagogical Partnership Programs" resource).

To highlight insights from experienced student and faculty partners and program directors who have launched pedagogical partnership programs, we weave these participants' perspectives into the main narrative across all the chapters and include extensive quotes. Some of these follow directly on and substantiate a point of discussion that precedes them, and some of them are drawn from different contexts to illustrate or corroborate a point being made. In both cases, these quotations are intended to offer glimpses into the lived experiences of partnership and the insights participants have gained, and thereby bring pedagogical partnership alive for you as readers.

Pronouns present a particular challenge in a guide written for this range of participants in pedagogical partnership by a collective of three people. Throughout we use "we" to refer to ourselves as authors and participants in SaLT. We use "you" to frame the questions that organize the chapters. Within the chapters, we write sometimes to a general audience (an implied and inclusive "you") and at other times to a particular constituency (e.g., "you as a student"). Our goal is to signal that there are some questions that might best be considered collectively, as a team (e.g., "How might you conceptualize facilitation of pedagogical partnership?") and others that will be the primary concern of one or another of the participants. Regardless of which pronoun might frame a question, we encourage you to be in dialogue with others involved in the development of your pedagogical partnership program as much as possible. As Cook-Sather, Bovill, and Felten (2014, 2) have argued, "Partnership is built on and through communication."

With this how-to guide, we offer an invitation to and a set of recommendations for individuals and institutions that aspire to realize the benefits of pedagogical partnership that we listed in the opening pages of this chapter. These include fostering the development of confidence, capacity, and empathy in faculty and students alike, thereby making them better able to work together to create productively challenging, equitable, and inclusive pedagogical and curricular approaches. The benefits include as well nurturing dialogue and deeper understanding across differences of position, identity, and perspective not only of faculty and students but also among others in institutions of higher education. These benefits, realized in the "as-if" spaces of pedagogical partnership (Cook-Sather and Felten 2017a), hold promise for the ways we can work together in higher education beyond pedagogical partnership programs—through the co-creation of pedagogical and curricular approaches that, as Ana Colón García (2017) notes in the quote that opens this introduction, develop capacity and foster a sense of belonging for all.

Over the years that we have worked to refine these guidelines for faculty, students, and academic developers, Alison has been invited to share versions of what we include in these pages at over sixty institutions in thirteen countries. All three of us have found that this growing interest intersects with increasing calls to create more equitable and inclusive practices in institutions of higher education, both to support the thriving of all members of the academic community and to redress the harms institutions of higher education can cause to underrepresented students in particular (de Bie et al. 2019; Marquis et al., under review). We welcome you to use these resources to create your own version of this work firmly grounded in principles of respect, reciprocity, and shared responsibility (Cook-Sather, Bovill, and Felten 2014)—to join the growing number of individuals and institutions seeking to realize the potential of pedagogical partnership.

1 WHY MIGHT YOU DEVELOP A PEDAGOGICAL PARTNERSHIP PROGRAM AND WHAT MIGHT GET IN THE WAY?

In this chapter we expand upon and develop the points we listed in the introduction regarding why you might develop a pedagogical partnership program. We offer research evidence on the benefits of pedagogical partnership programs to all faculty and student participants, faculty who are new to institutions, students who have traditionally been underrepresented in and underserved by institutions of higher education, and institutions that want to transform their cultures. We explore explicit and implicit purposes for developing a pedagogical partnership program, key assumptions and expectations that participants bring, and threshold concepts to partnership.

Why develop a pedagogical partnership program?

There are philosophical and practical reasons for developing a pedagogical partnership program, and there are also recognized challenges. Because pedagogical partnership remains countercultural in most institutions of higher education, we urge you to be conscious and intentional about why you value pedagogical partnership and equally conscious and intentional in how you go about developing a partnership program. As we mentioned in the introduction, the most persuasive reason to develop a pedagogical partnership program, from our perspective, is the potential it has to affirm and empower all those involved and support their development into versions of the selves they want to be. In this chapter, we expand on what pedagogical partnerships offer so that you can think through distinct and targeted areas of growth and opportunity you might want to address through the development of a program. In the box below, we offer student and faculty perspectives on the benefits of partnership that capture what we have heard from many participants:

> "I often tell people that I would have left Haverford were it not for the SaLT program. Although this is probably an exaggeration I am now unable to test, I do feel like I owe SaLT a debt of gratitude for making me feel like an integral part of the school and its processes. As a freshman at Haverford I felt out of the loop, uninvolved, small, superfluous. Starting my sophomore year with a pedagogical partnership through the SaLT program, I felt like I was not only working with this specific professor in the moment but also towards a far-away future Haverford in which all professors have had the same opportunity to think about their pedagogy within the space of the SaLT program. This made me feel like my work was important and would have a lasting impact, which contributed to my deepening connection to the school. It also taught me that my happiness is closely tied to how much I can imagine my work to have wider effect and guided me to participate in other activities that were fulfilling in similar ways."
>
> —Perez-Putnam 2016, 1
>
> "In academia, it is not often that we find someone who can hold a mirror up to us, making nonjudgmental observations about how we work and reflecting with us on our goals and performance. The Students as Learners and Teachers program through the Teaching and Learning Institute (TLI) at Haverford and Bryn Mawr Colleges provides exactly this kind of opportunity for professors."
>
> —Abbott and Been 2017, 1

The student quoted above touches on the potential of pedagogical partnership to foster in students a sense of belonging, to support faculty in generative reflection, and to contribute to the evolution of an institution into a place where members of the community feel a meaningful connection. Student partners also deepen their capacity to reflect, and faculty partners can also experience a deeper sense of belonging and connection as a result of participating in pedagogical partnership (Cook-Sather and Felten 2017b). As we discuss in greater detail in the "Outcomes of Pedagogical Partnership Work" resource, and as articulated by faculty and student partners in quotes throughout this book, participating in pedagogical partnerships reduces the isolation of teaching because faculty work in collaboration with someone else in the educational community, and it contributes to faculty recognizing the humanity of their students. Partnership affords both student and faculty partners the opportunity to be deeply seen, heard, and affirmed by another person on campus. The second quote above captures this potential for faculty—what another faculty partner described as mirrors, only better (Cook-Sather 2008).

These themes recur throughout this book, inspiring and informing the advice we offer. They are, to our minds, always important, but they are perhaps especially so at a time when participants in higher education represent an unprecedented diversity and, at the same time, differences of position, perspective, and identity are, in some contexts, causing rifts and tensions between students and faculty. We have seen how pedagogical partnership can bridge divides and alleviate tensions, and we want to share what we have learned about why and how to keep building such connections.

What is the research evidence on the benefits of pedagogical partnership programs?

Research offers numerous reasons for developing pedagogical partnership opportunities for faculty and student participants. These have to do with positive outcomes for:
- all student and faculty participants,
- faculty who are new to institutions,
- students who have traditionally been underrepresented in and underserved by institutions of higher education, and
- institutions that want to transform their cultures.

What are the benefits to all faculty and student participants?

An analysis by Cook-Sather, Bovill, and Felten (2014) of individual partnership efforts—when single faculty members have undertaken pedagogical partnership without systematic, institutional support—as well as institutionalized pedagogical partnership programs in the United Kingdom and the United States surfaced strikingly consistent benefits across contexts. By and large, faculty participants experience transformed thinking about and practices of teaching; changed understandings of learning and teaching through experiencing different viewpoints; and reconceptualization of learning and teaching as collaborative processes. The same analysis found that student participants typically experience enhanced confidence, motivation, and enthusiasm; enhanced engagement in the process, not just the outcomes, of learning; enhanced responsibility for, and ownership of, their own learning; and deepened understanding of, and contributions to, the academic community (Cook-Sather, Bovill, and Felten 2014, 103). These findings are echoed in other research studies and in reflective essays that individual faculty and students have authored. For instance:

- 93% of students who participated in partnerships with faculty at Birmingham City University in England reported that they had a greater sense of belonging at the institution (Curran and Millard 2016).
- Students who participated in faculty-student partnerships at Universiti Utara Malaysia, Sintok, Malaysia, experienced deeper learning of the course content, a more inclusive classroom dynamic, a sense of empowerment and competence, and more (Kaur, Awang-Hashim, and Kaur 2018).
- Through a course redesign project at Loughborough University in England, faculty and student partners experienced enhanced relationships, student partners developed deeper subject matter understanding, and faculty members developed deeper understanding of students' perspectives on learning the subject matter (Duah and Croft 2014).
- As part of his ongoing academic development, a senior lecturer in history at Massey University in Aotearoa New Zealand revised

both individual and departmental practices to be more responsive to student identities and learning needs (Griffiths 2018).

In published papers and conference presentations, student and faculty partners in different educational contexts and in different countries have articulated practically verbatim the same benefits of pedagogical partnership. We detail the most consistent of these in the "Outcomes of Pedagogical Partnership Work" resource. Here we focus on why you might want to create opportunities for participants to experience these benefits.

What are the particular benefits to faculty who are new to institutions?

While the benefits described above certainly extend to faculty who are new to institutions, there are particular challenges faculty face when they join institutions that pedagogical partnership has the potential to address in unique ways. There is plenty of long-standing research that documents the importance of supporting the orientation and development of new faculty (Boice 1992; Fink 1984; Lewis 1996; Sorcinelli 1994; Trowler and Knight 2000). But as faculty roles and responsibilities have shifted and as the factors affecting higher education have multiplied, supporting faculty new to institutions has become increasingly challenging (Austin and Sorcinelli 2013; McAlpine and Åkerlind 2010; Paris 2013; Turner 2015). A wide variety of approaches exists to support the complicated process of "'self-authoring' a professional identity as an educator" (Gunersel, Barnett, and Etienne 2013, 35) in which new faculty engage (Bok 2013; Brew, Boud, and Namgung 2011; McAlpine and Åkerlind 2012). Pedagogical partnership offers an additional approach with particular potential. As one faculty participant in the SaLT program put it: "The presence of my student consultant has turned out to be one of the most constructive factors in navigating my first semester at Bryn Mawr, one that will have lasting impact on my pedagogical commitments and academic identity as a teacher" (Oh 2014, 1).

The SaLT program affords incoming faculty at Bryn Mawr and Haverford Colleges three options for working in partnership with students. First, before they set foot on campus, they can enter into pedagogical partnership with student consultants through a summer syllabus development workshop, which includes dialogue with student partners regarding what students in that context hope to see included on syllabi. Second, in the week before classes begin, they meet and talk with students about what makes an engaging, inclusive, and effective learning experience at a one-hour session as part of new faculty orientation. Finally, during their first or second semester, they have the option to participate in semester-long, classroom-focused partnerships with student consultants. (See the "Options for Incoming Faculty to Work in Partnership through the SaLT Program" resource, and for a more detailed discussion, see Cook-Sather 2016a.)

As one student partner in the SaLT program explains, student partners can "contextualize and explain the dynamics that occur within the classroom and in the greater college community," and "they can be a window into the world of student life" (Pallant 2014, 1). Through working as dialogue partners and cultural guides, student partners can ease faculty members' transitions into new teaching and learning contexts. These opportunities can contribute to incoming faculty feeling more at ease, confident, and energized as they embark upon this new phase of their professional lives.

Confidence, energy, engagement—these are important for all new faculty but especially for underrepresented faculty as they strive to "establish 'home'" on a campus that may not historically have been a welcoming place (Mayo and Chhuon 2014, 227). In a reflection she offered as part of informal feedback on her experience, one new faculty partner in the SaLT program emphasized how she and her student partner, also with a background underrepresented in higher education, created a home for one another on campus: "I deeply appreciate the space that [my student partner] and I have created in which I can talk more about how I feel in the classroom rather than focusing on technical areas, that at least for me are less relevant in the search of becoming a better knowledge facilitator!"

While not every incoming faculty member embraces or appreciates these opportunities to work in partnership with students, the vast majority indicate that such partnership both eases their transition immeasurably and gives them an inspiring and empowering foundation upon which to build teaching and learning relationships with their own students. The partnership with a student makes the work of "'self-authoring' a professional identity as an educator" (Gunersel, Barnett, and Etienne 2013, 35) a shared endeavor, not the often isolating and enervating struggle that many faculty who have not participated in pedagogical partnership evoke to describe their early years as scholars. As a new faculty member wrote: "Working with my student consultant . . . was an important step in developing my own teaching style and translating my aspirations into a more tangible action plan. . . . I found that my partnership . . . proved instrumental in adjusting my course planning and in-class activities" (Kurimay 2014, 1).

At Bryn Mawr and Haverford Colleges, both SaLT and the institutional support it enjoys signal that it is legitimate to focus on teaching alongside research, even as a new faculty member. Virtually all higher education contexts that expect faculty be productive scholars are quite emphatic that new faculty establish and maintain their research agendas first and foremost. This is certainly important, since even colleges that value teaching tend to weigh research productivity more heavily in reappointment and promotion decisions. But what Alison has heard from many new faculty over the years is that teaching in a new context is the most difficult adjustment they face. Many come directly from graduate school, where they have been immersed in their research, and others come from dramatically different teaching contexts. Unless they find a way to manage the demands of teaching in their first job or new context, they cannot focus on their scholarship anyway.

Therefore, while devoting so much time and such substantial institutional resources to supporting faculty in pedagogical and curricular matters might seem both counterintuitive and countercultural in many college and university contexts, it actually supports new faculty in achieving greater satisfaction and success in both teaching and scholarship. Indeed, anecdotal evidence suggest that, since the advent of the SaLT program at Bryn Mawr and Haverford Colleges, fewer faculty have come up against problems at moments of review and promotion because of pedagogical challenges. Pedagogical partnership programs like SaLT not only provide energy and encouragement for new faculty as teachers, they can support new faculty in balancing or integrating the multiple dimensions of their institutional identities and responsibilities: as teachers, as researchers and scholars, and as members of a community they serve in various ways (on committees, through advising, etc.). As one new faculty member explained about his and his colleagues' experiences, participating in the SaLT program supported "not just our learning about pedagogy but our learning about ourselves, how we relate to students, and how we approach teaching as a part of our lives at the college" (Cook-Sather et al. 2017, 131).

What are the benefits to students who have traditionally been underrepresented in and underserved by institutions of higher education?

Supporting the success of a diversity of students is a topic of increasing discussion in higher education (Devlin 2013; Gale and Parker 2014; Gibson et al. 2017; Hockings 2010; O'Shea and Delahunty 2018; US Department of Education 2016). Research studies and reflective essays focused on the benefits of pedagogical partnership to students from groups who are traditionally underrepresented in and underserved by higher education point to the ways in which pedagogical partnership supports student success and, more generally, a sense of belonging (Colón García 2017; Cook-Sather and Agu 2013; Cook-Sather and Felten 2017b; Cook-Sather et al. 2019; de Bie et al. 2019; Gibson et al. 2017). Students' analyses of their experiences suggest that participation in pedagogical partnership has particularly powerful outcomes in relation to their academic engagement in their own classes and their sense of their evolution as active agents in their own development (Cook-Sather 2018b; de Bie et al. 2019).

Students whose educational backgrounds have not prepared them for the culture of higher education find that partnership affords them access to, experience with, and increased confidence in navigating academia. Students quoted in Cook-Sather (2018b, 927) describe gaining a deeper understanding of "the rationale behind an activity or behind an assignment"—an ability to discern the "pedagogical reasoning" in ways that "totally deepened my learning." The deep thinking about learning that student partners engage in helps them "recognize which strategies and teaching styles work for me and recognize when they aren't working for me." Concomitant with this deeper understanding is greater confidence in approaching faculty: "I have a lot more comfort talking to professors."

Student partners from underrepresented backgrounds also consistently talk about how participating in partnership "has given me confidence in my classes in new ways"; students feel "stronger and more empowered to give my voice"; they feel "a sense of ownership of my experience both inside the classroom and outside the classroom" (students quoted in Cook-Sather 2018b, 928). Students describe taking "more leadership roles as a result [of participating] in the program" (student quoted in Cook-Sather 2018b, 929). The leadership roles and the confidence to pursue them extend beyond students' time on campus. The extended reflection in the following quote captures the experience of an underrepresented student who built essential confidence through their experience of partnership and carried that with them into the work world:

> There is kind of an idea that when you go out for a job you should always be aiming for something that is higher than where you feel like you are, something that you are probably underqualified for, and I feel like participating in SaLT set me up to be more aware of what that would look like for me. It's really tough for women, for women of color, for LGBTQ folks; we usually apply for positions that we are overqualified for. As an example, white men go for things they are underqualified for. Like our president [Donald Trump]. They do that. They feel really comfortable with it. After SaLT, "consultant," "fellow," these are words not typically afforded access to people like me. So, having the experience, being able to say I do know these things, I can prove them, set me up to be more willing to go out for things that I wouldn't have gone out for before. It improved my confidence, my job seeking confidence. And it's true, I haven't had trouble getting jobs. My mom talks to me about that all the time. She says, "Of all my kids, you're the one I don't worry

about when it comes to finding a job." And the reason for that is programs like [SaLT] . . . I would not be in that same position if it wasn't for that same training and understanding. (Student partner quoted in Cook-Sather 2018b, 929)

That these benefits to underrepresented and underserved students have a profound impact both while students are undergraduates and after graduation is consistent with research that identifies predictors of students' post-graduation engagement and well-being. These predictors include having a professor who cares about students as people, makes them excited about learning, and encourages them to pursue their dreams, and having an internship or job in college that allows them to apply what they are learning in the classroom, be actively involved in extracurricular activities and organizations, and work on projects that take a semester or more to complete (Ray and Marken 2014, Gallup-Purdue Index Study). Pedagogical partnerships offer all of these experiences.

What are the benefits to institutions that want to transform their cultures?

Partnership "speaks to an institutional culture that values students as participants in knowledge construction, as producers of knowledge, within the university learning community." For many institutions of higher education, "this is a radical cultural shift" from an environment in which administrators, staff, and faculty make decisions to benefit students toward a mindset where students work "as colleagues, as partners, as trusted collaborators—with shared goals" (Matthews, Cook-Sather, and Healey 2018, 24). Because it is such a radical shift, it typically does not happen quickly. Indeed, such transformation in culture tends not only to be slow, it also tends to happen in expected ways, and might look different in different contexts.

Sophia Abbot, a former student partner in the SaLT program who went on to develop and lead Tigers as Partners, a student-faculty partnership program at Trinity University in the United States, argues that "the shift is not only that students can work as colleagues, partners, and trusted collaborators but also that faculty need not work alone" (personal communication). She relates a story about how such a shift can make a difference: "A professor I met with recently said the major shift for her following her partnership in Trinity University's program was that when students did really poorly on her most recent midterm, instead of sitting by herself and pondering what could be the issue, she went back into class and just asked them." So, Sophia argues, "this paradigm shift is one not only of seeing students as partners but of not seeing oneself as a silo (and it goes both ways! Partnership helped me to realize I could ask for help from my professors, and be open with them about my goals and needs)."

As Sophia's story illustrates, pedagogical partnership reconceptualizes the knowledge and capacities of all student and faculty partners. Such reconceptualization can take place regardless of participants' particular identities. At the same time, it releases faculty from the myth that they must be the sole expert on everything held in the classroom: content, pedagogy, and the students themselves. Student partners often articulate the importance of these kinds of reconceptualization. As one student argues: "Professors aren't just people on a pedestal who have to know everything and can do everything and will do everything. They are just people who are working really hard" (quoted in de Bie et al. 2019, 40). This student continued that, as a result of the destabilization of power dynamics in partnership work, "I feel so much more ownership over my experience as a student. I feel like I've been given a platform to say, 'No, I know things and I need things and other people also need things, and I can be in tune with that'" (quoted in de Bie et al. 2019, 40).

Positioning underrepresented students as pedagogical partners in particular recognizes those students as "holders and creators of knowledge" (Delgado-Bernal 2002, 106) who become "a resource for faculty learning" (Cook-Sather and Agu 2013, 272) and significantly diversify the identities of those doing educational development work. In so doing, it catalyzes a culture shift on college and university campuses. Pedagogical partnership programs that position underrepresented students as pedagogical partners complicate the institutional roles of student, instructor, and academic developer; mobilize the cultural identities of student partners from underrepresented groups; and contribute to the transformation of universities into more egalitarian learning communities that support equity-seeking students and culturally sustaining pedagogical practices (Cook-Sather et al. 2019; Gibson and Cook-Sather, forthcoming).

In the following quotes, we offer the perspectives of three differently positioned members of higher education communities in Canada, the United States, and Australia and how they perceive partnership as contributing to the transformation of institutional culture:

> "There's actually people looking at teaching and learning in all kinds of different [ways], including access and accessibility and all these sorts of things. Yeah, definitely can contribute to . . . a better campus, an inclusive campus."
>
> —Student partner in McMaster University's Student Partners Program (Response to survey)
>
> "The program helped us as students want to engage in the work and feel like we could engage in the work of making a more equitable campus."
>
> —Student partner in SaLT (Response to survey)
>
> "Defining and making sense of students as partners work is part of a cultural change process that needs to take place locally and enables a process of coming to a shared understanding."
>
> —Kelly Matthews, Associate Professor, Curriculum, Institute for Teaching and Learning Innovation, University of Queensland, Australia (personal communication)

What purposes can you articulate for developing a pedagogical partnership program?

In the sections above, we have offered a number of reasons why we advocate the creation of pedagogical partnership programs. Your reasons for engaging in partnership may be like ours or different from ours, and how explicit you are about those reasons will be political as well as pragmatic. Of the reasons you have, some might become explicit statements of principles and guidelines for practice, while others might remain tacit or implicit, explored in the closed and confidential spaces of partnership work rather than claimed publicly as commitments. In the spirit of this "how-to" guide, our advice is to be thoughtful and intentional, to try to be clear about and aware of what you are doing, and to think through the potential consequences of any given decision.

Your decisions about what to state publicly and what to keep more tacit will depend on: what you understand partnership to be; what emotions and attitudes those who will participate on your campus bring; what the aim, scale, and time frame of the project or initiative will be; and what conceptual frameworks you adopt to guide your understanding and practice (Healey and Healey 2018). In chapter 2, we elaborate on these questions, and you may want to address them to clarify for yourself what your purposes are. Here we review some common explicit and implicit purposes that partnership programs have to get your thinking started.

What explicit purposes of pedagogical partnership programs might you embrace?

Regarding your explicitly stated purpose or purposes, strive to identify what will resonate with or at least not alienate those in your particular context. A purpose that is likely to be of high interest and relatively low threat to most members of higher education communities is to facilitate dialogue across different positions and perspectives—students, faculty, and staff—with the goal of developing or revising pedagogical practices and curriculum. You might have very specific purposes in mind, such as developing pedagogical approaches that are responsive to underrepresented and underserved students or developing or revising curricula for particular programs or courses, such as first-year, introductory courses or capstone courses for majors.

A purpose that some members of higher education communities might welcome, and some might find more threatening, is to complicate and challenge traditional power dynamics, assumptions about who has legitimate knowledge about teaching and learning, and who should play an active role in developing and analyzing pedagogical practices and curricula. This is a more avowedly radical purpose, but it may well be a good fit for your institution. It might still inform the kind of curricular and pedagogical analysis and revision described above, but the reasons and processes for undertaking such analysis and revision would be framed in a very different way.

Among the purposes of pedagogical partnership articulated by particular programs are providing "an opportunity for faculty to reflect on their pedagogy, receive feedback from a student not in their course, and work collaboratively to meet teaching goals" (Reed College, Student Consultants for Teaching and Learning) and "developing a more inclusive learning environment" (Smith College, Student-Faculty Pedagogical Partnership Program). If you want to draw on scholarship, you could identify as your purpose ensuring that students "become full participants in the design of teaching approaches, courses, and curricula" (Bovill, Cook-Sather, and Felten 2011, 133) or transforming higher education contexts into more egalitarian learning communities (Matthews, Cook-Sather, and Healey 2018). The growing body of scholarship on pedagogical partnership can provide numerous, variously articulated rationales for developing programs, and drawing on published arguments often helps to "legitimate" such work.

What you call your program and what name you choose for student and faculty partners, questions we address in chapter 3, are closely related to the explicit purposes and public language you choose. These are significant questions and best considered ahead of time, in a dialogue that includes academic developers, student partners, faculty partners, and others who are committed to this work.

What implicit purposes of pedagogical partnership programs might you embrace?

Your implicit purposes, if you have them, may be more radical and even subversive. We include some of ours here to illustrate what we mean. From our perspective, when students are partners, positioned as those with legitimate knowledge about teaching and learning and invited to engage in dialogue and collaboration with faculty and staff, they cannot ever go back to being the kind of students they were before—being "only" students. The insights they gain, the empowerment they experience, the empathy they develop, and the capacity they build change them irreversibly. So even the most basic purpose of this work—to support dialogue across differences of position and perspective—is, to our minds, revolutionary. If you share this purpose, do you want that to remain implicit or become an explicit purpose of your partnership program?

The kinds of transformation faculty experience can also be life and practice changing. Some faculty, once they work with a student partner, never want to go back to teaching alone because they recognize how valuable the student partner's perspective and camaraderie are in contrast to the "pedagogical solitude" (Shulman 2004) in which faculty typically labor. Some faculty partners in the SaLT program and in programs like it request to work with a student partner semester after semester. Do you want that option—to replace pedagogical solitude with perpetual student-faculty partnership—to remain implicit or become an explicit purpose of your partnership program?

In our program, the explicit focus is on enriching and equalizing teaching and learning experiences through bringing the different perspectives of students and faculty to bear on curriculum and pedagogical practice, but implicit in that is the purpose of supporting both individual and collective empowerment. A former student partner, Olivia Porte, and Alison describe our conception of partnership this way: "Through a perpetually negotiated exchange within the spaces" that student-faculty pedagogical partnerships create, students and faculty, "who have different identities, positions, roles and responsibilities, strive to grasp—understand, take ahold of—what is offered by the other in the exchange" (Cook-Sather and Porte 2017). Would you want that kind of reciprocal exchange and mutual transformation to be an explicit or an implicit purpose of your program?

As Cook-Sather and Porte (2017) note above, through this perpetual process of reaching across differences of position and perspective and striving to grasp what the person across the space is holding out, participants in pedagogical partnership can enact Freire's (2005, 264) vision: "Through dialogue, the teacher-of-the-students and the students-of-the-teachers cease to exist and a new term emerges: teacher-student with student-teachers. . . . They become jointly responsible for a process in which all grow." Such freedom from traditional roles comes with greater responsibility and a different kind of investment on both faculty members' and students' parts. To what extent do you want that to be an explicit purpose and to what extent might it be more effective remaining implicit?

There may well be other implicit reasons that you have for wanting to develop or expand a pedagogical partnership program, but we recommend that you consider at a minimum the reasons we list here: repositioning students such that they cannot go back to being the kind of students they were before; repositioning faculty such that they do not want to return to pedagogical solitude; supporting both students and faculty in empowering themselves; and advocating a willingness to share power and responsibility in teaching and learning.

What are the assumptions and expectations that participants bring?

Explicit and implicit purposes for partnership are informed by assumptions and expectations. All participants are likely to bring assumptions and expectations based on their previous experiences, identities, norms for participation in higher education, and more. Here we note the primary assumption and expectation we have found that faculty and students bring, respectively, to their first pedagogical partnership and one that we have encountered in both faculty and students who engage in second or third partnerships. Following this section, we focus on assumptions and expectations that can become threshold concepts. We articulate these here in the hopes that you can address them ahead of time rather than have to wrestle with them as they invisibly inform—and sometimes impede—the development of partnership.

What is the key assumption and expectation faculty bring?

The most common assumption and expectation that faculty bring is: *I will be under surveillance.* Because, as Lynch (2010, 55) has argued, "surveillance, and the unrelenting measurement of performance, are institutionalized and normalized in everyday life," and because most classroom visits are for purposes of evaluation, many faculty are uncertain about what the student partner role will be and unfamiliar with how to enter into conversation with a student regarding personal insecurities, worries, or moments of joy in the classroom (Ntem and Cook-Sather 2018). The excerpts from faculty reflections below capture the worry that many if not most faculty feel before embarking on pedagogical partnership:

> "When I learned about the program, it sounded very watch-doggy."
>
> —Faculty partner
> (quoted in Cook-Sather, Bovill, and Felten 2014, 149)
>
> "[The prospect of entering partnership] produced the anxious expectancy of classroom observation as a (real or perceived) form of benevolent surveillance."
>
> —Reckson 2014, 1
>
> "The disconcerting presence in the classroom of a student consultant ... [was an] unnerving conjunction of counselor, coach, and court stenographer."
>
> —Rudy 2014, 2

Almost all faculty discover that pedagogical partnership does not at all turn out to be the surveillance they worried about and expected. The first faculty member quoted above found "it was totally the opposite when I met my student partner" (faculty partner quoted in Cook-Sather, Bovill, and Felten 2014, 149). The second found that her student partner offered "observation without judgment—a rare gift—and along with it, a sense of camaraderie and shared purpose" (Reckson 2014, 1). And the third faculty member came to see his partner as "a liminal and unexpected figure foreign to traditional teaching and central to raising pedagogical awareness" (Rudy 2014, 5). But program directors, faculty members, and student partners alike should be prepared for the initial expectation to be infused with fear of surveillance, and some faculty—very few, but some—never move past that fear.

If you are a program director or student partner already participating in or planning pedagogical partnership, we urge you to do everything possible to try to assuage this assumption and expectation on the part of faculty partners. All participants are working against institutional structures and human fear born of vulnerability, so reassurance, patience, and support are key. The discussion we offer in chapter 4 of the shared responsibilities of facilitating pedagogical partnerships can help address this particular assumption and expectation, particularly the importance of bringing an open mind to everyone's contribution; building trust; co-creating an approach to the collaboration; communicating; being present to and mindful of others; and advocating.

What is the key assumption and expectation students bring?

The key assumption and expectation students bring is some form of: *I don't have anything to offer but I need to find something to critique.* The first part of this formulation springs from institutional norms that position students as recipients not producers or co-creators of knowledge about learning and teaching, and the second part springs from the commonly embraced purpose of much higher education: to develop critical ways of thinking. One student partner captured both of these in her perspective on joining the SaLT program:

> At first I was kind of skeptical because you are a student and these profs have been doing this for quite some time they have advanced degrees, you're a kid with some college. And you are trying to come in and say, "Do this better, do that." And you could easily be dismissed. (Quoted in Cook-Sather and Agu 2013, 280)

This student's words reflect a lack of recognition of the knowledge she and other students bring—not knowledge that eclipses or replaces faculty knowledge and experience, but other, complementary forms of knowledge and experience. Her reflection also captures the misperception student partners have initially that they are supposed to say, "Do this better, do that." A kind of analogue to the faculty fear that they will be under surveillance, this assumption that student partners should tell faculty partners what to do is one that needs to be countered from the start. As we discuss in chapter 4, student partners affirming what they think is working well and why in faculty partners' practice is an essential mode of engagement in the SaLT program, but such practice needs to be scaffolded, learned, and reinforced (Cook-Sather et al. 2017). We return to this point in the section below on threshold concepts.

What key assumption and expectation do both faculty and students bring?

Returning student and faculty partners can assume and expect that ***their new partner/ship will be like their previous partner/ships.*** This is a function of human minds—to expect things to be as they have been—but it is important for all participants involved to approach each new partnership as new. It is impossible not to bring prior experiences and associated assumptions and expectations, but those need to be acknowledged as such, not taken as templates or necessities. In a conversation among faculty partners that Alison facilitated at Smith College, Johanna Ravenhurst, program coordinator in Smith College's Sherrerd Center, where their partnership program is based, wrote this in her notes:

> "No two partnerships are the same"—this is especially important to keep in mind when faculty or student partners start a second partnership with a new pedagogical partner. It is important to share your hopes and expectations with your partner at the beginning of the semester. You may be surprised by theirs. Try not to assume you are entering the partnership for the same reasons/with the same expectations. (Personal communication)

All program directors, but experienced faculty and student partners as well, play an important part in reminding one another that every partnership is unique, might warrant different approaches, will develop through a different kind of dynamic between the partners, and will yield new insights.

What are the threshold concepts to partnership?

The three assumptions and expectations noted above can typically be addressed early on in pedagogical partnerships because experience in partnership tends to counter them. Other assumptions and expectations can persist through and despite experience. These are what we call threshold concepts to pedagogical partnership: concepts that, if not addressed, can block or hinder the development of partnership. They need to be made explicit and grappled with if the potential of pedagogical partnership is to be realized. To illuminate these threshold concepts to partnership, we start by defining the term, then we briefly discuss student-faculty pedagogical partnership itself as a threshold concept, and then we note the specific threshold concepts within pedagogical partnership we have seen. We elaborate on these threshold concepts in the "Threshold Concepts in Pedagogical Partnership" resource.

Over ten years ago, two scholars developed the notion of "threshold concepts," which they defined as "conceptual gateways" or "'portals' that lead to a transformed view of something" (Meyer and Land 2006, 19). They applied this notion to concepts such as supply and demand in economics: concepts that must be understood if learners are to move beyond a superficial understanding of the subject. Important to understand about threshold concepts is that they can seem counterintuitive, and it is possible for learners to complete whole courses of study without mastering them (and, indeed, sustaining their limited and even false understandings). Because they require a shift in understanding, and an accompanying "shift in learner subjectivity," threshold concepts can be "troublesome," "transformative," "irreversible (unlikely to be forgotten, or unlearned only through considerable effort), and integrative (exposing previously hidden interrelatedness)" (Land et al. 2005, 53).

The notion of threshold concepts has proven useful in the realm of academic development in general (see King and Felten 2012), and several scholars have identified student-faculty pedagogical partnership as a threshold concept (Cook-Sather 2014; Cook-Sather and Luz 2015; Marquis et al. 2016b; Werder, Thibou, and Kaufer 2012). As Marquis et al. (2016b, 6) explain, "passing through the partnership threshold entails coming to understand staff and students as collegial contributors to teaching and learning, with complementary roles, responsibilities, and perspectives, and *realizing* this understanding within actual teaching and learning practices."

Within the larger notion that student-faculty partnership itself is a threshold concept, there are particular ideas that can constitute threshold concepts to partnership. Most of these ideas stand in stark contrast to traditional assumptions, fears, vulnerabilities, and resistances (Ntem and Cook-Sather 2018), and they require holding seemingly contradictory or at least complex ideas in one's mind. Below we list the threshold concepts we have most often experienced or perceived, and in the "Threshold Concepts in Pedagogical Partnership" resource, we discuss these in detail and offer participant perspectives on them:

- Students have valuable knowledge of and important perspectives on teaching and learning.
- Student partners are not subject matter experts.
- Reciprocity in partnership does not mean exchanging exactly the same thing.
- Faculty partners do not have to do whatever students say.
- Partnership is not about finding what is wrong and fixing it.
- Pedagogical partnership is about exchange, not change for the sake of change.
- Partnership is about sharing power, not giving it up or taking it away.
- Partnership is a process, not a product (although it can lead to products of various kinds).

YOUR TURN

Considering your goals:

If someone asked you why you want to develop a pedagogical partnership program, what would you say?

With whom on your campus would you share your explicit reasons for wanting to develop a pedagogical partnership program, with whom would you share your implicit reasons, and why?

Considering the research:

Which of the research findings on the benefits of pedagogical partnership programs do you find most compelling?

Which do you think would be most compelling in your context?

What areas do you think warrant further investigation?

Considering assumptions, expectations, and threshold concepts:

Which assumptions and expectations about partnership articulated in this chapter did you find yourself sharing?

Were there assumptions and expectations you found yourself thinking about that weren't mentioned but that either you or others in your context would need to tackle?

Which of these, if any, might be threshold concepts in your context?

2 HOW DO YOU KNOW WHAT KIND OF PARTNERSHIP PROGRAM IS RIGHT FOR YOUR CONTEXT, AND WHY MIGHT FACULTY AND STUDENTS WANT TO PARTICIPATE?

We noted in the introduction that there is a wide variety of approaches to and kinds of pedagogical partnership developing around the world, and we discussed in chapter 1 a range of reasons for developing partnership programs, explicit and implicit purposes of pedagogical partnership programs, and threshold concepts to pedagogical partnership. To give a sense of the range of approaches to pedagogical partnership and also to situate the type of program we focus on in this book, we provide some guiding questions that will help you decide what kind of program might be right for your context. We also include brief overviews of the five programs we mentioned in the introduction—the Student Partners Program at McMaster University in Canada; Co-create UVA at the University of Virginia in the United States; a unique approach to introducing partnership at Queensland University in Australia; a partnership program at Kaye Academic College of Education, Be'er Sheva, Israel; and an approach to curriculum co-creation at Victoria University of Wellington, Aotearoa New Zealand. We discuss as well why faculty and students might want to participate in pedagogical partnership programs, and we provide an overview of how programs like SaLT have developed at other institutions.

What are the questions you might ask yourselves to decide what kind of partnership program is right for your context?

Healey and Healey (2018) propose that those embarking upon the process of developing partnerships between and among students, faculty, and staff consider four areas. We present these considerations here as questions and, depending on what is possible and what is non-negotiable in your context, you can choose to address them in the order that makes most sense to you.

Questions to Consider in Developing Pedagogical Partnership Projects and Programs

What is the aim, scale, and time frame of the project or initiative?	What are the conceptual frameworks that will guide understandings and practices?
What are the emotions, attitudes, behaviors, and values of the participants in pedagogical partnership?	What is the meaning of partnership, or how will you define what it is that you hope and plan to do?

The kind of program and the approach you take to developing it will depend on how you answer these questions. For instance:

Aim, scale, and time frame of the project or initiative: The underlying vision or aim of the pedagogical partnership project, as well as the imagined scale and time frame, will help create parameters and clarify purposes for partnership work. Will the program feature only pedagogical partnerships focused on classroom-based practice and curricular design and redesign, like SaLT, or will it include a wider range of approaches, like Co-create UVA (Doktor et al. 2019) and the Student Partners Program at McMaster University (Marquis et al. 2016b; Marquis, Black, and Healey 2017)? Will it be a pilot or a program focused on a particular, time-bound classroom or institutional challenge, or will it provide a structure through which students in partnership with faculty, staff, and administrators continually identify, research, and work to transform practices at the institution, such as the Students as Change Agents program at the University of Exeter in England (Dunne and Zandstra 2011; Dunne et al. 2014) or the Wabash-Provost Scholars Program at North Carolina A&T in the United States (Cook-Sather, Bovill, and Felten 2014)?

Conceptual framework: Different ways of theorizing partnership—through constructs or metaphors, for instance—can serve to remind participants what the goals of partnership are and guide both thinking and action (Cook-Sather 2017; Matthews, Cook-Sather, and Healey 2018; Matthews et al. 2018). For instance, theorizing pedagogical partnership as a structure that supports students and faculty in "processes of translation that lead to transformed perceptions of classroom engagement, transformed terms for naming pedagogical practices, and, more metaphorically, transformed selves" (Cook-Sather and Abbot 2016, 1) allows you to attend to the development of ways of perceiving, ways of naming, and ways of being that partnership can transform. If you think of engaging in pedagogical partnership as a process of crossing a threshold, as we discussed in chapter 1—of striving to redefine roles in a way that is, for many participants, troublesome, transformative, discursive, irreversible, and integrative (Meyer and Land 2006; Cook-Sather and Luz 2015; Marquis et al. 2016b; Werder, Thibou, and Kaufer 2012)—then you can focus on supporting participants in managing those challenges, based on what we know about how students (Land, Meyer, and Flanigan 2016) and faculty (Cook-Sather 2014a; King and Felten 2012) grapple with threshold concepts.

Meaning of partnership: Many program directors, faculty, and students embrace this definition of pedagogical partnership: "a collaborative, reciprocal process through which all participants have the opportunity to contribute equally, although not necessarily in the same ways, to curricular or pedagogical conceptualization, decision making, implementation, investigation, or analysis" (Cook-Sather, Bovill, and Felten 2014, 6-7). If partnership is "a way of doing things, rather than an outcome in itself" (Healey, Flint, and Harrington 2014, 7), it makes sense to emphasize "the relational and social elements of mutual learning"

(Matthews 2016, 1; 2017a). In what ways will these—or other—meanings of partnership guide the structures and practices that you as program director, faculty partner, or student partner develop?

Emotions, attitudes, behaviors, and values of partnership: Among the attitudes and behaviors we argue are essential for successful pedagogical partnership are: bringing an open mind to everyone's contribution; building trust; co-creating an approach to the collaboration; communicating; being present to and mindful of others; and advocating. We discuss these in detail in chapter 4. In terms of emotions, anyone who has undertaken pedagogical partnership work knows that it demands intense emotional as well as intellectual engagement. Felten (2017) has asserted that without attending to emotions, we cannot understand either the experiences of or outcomes for individuals in partnerships, or the interactions and relationships between individuals in partnerships (see also Hermsen et al. 2017). Confirming this assertion, one student partner noted how "emotionally vulnerable" student partners make themselves as they "give so much of themselves in their partnerships to make professors understand, to give professors perspective on their experience" (student partner quoted in Ntem and Cook-Sather 2018, 92). Faculty partners, too, experience a range of positive and negative emotions through partnership (Cook-Sather, Ntem, and Felten in preparation). How will you support the emotional work required to engage in partnership and help participants develop the attitudes, behaviors, and values associated with partnership? These are questions we return to in chapter 8.

We recommend spending time addressing these questions with those on your campus who are involved or hope to be involved in developing a pedagogical partnership program. Perhaps have differently positioned people—students, faculty, program directors, others—address the questions separately, and then discuss your responses as a group. Also, as we discuss in chapter 3, we recommend that you talk with others on campus who may already be engaged in partnership, in a wide variety of forms, and consider how to build on or complement those existing approaches. Values and commitments emerge through such dialogues, as Floyd Cheung, founding director of Smith College's pedagogical partnership program, articulates:

> Our student-faculty partnership program not only supports colleagues in improving their teaching but does so with an eye on enhancing inclusivity by foregrounding the perspectives of students from underrepresented backgrounds. Such students, we believe, can help professors see their curricula and teaching practices anew. In conjunction, these students are valued and empowered in ways that most had never imagined.
>
> —Floyd Cheung, director,
> Sherrerd Center for Teaching and Learning,
> Smith College, United States
> (personal communication)

What is the range of pedagogical partnership programs currently under development?

As indicated in the section above, every pedagogical partnership is context specific. The SaLT program is no exception, and in the "History and Structure of the SaLT Program" resource we provide the details of our context and the way the SaLT program is structured. Here we provide examples of programs that have developed in contexts that are quite different from that in which SaLT developed as well as from one another. We asked the directors or developers of pedagogical partnership programs at McMaster University in Canada, University of Virginia in the United States, University of Queensland in Australia, Kaye Academic College of Education in Be'er Sheva, Israel, and Victoria University of Wellington in Aotearoa New Zealand to describe the kind of institution in which they work, what their partnership program does, why they chose their particular structure over another, and what their program does not (yet) accomplish. Their detailed responses to our questions are included in the "Five Stories of Developing Pedagogical Partnership Programs" resource, presented in their own voices. Below are short summaries of each of their stories.

Story 1: Student Partners Program, McMaster University, Hamilton, ON, Canada

Under the leadership of Beth Marquis, Associate Director (Research) at the Paul R. MacPherson Institute for Leadership, Innovation and Excellence in Teaching, and her colleagues at McMaster University, the Student Partners Program (SPP) has developed several overlapping strands: supporting student-faculty co-inquiry on Scholarship of Teaching and Learning (SoTL) projects; engaging students as course design/delivery consultants who partner with faculty to design, re-design, or review courses faculty partners are teaching (modeled on the SaLT program); and connecting students with faculty and departments working on program-wide curriculum development or review. Furthermore, at this medium-sized (~30,000 students) medical doctoral, research-intensive university that consistently ranks among the top institutions in Canada for research intensity, student partnership has been integrated into a major fellowship program supported by the teaching and learning institute. In all cases, the aim is to develop collaborative partnerships wherein students make meaningful contributions to the intellectual development of the work they undertake. Cherie Woolmer, Postdoctoral Research Fellow at the MacPherson Institute, reflects on why the Student Partners Program might have developed and flourished so quickly:

> McMaster's Student Partners Program has grown significantly over a relatively short period of time. A key part of this, I think, has been a conscious decision to allow partnerships to flourish in a variety of contexts that have been identified, and are therefore meaningful, to colleagues across the university community. Partnerships are enacted through the connections and relationships built between individuals working on shared projects and initiatives; this is where I see the values of partnership become real and transformative for people involved in the program. Scaling up such activities in a way that retains this space for individuals to connect through meaningful dialogue is not without its challenges. For

example, we have to be mindful of how we can ensure equity as demand grows; encourage participation of a wider group of faculty, staff and students; and influence institutional discourses about impact and success to ensure they capture the value and benefit of partnerships in meaningful ways. Facilitators in the MacPherson Institute play a key role in mediating these tensions to ensure that we continue to enact the principles on which the program was founded.

—Cherie Woolmer, Postdoctoral Research Fellow, MacPherson Institute, McMaster University, Canada (personal communication)

Story 2: Co-create UVA, University of Virginia, United States
Dorothe Bach, faculty co-creator, Center for Teaching Excellence, and Keaton Wadzinski and Jacob Hardin, student co-creators at ReinventED Lab, a student-led organization, developed the partnership program at the University of Virginia (UVA), a large public research institution with a strong commitment to undergraduate education. Co-create UVA was founded in 2014 as a partnership between ReinventED Lab and the Center for Teaching Excellence. The program consists of multiple initiatives, including six to eight paid undergraduate student teaching consultants, student-facilitated design thinking workshops, student-faculty luncheons at new faculty orientation, and course development grants for faculty and student teams. (See Doktor et al. 2019 for a full discussion.) One of the student co-creators reflects on the profound experience the development of Co-create UVA was for him:

> Participating in Co-create UVA was the most profound experience during my entire time at the University of Virginia. Never before had I been asked to think about the way that I, or my peers, learned. The level of metacognitive thinking and agency that came with coordinating an effort like Co-create UVA gave me the confidence to pursue a career in education innovation. I worked

regularly with professors and faculty at the Center for Teaching Excellence as a program coordinator and as a consultant, giving real feedback to real assignments, syllabi, and courses that were being taught at the university. I began my work as a consultant thinking that professors would come to us for advice to indulge us as proactive students, but the genuine conversations that happened proved otherwise. I wish every student could feel what we felt as undergraduate consultants. We really made a difference.

— Jacob Hardin, student co-creator, ReinventED Lab, University of Virginia, United States (personal communication)

Story 3: National Australian Learning and Teaching Fellowship on Engaging Students as Partners, University of Queensland, Brisbane, Australia

At the University of Queensland (UQ), a large (~50,000 students), comprehensive "Group of Eight" university in Australia and one of the oldest universities in the country, Kelly Matthews, Associate Professor, Curriculum, Institute for Teaching and Learning Innovation, was the recipient of a National Teaching Fellowship in 2015 to develop "Students as Partners: Reconceptualising the Role of Students in Curriculum Development." The fellowship supported a range of activities through the Institute for Teaching and Learning Innovation at UQ, including establishing an Australian community of scholars with international ties; mapping students as partners activities across Australia; piloting student-academic partnership activities at UQ; developing guiding principles and case studies; and facilitating workshops and roundtables. Matthews reflects on her intentional choice to develop partnerships with students:

What is unusual, at least in Australia, was my deliberate choice to engage with students on the fellowship activities as a central part of learning about *students as partners* through partnerships. Because I see my work as creating community, I have a long-term view with some clear goals in mind... but lots of room to follow opportunities as they arise.

—Kelly Matthews, Associate Professor, Curriculum, Institute for Teaching and Learning Innovation, University of Queensland, Australia (personal communication)

Story 4: Kaye Academic College of Education, Be'er Sheva, Israel

Kaye Academic College of Education is an institution of higher education in southern Israel for teacher education and the professional development of 5,000 kindergarten, elementary, and high school teachers each year who are preparing to serve the Jewish and Bedouin population of the Negev Desert. College President Lea Kozminsky, Partnership Coordinator Ruth Mansur, student partners, and twelve student-faculty pairs launched a pedagogical partnership program at the beginning of the 2018-2019 academic year. The goal is to include students' perspectives in their teacher education process, and thus to improve their current pedagogical practices and contribute to the conceptualization of learning and teaching as collaborative processes. Student partners Iska Naaman and Moria Propost describe their experiences of participating in this launch:

> The project is very important as I feel that I am the voice of the students, a partner in teaching, and can express my views and raise various points of view. In addition, the project develops my pedagogical professionalism. The connection between Doron (the lecturer) and myself is based on respect, listening, and sharing. He answers my questions very seriously, reveals to me his considerations regarding the course, both the pedagogical considerations and the teaching methods he uses.

— Iska Naaman, student, Kaye Academic College, Israel (personal communication)

> As a student, I have the opportunity to be exposed to new knowledge and understand the logic that lies behind Dini's (the lecturer) actions. My relationships with her are based on professionality, respect, honesty, and open communication. Following my first meeting with her, I was surprised to see that she had already decided to implement what we had discussed and let the students become more active. I benefit from this project by gaining confidence as a future teacher, and also enriched my knowledge regarding implementing methods of teaching.
>
> — Moria Propost, student,
> Kaye Academic College, Israel (personal communication)

Story 5: Victoria University of Wellington, Aotearoa New Zealand
Victoria University of Wellington is a mid-sized (~22,000 students) research-intensive university in Aotearoa New Zealand. Senior Lecturer Irina Elgort, Associate Professor Kathryn Sutherland, and student mentors and undergraduates Isabella Lenihan-Ikin and Ali Leota are leading the development of Ako in Action, following the introduction in 2017 of Te Rautaki Maruako, the university's new learning and teaching strategy. This new strategy embeds a bicultural approach to learning and teaching that recognizes the value of *akoranga*, translated in the strategy as "collective responsibility for learning." Students and staff work in partnership on the two key components that comprise Ako in Action: observations of teaching, and consultations on the design of learning and teaching. Kathryn Sutherland explains the values that inform their program's approach:

> The values embedded in our learning and teaching strategy draw from Te Tiriti o Waitangi (the Treaty of Waitangi) and represent New Zealand's, and our university's, commitment to partnership. These values lend themselves to the co-construction and co-design of reflective, collaborative, and dialogic teaching and learning experiences. By honouring the students' participation

through scholarships – rather than by paying them as employees – we allow them to retain their identities as students. We ask everyone participating in Ako in Action to think of themselves in partnership; it is not just "students as partners" but also "academics as partners" and "professional staff as partners" and "Centre for Academic Development staff as partners."

—Kathryn Sutherland, Associate Professor, Victoria University of Wellington, Aotearoa New Zealand (personal communication)

Why might faculty and students want to participate in a pedagogical partnership program?

The brief overviews above capture some sense of how five different partnership approaches were conceptualized in different institutional contexts. The wide range of reasons individual faculty and students might participate in such programs can shape the opportunities offered as well as the evolution of the program. In the section below, we describe the three main reasons faculty choose to participate in the SaLT program.

Why might faculty members want to participate?

In the SaLT program, faculty can choose to participate in three basic ways in the two program options (classroom-focused partnership and curriculum-focused partnership) for distinct but often related reasons. All incoming faculty members may choose to engage in a student-faculty partnership that is linked to a pedagogy seminar in exchange for a reduced teaching load in their first year at Bryn Mawr or Haverford College (see Cook-Sather 2016a). Through these partnerships, faculty and student partners often combine classroom- and curriculum-focused work, although their main focus tends to be pedagogical. The reason most faculty choose to participate in partnership at this point is to get oriented to a new cultural context. They may have completed their graduate work at research-focused institutions and feel unfamiliar with the norms and practices of liberal arts colleges. Or, they may have worked at a liberal arts college with a very different ethos and want to learn about student culture at Bryn Mawr and Haverford. A student partner who worked with a faculty member who had switched institutions after a number of years of teaching explains how partnership can support such a transition between institutional cultures:

> The first issue we addressed was that my faculty partner was not sure of what to expect with regards to interacting with students. For instance, she wondered if covering the guidelines for papers might imply that she didn't think the students were smart enough; she worried that their intelligence might be offended if she said a certain thing; etc. The way we worked through these issues was that I told her what I thought was "normal" for Haverford, and then she would ask the class during the week what they thought about the way she was interacting with them. This strategy of opening up the classroom for discussions was one that I felt was crucial in giving the students a say in what they wanted, while still allowing my faculty partner to make clear what she wanted from the class. (Wynkoop 2018, 2)

Once faculty have participated in a partnership in their first year, a proportion of them continue with their student partners, or with different student partners, either maintaining a focus on pedagogy (see, for example, Schlosser and Sweeney 2015) or switching to a curricular focus (see, for example, Charkoudian et al. 2015). The reason they choose this option is to deepen and extend their work, either with the same student partner or a different one (see chapter 8 for a discussion of the benefits and drawbacks of staying with the same pedagogical partner over time). Lou Charkoudian, assistant professor of chemistry at Haverford College, explains why she wanted to work in a second partnership and what the focus of the partnership was:

> I came up for air in December of 2013 after finishing my first semester as an assistant professor of chemistry

at Haverford College. After carefully stacking 78 graded organic chemistry final exams on the top shelf of my office, I sat down to reflect on what had been a whirlwind experience. While I had participated in the Teaching and Learning Institute at Bryn Mawr and Haverford Colleges, and worked closely with a student consultant throughout the semester, this was the first time I was relaxed enough to ask myself some fundamental questions: *Did the overall structure of the course make sense? Did my forms of assessment align with my course objectives? What could I do to improve this class for future students?*

Indeed, I was already thinking ahead to the Fall 2014, when I would be teaching this class for the second time. I wanted to make informed improvements to the course while the material was fresh in my mind. I had gathered some useful information from the end-of-semester evaluations, but what I really craved was a dynamic discussion with my former students. After all, they were the ones who sat through each lecture and worked through each assignment. They held the insights that I needed to make mindful revisions to the course materials and pedagogical approaches. (Charkoudian et al. 2015, 1)

Finally, the third way that faculty can choose to participate in SaLT is by simply asking to work with a student partner, regardless of where the faculty member is in their career. Some faculty members request student partners every semester; others go several years after their initial participation in SaLT and then request a student partner. Still others spend most of their career at the colleges without working in a pedagogical partnership and then decide that they want or need to. This last option has become increasingly important as the socio-political climate in the United States has become more tense and divisive. A student partner describes the experience of working in partnership with an experienced faculty member:

> The reason my partner wanted to be part of the SaLT program was clear. For the first time in his thirty plus year career, he was unsure about whether he was fit to teach his subject matter. He worried that his class was not inclusive enough and that he lacked an understanding of what his students were experiencing that was necessary to create a successful learning environment. My partner also wanted to know if there was a way that he could create a curriculum that would make him more "in touch" with his students. It was then and there that I realized that my partner had lost trust in himself. . . . He had been blindsided by an experience the previous semester to do with tensions in his class around race and had lost clarity on how to move forward. This was the root of everything. It was by learning this that I was able to further individualize everything I suggested: each discussion, idea, and approach. It was also by learning this that I was able to continue working to gain his trust, while also helping him regain his self-trust. Understanding the history and personal reasons someone has for joining a partnership can be incredibly beneficial to all components of a partnership but especially for building trust. (Brunson 2018, 2)

In the SaLT program, faculty need only contact Alison and let her know of their interest. Any faculty member who wishes to work in partnership focused on pedagogy or curriculum may do so, from those new to the college through those on the eve of retirement, from those on the tenure track to those visiting for a year or passing through as postdocs. With the exception of the faculty who participate in the seminar option during their first year, there is no financial compensation for faculty who participate in SaLT.

Why might students want to participate?
We frame our discussion of why students might want to participate in pedagogical partnership with a quote from Sophia Abbot, former student

partner in SaLT, and former fellow for collaborative programs through the Collaborative for Learning and Teaching at Trinity University, Texas, where she started a pedagogical partnership program:

> Students who participate in student-faculty pedagogical partnership programs gain access to the behind-the-scenes workings of the university, helping make the language and goals of professors more legible. Participating students also impact their faculty partners by increasing professors' awareness and understanding of the diversity of perspectives and experiences present in their classrooms and helping them to see different ways of presenting ideas and information. Finally, partnerships between students and professors can result in more equitable and inclusive courses.
>
> —Sophia Abbot, former student partner in SaLT, fellow for collaborative programs at Trinity University, United States (personal communication)

In SaLT, the student partner role is also voluntary, but it is compensated, and students seek out the role for a variety of reasons. Some are simply looking for a well-paying campus job and stumble upon it listed among other campus jobs, but most are seeking a meaningful form of engaging with the campus, faculty, and other students. Many student participants in SaLT are referred to, or first hear about, the program from friends who have participated in the past.

Some student partners are drawn to the role because they are seeking a greater sense of connection to professors and the academic community. Melanie heard about the SaLT program from a friend and chose to apply based on her desire to actively build relationships with faculty at Bryn Mawr. After taking most of her courses for two years on other campuses as part of a consortial major shared across several institutions, she felt disconnected from Bryn Mawr's academic community. By becoming a student consultant, she built relationships with professors as people and made space for herself in the college's academic life. Student partners get to connect or reconnect academically with individual faculty and with departments by actively fostering relationships and maintaining a connection with the campus as a whole. The following quote is an example of what students write on their applications regarding why they want to join the SaLT program:

> It would be a truly invaluable experience to work one-on-one with a professor, and expand my understanding of my academic experience. Being a Student Consultant would provide me with the opportunity to work closely with a faculty member to better understand the experiences of both students and educators in the classroom. As a student, I am seldom able to witness firsthand the thought process behind the way in which my professors structure their classes and its content. Normally, I only experience the classroom through my perspective. However, through my work as a Student Consultant, I would be able to engage in meaningful conversation with professors about their pedagogy, allowing me to reflect on the experiences I have had within the classroom. (Student partner, excerpt from application to SaLT program)

Anita and other student partners have indicated that moving beyond traditional hierarchical power structures in educational institutions may also motivate students to participate (Cook-Sather et al. 2019). Participating in student-faculty partnership shifts those power dynamics to more of a level field of collaboration by operating outside the hierarchies that limit faculty and student relationships. The student partner role also provides an opportunity to connect with faculty in a way that creates sincere relationships through deepened understanding of both roles. The student partner role emphasizes the value of student perspectives and elevates student expertise; this validation is attractive to students who have opinions about their educational experiences but limited opportunities or agency to voice and act on them.

Some students include this reasoning in their applications. One student wrote: "The experience [of being a student consultant] would provide a lot of insight into how classroom practices are created and how professors navigate classroom culture among college students." This student specified that her interest in the role was informed by the importance to her of culturally responsive practice: "I am also interested in the ways classroom culture encompass understandings of diversity, inclusion, and positionality and how to support and have conversations that center and accommodate for these factors."

Anita has noted that students see this role as offering a rare opportunity that empowers them with the right to analyze education from various angles. Student partners are able not only to be activists but also to ask constructively critical questions that assess pedagogical structures and the effects of those structures on the student experience. This role encourages students to be positive "agents of change" in their own education and to be advocates for their peers by improving the student experience at their institution. The opportunity to think about learning from a different angle gives students a new frame for their own courses and serves as useful preparation for those who plan to be teachers themselves. Some students participate as a way of preparing themselves to be future educators who have built confidence in advocating, affirming, and analyzing situations. We discuss these outcomes in detail in the "Outcomes of Pedagogical Partnership Work" resource. A recently graduated student consultant, Fatoumata Sylla, explains how participating in partnership changed her perceptions:

> In my first few years of college, I had a relatively skewed perception of professors and my positionality in relation to them. My educational background had taught me that within the realm of academia and learning, there exists a clear hierarchy: the professor sits at the top of this hierarchy and students below them. This mindset, though conventional, serves as a roadblock to what I regard as effective learning/ mutually beneficial classroom dynamics. Through my work as a consultant in the Students as

Learners and Teachers (SaLT) program at Bryn Mawr and Haverford Colleges, I've had the opportunity to critically reflect on my past learning experiences and evaluate how they have impacted my conceptions of socially responsible teaching. Through a process of reflection on my own education and using my past experiences to inform and guide me through my SaLT partnerships, I've realized that there is one essential and key element that must be present in any meaningful teaching and learning interaction; this element is trust. Trust, between a student and a professor, allows for several channels of dialogue to be opened, therefore allowing for more enriched, holistic, and socially conscious educational engagement. (Sylla 2018, 1)

How have SaLT and programs like it expanded beyond student-faculty partnerships?

Pedagogical partnerships are often collaborations between students and faculty members, but SaLT and programs like it can also support partnerships between students and other members of educational institutions, such as librarians, instructional technologists, and administrators. The SaLT program itself grew out of a model in which teams of four—a faculty member, a student, a librarian, and an instructional technologist—worked together to revise a course (Cook-Sather 2001). In the current iterations, student partners work with faculty and librarians.

For instance, one faculty member in the natural sciences collaborated with her own student partner and a science librarian who was also working with a student partner to develop a lecture and group activity on research proposal preparation. The faculty member and her student partner brainstormed some active learning, group-based activities for students based on the faculty member's learning goals and the final research proposal. Then the faculty member brought these ideas to the librarian, and they drafted an active learning guide that students could fill out during the lecture and group activity. Working with her student partner, the faculty member also developed an evaluation form for students to fill out during the last ten minutes of class that was collected and summarized by the student partner.

About this experience, the librarian explained that her student partner "was truly embedded in the process. She didn't just observe the instruction session; she was part of the planning activities as well" (personal communication). Furthermore, the librarian's student partner offered feedback on the session that the librarian conducted in the faculty member's class. As the librarian explained: "Her comments were invaluable! The strength of [her] feedback lies in her blow by blow account of my presentation; in other words, she allowed me to see the layout, timing, and content of my presentation through someone else's eyes." The student partner who worked with the librarian explained that she "gained a greater sense of the scaffolding librarians had done (really laying out the research goals for students)." This not only gave the student partner insight into the work that librarians do but also affirmed her as a student scholar, which gave her a lot more insight on how the institution saw her as a potential scholar. As she put it: "it felt empowering to have my perspective be so valued by the librarians who in many ways had architected my academic experience." Ferrell and Peach (2018) describe a similar librarian-student partnership at Berea College.

SaLT has also supported partnerships between students and administrators specifically to explore issues of equity and inclusion more broadly across their campus. On both Bryn Mawr's and Haverford's campuses, student partners have worked with the directors of access and disability services in a collaboration led by an experienced student partner, who organized and facilitated the partnerships and the regular meetings of student partners. This collaboration sparked more conversations on both campuses regarding accessibility in the classroom, and student partners in this collaboration worked to collect and document student and faculty experiences with access in the classroom. This work resulted in the creation of a living online resource for faculty and student partners to refer and contribute to.

A similar partnership developed at Ursinus College. Building on the success of their traditional faculty-student partnerships, the Teaching and Learning Institute at Ursinus College used funds awarded to them from the Arthur Vining Davis Foundations (through the Pennsylvania Consortium for the Liberal Arts) to create partnerships between student consultants and administrators or department chairs. As Diane Skorina, staff co-director of Ursinus' Teaching and Learning Institute, explained: "We reached out to administrators and chairs who we thought would most benefit from a student consultant's perspective on issues of inclusion and equity on campus, with the aim to bring student perspectives beyond the individual classroom to people who can be somewhat distanced from the student experience due to heavy administrative responsibilities" (personal communication). The most successful partnership, according to Skorina, was created between an experienced student consultant and the director of disability services. This yearlong partnership resulted in the development of a two-credit disability studies course that will be proposed to the faculty through Ursinus' academic council. The student, the director, and the Teaching and Learning Institute also brought a speaker to campus to give greater exposure to issues around inclusion and equity related to disability.

Where can you learn more about other colleges' and universities' approaches to developing pedagogical partnership programs?
The "History and Structure of the SaLT Program" resource details the context of the SaLT program and the way it is structured, and the "How the SaLT Program Got Started" resource narrates the evolution of the program. The "Five Stories of Developing Pedagogical Partnership Programs" resource offers greater detail about how partnership programs developed at McMaster University in Canada, University of Virginia in the United States, University of Queensland in Australia, Kaye Academic College of Education in Be'er Sheva, Israel, and Victoria University of Wellington in Aotearoa New Zealand. Finally, the "Selected Reading Lists" resource includes publications that describe other programs and projects.

YOUR TURN

Addressing key questions:

Who on your campus is interested and invested in the idea of partnership? Might you gather such individuals and groups together and address some or all of these questions:

What is the aim, scale, and time frame of the project or initiative?

What are the conceptual frameworks that will guide understandings and practices?

What are the emotions, attitudes, behaviors, and values of the participants in pedagogical partnership?

What is the meaning of partnership, or how will you define what it is that you hope and plan to do?

Looking to existing models:

Which aspects of the approaches taken at the following institutions might you want to build on or emulate?
- McMaster University in Canada
- University of Virginia in the United States
- University of Queensland in Australia
- Kaye Academic College of Education in Be'er Sheva, Israel
- Victoria University of Wellington in Aotearoa New Zealand

What other institutions might provide models for a pedagogical program that would work in your context?

Learning about student and faculty interests and goals:

What questions might you include in surveys or focus groups to learn why faculty and students might want to participate in a pedagogical partnership program?

Are there places on campus where partnership is already happening that you could connect to or build on?

What is missing on campus that partnership could help address?

Imagining:

How have SaLT and programs like it expanded beyond student-faculty partnerships?

In what other ways might existing partnership programs be further developed and expanded?

3 HOW CAN YOU SITUATE AND STRUCTURE THE PROGRAM, HOW DO YOU GET STARTED, AND HOW MIGHT YOU PLAN FOR SUSTAINABILITY?

Reflecting on the first of these questions, Susanna Throop, who was the second director of the Teaching and Learning Institute at Ursinus College following its founding by Meredith Goldsmith, explained that their partnership program is embedded within a larger office dedicated to advancing faculty development. She specifies that the program is "in Academic Affairs, but not in the Dean's Office, because we consider it very important for the program (and participation in it) to be separate from promotion and tenure decisions" (personal communication). About whom the program is designed to serve, she continues: "While the students are indeed learning from the experience of being partners, the program exists to support faculty, and the students are employees in the program. Their work is considered work; they are consultants for their faculty partners." The clarity with which the program at Ursinus is situated has likely contributed to its success. But not everyone makes the same choices, and there are many models of success.

In this chapter, we pose questions that help you explore how you might situate and structure a partnership program in your context, how you can get started with launching your program, and how might you plan for sustainability.

How can you situate and structure the program?

How you address this question will depend in part on how your institution functions, where the existing support structures are, and where the spaces exist that you might fill. Your answer will also depend on what you imagine and can co-create. As with any new creation, how it is situated, what it is called, who participates, and what new structures you create will all influence, in predictable and unpredictable ways, what emerges.

How will a pedagogical partnership program fit into the larger institution?

Most partnership programs are situated in teaching and learning centers and are one among a number of options for academic development for faculty, staff, and students. SaLT is somewhat anomalous in that it is not located in a teaching and learning center (because neither Bryn Mawr College nor Haverford College has one); it is a free-standing program linked by association and commitment with the Education Program, because that is where Alison holds her faculty appointment, and functioning in collaboration with the Provost's Offices on both campuses, out of which comes much faculty support. As we detail later in this chapter, there are numerous ways to launch a partnership program, but it is first important to think about where it will be located and what other programs or centers it will be connected to.

Who will the program director report to?
This will depend on how the institution and the center or department is structured. Most program directors report to provosts, deans, or vice presidents, but it is essential that such reporting be kept separate from the confidential nature of the partnership work. If your program is located within a teaching and learning center and the program director of the pedagogical partnership program is one staff member among many, that person will likely report to the center director. If you have a more distributed model, such as the one at Bryn Mawr and Haverford, the program director may end up reporting directly to a dean or provost. Consider the implications of any reporting structure, how long directors of the pedagogical partnership program will stay in the role, and who will run the program when the director is on leave, departs, or retires.

Where should the pedagogical partnership be located?
It is important to understand how "partnership" is conceptualized beyond your campus and also how it is already conceptualized on your campus,

if at all, so that you can be intentional and even strategic about situating a student-faculty pedagogical partnership program. Similarly, try to get a sense of whether there are any territorial issues you need to consider and what kinds of collaborations might be possible.

Many programs start out by looking both outward and inward for models or approaches to working in pedagogical partnership, as we discuss in the "Steps in Launching Pedagogical Partnership Programs" resource. For instance, a number of institutions have sent groups of faculty and administrators to visit campuses where pedagogical partnership programs are already in operation to meet and talk with various stakeholders, including students, faculty, program directors, deans, and provosts. These same institutions and others have done a kind of inventory of what already exists on their campuses. Kathryn Byrnes, Baldwin Program Director at the Center for Learning & Teaching at Bowdoin College, reflects on her initial steps toward developing a partnership program:

> This is my first year in this role and my plan is to gather students who already work in classes as learning assistants, teaching assistants, writing assistants, or graders to learn about their experiences with the "student partnership" models as they exist at Bowdoin. I think that a re-imagined preparation for students working with faculty and a more concrete and robust model of student partnerships could really benefit the learning and teaching happening at Bowdoin.
>
> —Kathryn Byrnes, Baldwin Program Director,
> Center for Learning & Teaching, Bowdoin College,
> United States (personal communication)

As Byrnes describes, it is worthwhile considering what other centers or programs on your own campus work closely or in collaboration with students, such as writing centers, peer-tutoring programs, or other mentoring programs. How do they conceptualize partnership? What are similarities and differences between what they are already doing, and therefore what is more familiar on campus, and what you want to do, which will likely be unfamiliar and potentially confused with existing centers, programs, and roles?

What relationship will the program have to other programs, such as those focused on academic support for students?
As suggested above, there may already exist on many campuses roles such as writing fellow, peer mentor, teaching assistant, and others that might or might not be understood as forms of partnership between faculty and students and that might or might not provide models you want to emulate. It is important to learn about what this range of programs and roles is and how both are understood on your campus. With that kind of understanding, you can identify the ways in which you want to seek links with existing programs and ways in which you might want to distinguish what the pedagogical partnership program aims to do. Such connecting and distinguishing is both a conceptual undertaking and a communicative one: you need to be clear on your own aims, and you need to strive for productive communication with others on campus so that you do not inadvertently stray into their "territory" or give the impression that you are trying to replace them.

Here is one way in which such overlap and distinguishing can play out. Some offices on campus might already engage in practices, such as gathering midterm feedback, that could overlap with those a pedagogical partnership program might take up. Find out how they go about engaging in their practices, who is involved, etc. It may be that this practice, enacted in one way in one office and in a different way in your partnership program, can offer faculty useful choices, such as between whether a staff member from an office of academic support or a student from your pedagogical partnership program gathers feedback. But understanding and communicating about these differences is essential to contributing to, rather than disrupting, systems that are striving to be functional.

What is pedagogical partnership for faculty?
As our various points of discussion thus far suggest, becoming a faculty partner entails reframing faculty-student relationships, rethinking who has what kind of relevant knowledge regarding teaching and learning,

sharing power, and emerging from what Lee Shulman (2004) called "pedagogical solitude" (as concept or practice) to collaborate with students in classroom- and curriculum-ed work. Faculty partners need to be confident and receptive, courageous and humble, clear and communicative, and willing to engage in deep, ongoing reflection and dialogue. These processes are alternately—and sometimes simultaneously—exhausting and invigorating.

In addition to how faculty members think about themselves as pedagogical partners, they will want to consider how others view partnership. What will colleagues make of the kinds of shifts we describe above? How will such partnership be situated in relation to other roles faculty have on campus, such as participation in committee work? How will pedagogical partnership be perceived at moments of review for reappointment or promotion?

In chapter 1 we discussed assumptions, expectations, and threshold concepts regarding pedagogical partnership, and how you conceptualize the role of faculty partner is bound up with all of these. You may want to return to that discussion to revisit questions of trust and surveillance and how the frame of pedagogical partnership makes it different from formal review. You may want to consider the possible misconceptions of pedagogical partnership—as one-way mentoring of a student, as being shadowed by a student, as working with a TA, as abnegating power and responsibility or losing control. It is easy to slip back into these kinds of assumptions that permeate so much of higher education.

The bottom line is that pedagogical partnership is what faculty make of it. While the same is true for student partners, students take on the role of pedagogical partner for compensation or course credit and so have a certain kind of responsibility to invest. Furthermore, regardless of the ways in which partnership works to support a sharing of power, the reality of most institutions of higher education is that faculty are in positions of greater institutional power, and so it is they who must initiate and sustain the sharing of power if it is indeed going to be shared. Finally, it is the faculty member's classroom, curriculum, or pedagogy that is the focus of the kind of partnership we focus on in this book. The extent to which faculty open up the literal spaces of their classrooms, the planning and revision spaces in relation to their curriculum, and what one student partner called their "pedagogical thinking space" (Ntem and Cook-Sather 2018, 87) will shape the extent to which the student partners can engage in the partnership.

Pedagogical partnerships are most successful if faculty adopt open and receptive attitudes such as this: "I've partnered with several students over the course of the past six years, and, in each partnership, the conversations I had with them were expansive, inspiring, and exciting. I often came away from my discussions with new ideas, or having revised some approach I had planned . . . [and this] felt like inspiration, arrived at together" and this: "I wanted constructive criticism to improve my teaching. So, I welcomed ALL comments to improve my pedagogical techniques" (Survey responses, Abbot and Cook-Sather, under review).

How do you ensure that pedagogical partnership is separate from faculty review and promotion?
While it is likely that the partnership program will collaborate in some ways with the offices of the provost, deans, vice-president for academic affairs, or other high-level administrative bodies on campus—around new faculty orientation, for instance—it is essential, as Susanna Throop, director of the Teaching and Learning Institute at Ursinus College, noted at the opening of this chapter, that the partnership program not be located in a program or office that oversees processes of review and reappointment. We agree strongly that the partnership program should be a space in which faculty and student partners can explore, experiment, be vulnerable, take risks, and otherwise engage in the messy, unpredictable, error-filled processes of learning and growing. If pedagogical partnership programs are linked to processes of review, reappointment, and promotion, faculty are less likely to engage in the ways described above.

In addition, we recommend that participation in the pedagogical partnership program be voluntary. Student partners may seek out this role as a campus job, as connected to a career aspiration or an informal but passionate interest, or as an area of intellectual as well as practical exploration. It is equally important that faculty partners choose to participate in pedagogical partnership for their own personal and professional reasons.

Finally, we feel strongly that all participants in the program—program directors, faculty partners, and student partners—ensure that the work student and faculty partners do is confidential, also not to be connected with processes of review for reappointment or promotion unless faculty partners choose to reference or include it. Some faculty partners request letters from their student partners for their review processes. It must be their choice to do so, however, not an option for student partners or program directors to reveal any of what unfolds in pedagogical partnerships without participant permission (and unless there are real concerns or dangers: see chapter 8).

How might you conceptualize, name, and compensate student and faculty partners' work?

Part of developing a pedagogical partnership program is figuring out what is already in place and what you need to pay attention to as you proceed. Another part is imagining what you want to develop and attending to how the choices you make will inform what follows.

How can you ensure that students are involved from the beginning in conceptualizing and developing the pedagogical partnership program?

As we discuss in our description in the "How the SaLT Program Got Started" resource, students were involved from the beginning in conceptualizing the program, recommending who should participate in the launch, naming the program, and naming their role (see also Cook-Sather 2018a). To be consistent with the spirit of this work, it is important to consider how students can be at the table, alongside faculty and program directors, and perhaps others, from the beginning.

We have already mentioned other programs' approaches to including students as partners in conceptualizing and launching programs. We noted, for instance, that Co-create UVA was founded in 2014 as a partnership between student-led organization ReinventED Lab and the Center for Teaching Excellence at the University of Virginia. The Student

Partners Program at McMaster University was initially developed via a collaboration between staff and faculty at the MacPherson Institute and students in the Arts & Science program on campus. Another example of co-creation from the outset is the efforts of Kaye Academic College of Education in Be'er Sheva, Israel, where the faculty and administrative leaders of the initiative to launch a pedagogical partnership program are including student participants and collaborators from the beginning.

There are many ways to ensure that students are active partners from the outset. Conducting focus groups to gather a wide variety of perspectives, ensuring that there are positions for students on advisory or steering committees, and creating new roles, such as the postbaccalaureate fellow (see the "Creating Post-Bac Fellow Positions to Support the Development of Pedagogical Partnership Programs" resource), are just a few possibilities. Without these intentional efforts, students might not be present at all or might be relegated to roles from which they might have input but do not have any real agency or influence as the program develops.

What options should you consider for compensating student partners?
Student partners in most pedagogical partnership programs are compensated in one of three ways. Meredith Goldsmith and Susanna Throop, who have both served as directors of Ursinus College's student-faculty pedagogical partnership program, suggest that program directors ask themselves this question: Do I consider the work that student partners are doing primarily labor or learning? It is, of course, both, but the point is to clarify for yourself how you situate partnerships within the structures of your institution. At Berea College, for instance, student labor positions are part of the academic program for accreditation purposes and are clearly aligned with academics in many cases, so such a question needs to be addressed differently from how it might be addressed in institutions where student work and student academic pursuits are more clearly distinguished.

One way to compensate student partners is through situating the position as a campus job with hourly pay. Like other jobs on campus, the student partner position can be advertised through the student employment office. In the SaLT program, we generally use this approach, paying students for every hour they spend observing their faculty partners' class sessions, typing up their observation notes, meeting weekly with their faculty partners, working with their faculty partners and other students to develop or revise courses, and meeting weekly with Alison and other student partners. This approach may be of particular benefit to students who need to work:

> Instead of having lower-income undergraduates serve as personal maids for their peers, colleges could provide on-campus jobs that foster skill acquisition, contact with faculty and administrators, and opportunities for enrichment. Bryn Mawr and Haverford Colleges, for example, host the Students as Learners and Teachers (SaLT) program, where students are paid to collaborate with faculty as "pedagogical" partners to enhance innovative teaching at the colleges. (Jack 2019, 177)

Ursinus, Reed, Oberlin, Lewis & Clark, and Lafayette Colleges and McMaster University have also taken this approach. As Susanna Throop, director of Ursinus College's partnership program, explains: "The move to hourly pay [for the work student partners do] was deliberate for us, and I think this is another way in which institutional culture gets reflected in such programs" (personal communication). At McMaster University, they had wanted to consider a stipend or scholarship model (instead of or in addition to pay), but it proved impossible within their institutional structures. This example illustrates once again that it is important to consider not only how institutional practices and policies might shape what is doable but also how your particular values and commitments intersect with those.

A second way to compensate student partners for their time is to situate the work in the academic arena. One option here is to offer a quarter- or half-credit course in which student partners enroll. Some program directors, such as Floyd Cheung at Smith College, have proposed new courses to be approved by the appropriate faculty and administrative body (see the "Sample Student Partners Course Syllabus" resource for a version of the syllabus Alison designed for Floyd and the student partners at Smith College). Another option is to offer the possibility of an independent study supervised by the director of the partnership program, which may not need to go through a formal course approval process. In these cases, students not only do all of the work described above but also read selected texts and engage in reflective and analytical writing. Some student partners in the SaLT program have chosen the option of completing an independent study, either for a grade or for credit/no credit. Student partners at Smith College complete a 2-credit course taken for an S (Satisfactory) or U (Unsatisfactory) (a "normal" course at Smith carries 4 credits), and student partners at Berea College complete a quarter-credit course (which corresponds to a 1-credit course in a 4-credit system).

A third way to compensate student partners is through scholarships. Two benefits of this approach are that they shift the dynamic between student partners and program directors out of the employee/employer dynamic and that, in some institutions, such scholarships are exempt from taxes. Victoria University of Wellington in Aotearoa New Zealand is developing this model as they expand their approaches to pedagogical partnership. In their program, students' participation is honored through scholarships—rather than by paying them as employees—so that they retain their identities as students.

How student partners are compensated will situate them in relation to other student positions on campus, such as TAs, so it is worth considering, if you have the flexibility, which model makes most sense for students. Furthermore, some students might also have restrictions connected to paid work—some may need to spend their time in paid positions for financial reasons, but others (e.g., some students with disabilities on McMaster's campus) have restrictions about how many hours they can spend in paid positions while receiving particular grants to support their education. Colleagues on campuses such as McMaster's have tried to figure out ways to be flexible, while still ensuring equitable compensation.

Also, consider which approach might fit in with, complement, or be in tension with other student positions on campus. Many student partners spend a good deal of time explaining that they are not TAs. For some this may just be a matter of title, but for others it might be a matter of status or credential. For these reasons, whether you conceptualize student partners' work as labor or learning or both and what you call the pedagogical partnership program and the position of student and faculty partner within it (e.g., student consultant, student as change agent, student and faculty partners), as discussed below and in the "Choosing Names for Partnership Programs and Participants" resource, are questions that warrant deliberation.

An additional consideration regarding compensating student partners is that many students need to have predictable and reliable work hours. Some partnerships might take more time than others. Program directors need to ensure that student partners are guaranteed a minimum number of hours and that the program makes an effort to find more work for consultants if their partnerships are not reaching that minimum.

What options should you consider for compensating faculty partners?
The issue of how to compensate faculty for their participation raises a different set of questions from those to consider around student partner compensation. While faculty partners must consider how to integrate partnership into their work and their schedules, they do not, like student partners, take on an entirely new position when they participate in partnerships focused on classroom practice or curricular design and redesign. At Bryn Mawr and Haverford Colleges, only new faculty who simultaneously participate in weekly seminars and pedagogical partnerships with students are compensated (with a reduced teaching load in their first year). Faculty who participate at other points in their careers are not compensated financially. Some institutions take up the stance that it is the responsibility of faculty members to develop their pedagogical and curricular approaches, and so additional compensation is inappropriate.

Other institutions compensate faculty for participating in pedagogical partnerships either through course development grants or other kinds of fellowship schemes, and indeed, at Bryn Mawr and Haverford Colleges, faculty can combine grants for curricular innovation, for instance, with collaboration with a student partner. At Berea College, faculty members participate in the program as members of a grant-funded community of practice that complements their work with their individual student partners. Faculty participants meet with each other once every three weeks or so for an hour to discuss their experiences in the program. Over the course of three semesters, faculty participants at Berea have unanimously found these faculty meetings very beneficial, deepening the developmental opportunities of the program, as this extensive set of responses, provided by Leslie Ortquist-Ahrens, the director of Berea's partnership program, with permission of the faculty, documents:

> "I really appreciated getting feedback from other faculty and hearing how they worked with their partners, and also hearing a bit more about how other people run their classes in general (how they get feedback on the effectiveness of their teaching, different kinds of activities to engage students, etc.). This was a good skill-sharing opportunity [especially for me as a new faculty member]."
>
> —Lex Lancaster, Art History

> "I enjoyed the sense of shared purpose and community in these meetings. As a veteran in partnership, I think that I probably didn't 'need' these meetings in the way that a novice participant would. Had I been new to the program, I would have found them a critical space for support and encouragement."
>
> —Anne Bruder, English

> "I had to miss about half the sessions [due to a conflict with department meetings]. Some content was nice and useful but the true benefit to me was the reminder that this is not just me and my partner. I liked that the meetings that I was able to attend forced me to engage in reflection that I would otherwise not have engaged in."
>
> —Volker Grzimek, Economics

"I loved attending the meetings because hearing others share made me dig in even deeper and commit even further. There were faculty partners who truly valued and listened to their student mentors [*this participant always referred to her partner as her "mentor"*], and from them I drew inspiration, taking away ideas of ways to communicate and work with my own mentor. There were other faculty who seemed to not trust or value their mentors as much as I did mine, and they were helpful, too, because they forced me into this entire interior monologue where I railed against their attitudes and defended the program against their skepticism. It's funny, but whenever you're forced into one of those imaginary arguments, in your head alone, because you're too polite to engage for real, it forces you to take a firmer stance. So thanks are due to the non-believers, right?"

—Amanda Peach, Library

"I attended all the faculty meetings. It was great to hear about others' experiences, and bounce ideas around. I got some excellent ideas that I'm going to try in my classroom. I also really enjoyed the activity where we had to stand in different places in the room based on our response to a question. I'm going to use that. Thanks for that!"

—Beth Feagan, General Education

"The meetings allowed us to see the spectrum of how the partnerships have developed between students and faculty. I was able to take away a better understanding of how feedback helps me in the classroom. I also was exposed to the possibility of having the students take a more active role in the direction the course could take. I will consider this in upcoming classes."

—Ric Hale, Accounting

While faculty participants at Berea receive a small stipend for a semester-long commitment, the intrinsic motivation that brings them to the work constitutes the major incentive, and many are surprised at the end of the term to receive the stipend, despite the fact that the call for participation included it as a benefit of participation. The program at Berea is conceived as much as a formal component of the overarching faculty development program through their Center for Teaching and Learning as it is a program for offering growth opportunities for students.

As you are conceptualizing and planning for your program, discuss these questions explicitly: How can you ensure that students are involved from the beginning in conceptualizing and developing the pedagogical partnership program? What options should you consider for compensating student partners? What options should you consider for compensating faculty partners? Remember that whatever choice you make initially may set a precedent or might be framed as a pilot approach that will later be folded into existing structures or serve to create a new structure.

What might you call what you want to do?

Naming is a form of bringing into being. Van Manen, McClelland, and Plihal (2007) have written about this phenomenon in relation to naming in teacher-student relationships. In reflecting on the power of naming, they evoke the semiotic analyses of Derrida and Gusdorf: "What occurs when one gives a name? asks Derrida (1995). What does one give? One does not offer a thing. One delivers nothing. And yet something comes to be" (85). What "comes to be" is the perception of a presence and the recognition of a relationship that were not there previously. That is why, van Manen et al. (2007) contend, "Gusdorf (1965) suggested that 'to name is to call into existence' (p. 38)" (85).

What you call your program, practice, and participants will make a difference in how they are received and experienced. The name you choose should reflect your understanding of what you are doing and your commitment in doing it. Even the term "partnership" itself, or the phrase "students as partners," can be problematic for some (Cook-Sather et al. 2018). For instance, in Aotearoa New Zealand, the term "partnership" signals for many Māori the failed promise of a treaty between the British Crown and the indigenous population of the country, so while the principles that underlie partnership—respect, reciprocity, and shared responsibility—resonate with Māori values in teaching and learning, the term "partnership" is vexed. (See Cook-Sather 2018c and Berryman, Bourke, and Cook-Sather, in preparation, for discussions of this.) Every country and context will have its own particular associations with terms and names.

We suggested in chapter 2 that, as you explore various approaches to and models of pedagogical partnership you might want to embrace and enact, you will want to ask yourself a variety of questions about what you understand partnership to mean: what the aim, scale, and time frame of the project or initiative might be; what conceptual framing of partnership you are assuming or explicitly adopting; and what the emotions, attitudes, behaviors, and values of the participants in pedagogical partnership are and could be (Healey and Healey 2018). Connected to these questions, you may also want to ask yourself: What language should we use to describe the partnership practices, program, and participants we want to support?

What language should you use to describe the partnership practices you want to support?
The language you use to describe partnership approaches can either affirm or undermine the ethic of reciprocity (Cook-Sather and Felten 2017a) that informs what we argue pedagogical partnership should be. Cook-Sather, Bovill, and Felten (2014, 136) caution: "Our often unconscious use of certain terms can send unintended but unfortunate messages to students and faculty alike about what the work is about." Think about the language you use from the very first conceptualization stages. For instance, consider this: You are working to articulate your reasons for wanting to start a pedagogical partnership program. As you list your reasons, "if you talk about 'giving students voice' and 'using' students as consultants, you may convey a message that students have voice only when . . . faculty bestow it upon them and that students are a means to an end" (Cook-Sather, Bovill, and Felten 2014, 136).

You might also want to consider the ableist assumptions behind some of the language of pedagogical partnership. As one former student partner in the SaLT program, Sasha Mathrani, noted in a personal communication: "I have realized that a lot of language about empowerment can be ableist—being 'seen' or 'heard,' for example." Several faculty members quoted throughout this guide unintentionally use these metaphors that potentially reinforce racist and ableist assumptions about knowledge: not-knowing as darkness and blindness; knowledge as lightness, seeing. While phrases such as "following blindly" or "I was blind to it" are not intended to be derogatory, they nevertheless have this effect (see Vidali 2010).

Such often-unintentional uses of language can not only be harmful to people but can also undermine the goals of partnership, reinforcing existing hierarchical, unequal, and discriminatory dynamics. In contrast, phrases such as "seeking student perspectives on questions of teaching and learning" or "inviting students to consult on approaches to pedagogical practice" or "collaborating with students to design courses" still recognize that faculty have more power and agency than students in some arenas of higher education, since faculty are doing the seeking, the inviting, and often the grading, but at least the intention is to work in partnership (Cook-Sather, Bovill, and Felten 2014, 136). Likewise, it's important to be careful about the terms used to signal perception and knowledge.

What language and ways of naming programs, practices, and people in your institutions already exist, and what do they convey about those entities? In some cases, the language of student-faculty partnership "aligns with institutional mission and values, allowing you to frame your work as returning to the fundamental goals of your department or university" (Cook-Sather, Bovill, and Felten 2014, 20). In other cases, you might want to work intentionally against traditional norms and practices.

What do you want to capture and convey in the name of your program?
In the "History and Structure of the SaLT Program" resource and the "How the SaLT Program Got Started" resource we offer different versions of the story of how the SaLT program got its name—through a discussion among students, faculty, and administrators who launched the program. Each of the participants in that conversation brought a different identity, set of experiences, and perspective to the decision-making process. Each

had a different take on what would feel most appropriate to students who would take on the role and students who would experience student partners working with faculty. Each had a different take on how different names would or would not resonate on campus—strike the right balance between affirming values and practices already in place and expanding into a new practice. And each had a different sense of what might be comprehensible beyond campus—to prospective employers and others. In choosing "Students as Learners and Teachers," this group wanted to link two roles that are typically divided and distinguished in a way that would not seem too aggressive or threatening within the institution but would also signal to the wider world that we were challenging traditional roles. In the "Choosing Names for Partnership Programs and Participants" resource, we discuss other choices that programs have made.

What name should you choose for faculty and student partners? Just as it is important to consider how you name your program, it is important to consider what to call faculty and student partners. For reasons of hierarchy and power, as well as the nature of the positions that faculty members keep and that students take up through pedagogical partnership, student partners may need a different level of naming from their faculty partners.

In the SaLT program, faculty partners must certainly consider and cross the thresholds we discussed in chapter 1, but their basic position as faculty does not change. They are still the ones primarily and ultimately responsible for the pedagogical and curricular approaches they take, even if they have co-created those with student partners, and the focus of their partnerships is their own pedagogical and curricular approaches. The focus for student partners is also their faculty partners' pedagogical and curricular approaches, not their own practice as learners, although those are certainly affected by pedagogical partnership, as we discuss in the "Outcomes of Pedagogical Partnership Work" resource. Furthermore, they take on a new position, in addition to their role as student. These differences distinguish their participation in pedagogical partnership work from that of their faculty partners.

This is the case for virtually all the pedagogical partnership programs of which we are aware that focus on pedagogy and curriculum. If this is the way pedagogical partnership is likely to look in your context, then "faculty partner" may suffice as a name for the faculty role, or you may want to develop a name that references either the focus of the partnership work or the school identity. As Sophia Abbot, the creator and coordinator of the pedagogical partnership program at Trinity University, explains: "In Tigers as Partners (TaP), all participants are 'Tiger Partners' but students also hold the title of 'TaP student consultant' to legitimize their work for the external world" (personal communication).

Because of the shift in position and focus as well as role that student partners make in pedagogical partnership, we encourage you to consider how you want to conceptualize and name that shift. Language that informs such conceptualizations includes students as co-creators, consultants, partners, and change agents. All of these signal that students "become full participants in the design of teaching approaches, courses and curricula" (Bovill, Cook-Sather, and Felten 2011, 133), but they foreground different terms for that participation, some of which become names of programs and some of which become the terms used to define the student partner role.

What you choose to call student partners will depend on:
- what other positions exist for students from which you wish to distinguish this position (e.g., TA, peer mentor, research assistant);
- which ongoing debates regarding culture and practice within higher education are relevant to your context (e.g., students as consumers or customers);
- what the name will signal within your context (the intended—and unintended—effect the name might have for student partners themselves, for students who are not partners, and for faculty and staff within the culture of your institution); and
- what the name will signal beyond your context—how those outside that culture (e.g., prospective employers, readers of published works) will understand it.

As we did to decide on the name for student partners in the SaLT program, you might want to convene a group of people who are interested in developing a pedagogical partnership program on your campus and discuss what name they all think would best capture the spirit of what you want to do, fit well with campus culture, and be comprehensible to relevant constituencies (e.g., prospective employers) beyond campus. The "Choosing Names for Partnership Programs and Participants" resource also includes a discussion of some of the most common names for students: student consultants, student partners, and students as change agents.

What might descriptions of partnership opportunities and positions include?

Colleges and universities that have developed pedagogical partnership programs include descriptions of the goals of the program and options for participation on their websites. For instance, Reed College's website explains: "Interested faculty members are paired with a student with whom they work to improve aspects of their teaching in one of their courses. This partnership provides an opportunity for faculty to reflect on their pedagogy, receive feedback from a student not in their course, and work collaboratively to meet teaching goals. Student consultants observe a class throughout a semester, take detailed notes during class, and meet weekly with their faculty partner to communicate their candid and confidential observations."

From such descriptions, faculty and students can infer what will be involved in participation. In the case of the SaLT program and others like it, it is only the student partner who assumes a newly defined institutional position, even as both student and faculty partners need to rethink their roles. Therefore, we include a description of the student partner position and application process for the SaLT program on our website. See the "Advertising Student Partner Positions" resource for a description of the SaLT student consultant position and the position description that Sophia Abbot developed for the Tigers as Partners program at Trinity University.

For programs such as SaLT, application processes are not intended to serve gatekeeping functions. Rather, they are intended to initiate the reflective process that is essential to the role of student partner. The questions on the SaLT application—"Why do you want to be a Student Consultant?" and "What do you think would make you an effective Student Consultant?"—elicit thoughtful responses from applicants that initiate or deepen conscious, empathetic, helpfully critical awareness, which signals essential qualities for any student partner. (See the "SaLT Program Student Consultant Application Form" resource for full application form.) Students write things like this on their applications:

> I'm interested in becoming a Student Consultant because I'm intrigued by the idea of student as teacher and teacher as learner. I believe students should not be limited in their role as students. As active learners, students can be useful and support their teachers in order to help teachers see and think from different angles. Similarly, teachers are also students. Facing every new student, teachers make changes to their strategies along the way while learning more and more about their students. (Student partner, excerpt from application to SaLT program)

As you develop your pedagogical partnership program, consider how you want to conceptualize faculty and student positions, whether each needs a position description or just the student partner, and where to locate both program and position descriptions. Such position descriptions are related to but distinct from expanded descriptions and discussions of roles and responsibilities of student and faculty partners, which we detail in chapters 4, 5, 6, and 7.

How do you get your program started?

Different programs take different approaches to getting started. Consider what the goal of the partnership program is and from what level of the institution the impetus for it will come. As Takayama, Kaplan, and Cook-Sather (2017) argue in "Advancing Diversity and Inclusion through Strategic Multi-Level Leadership," there are many ways to develop initiatives, including engaging in university-wide leadership efforts (the macro level); interactions and initiatives within the school, college, or department (the meso level); and efforts by individual instructors and activists (the micro level). In the "How the SaLT Program Got Started" resource and in the "History and Structure of the SaLT Program" resource, we offer the history of our own launch. In the "Steps in Launching Pedagogical Partnership Programs" resource, we offer an overall set of steps you might consider taking that draws on examples of programs that were launched at a variety of other institutions. We recommend taking at least the following steps when preparing to launch a pedagogical partnership program:

1. Get a sense of what is happening elsewhere within and beyond your campus walls.
2. Create forums for dialogue and exploration among campus stakeholders.
3. Invite a pilot cohort of faculty and students.
4. Bring in people with experience to help guide the launch and to share experiences and advice.
5. Develop structures to support faculty and student participants.

In relation to these, you will want to consider scale and networks. "Scaling up" such work is as great a challenge as developing partnerships in the first place. There are various ways to think about scale, which we discuss in the section on sustainability below.

1. Get a sense of what is happening elsewhere within and beyond your campus walls

A first step to take is to try to get a sense of what is happening elsewhere within and beyond your campus walls in relation to partnership. If your institution has the resources, you might visit other campuses, but certainly contact people who have already undertaken the launch of pedagogical partnership programs. For instance, when Reed College was considering how to structure its soon-to-be created teaching and learning center, they sent a group of faculty and administrators to visit programs around the country. Every institution for which Alison has ended up serving as a consultant sent out preliminary inquiries regarding how to conceptualize and develop such a program.

2. Create forums for dialogue and exploration among campus stakeholders

A good way to foster such dialogue is to create a reading group or teaching circle so campus stakeholders can explore the concept and practices of pedagogical partnership before trying to put them into practice. Several campuses have used *Engaging Students as Partners in Learning and Teaching: A Guide for Faculty* (Cook-Sather, Bovill, and Felten 2014). After campus stakeholders have discussed ideas, you might have a book talk. This is the approach the Sherrerd Center for Teaching and Learning at Smith College in Massachusetts took.

3. Invite applications for a pilot cohort of faculty and students

We recommend starting small, inviting a hand-selected group of students and faculty who are established, confident, receptive, collaborative, and willing to experiment; they will increase the likelihood of success and model engagement for student and faculty colleagues. You may want to take into consideration how to include a range of perspectives and identities. For instance, Berea College's pilot included new as well as senior faculty members; faculty from different disciplinary divisions; faculty from historically underrepresented groups, etc.

4. Bring in people with experience to help guide the launch and to share experiences and advice

A fourth step is bringing people to campus who have expertise or experience in launching pedagogical partnership programs. Because such programs are still relatively unusual, students, faculty, and others might have trouble imagining what pedagogical partnership is, and hearing from people who have engaged in and facilitated partnership can both offer examples and reassure people. Florida Gulf Coast University and numerous other institutions have invited Alison to offer an orientation to faculty and student participants who were selected to launch their pilot pedagogical partnership programs, and both Alison and Melanie visited Muhlenberg College as they were considering developing a partnership program.

5. Develop structures to support faculty and student participants
A final step is developing structures to support faculty and student participants. Some such structures can be developed in advance, and others need to evolve in response to participant need and as appropriate for the institutional context. Alison designed a credit-bearing course for student partners and developed and facilitated a two-day summer institute for faculty participants at Smith College. (See the "Summer Institute for Faculty Participants in Pedagogical Partnership" resource). Berea College developed a quarter-credit course (equivalent to a 1-credit course elsewhere) that would combine learning about student-faculty partnerships, about teaching and learning, and about conducting observations and providing feedback. They also created a post-bac fellow position, which we discuss in the next section, "What [temporary] positions might you create to help launch or develop a partnership program?", in the "Creating Post-Bac Fellow Positions to Support the Development of Pedagogical Partnership Programs" resource, and in the "Three Stages of Backward Design for Creating Post-Baccalaureate Pathways to Educational Development" resource.

See the "Steps in Launching Pedagogical Partnership Programs" resource for more detail on how each of the institutions mentioned above developed its partnership program.

What [temporary] positions might you create to help launch or develop a partnership program?

In keeping with the spirit of collaboration, redefining of roles, and sharing responsibility, Alison has encouraged several institutions to create full-time, post-baccalaureate fellow positions for recent graduates who have experience as student partners and are uniquely positioned to support the launch and development of pedagogical partnership programs at their own or other institutions. Such positions are helpful to program directors who do not have the bandwidth to start or sustain the program entirely on their own and who need or want a partner who knows what this work is like from the inside. Some such positions have been created with funding from the Mellon Foundation; others have found support from other internal or external sources. Positions like that of post-bac fellow are ideal for confident, independent, flexible, and adaptable recent graduates. Table 1 shows the range of institutions that have created such positions and their different goals in doing so.

We put the term "temporary" in brackets because some institutions may have funding to support only a year or two of such a position in order to get the pedagogical partnership program launched. In other contexts, while such a position might be inhabited by a particular person temporarily, it can become a permanent fixture of the university, as is the case at Trinity University. If the latter approach is your goal, a question to consider is: How might a post-bac fellow position be conceptualized as a permanent rotating position for continued leadership and input from recent graduates?

In keeping with our previous discussions of naming, it is worth considering what you call this position. Several institutions call it Post-baccalaureate Fellow since the term "fellow" is familiar in higher education. As we note below and discuss in detail in the "Creating Post-Bac Fellow Positions to Support the Development of Pedagogical Partnership Programs" resource, both the experience of the person holding the position and the perceptions of others trying to make sense of it are enhanced by a clear definition of the responsibilities attached to such a position.

In the "Creating Post-Bac Fellow Positions to Support the Development of Pedagogical Partnership Programs" resource, we offer detailed recommendations for how program directors and potential post-bac fellows can identify the qualities and qualifications recent graduates need to flourish in the role. We also outline challenges post-bac fellows may experience as they transition between roles or institutions, and we share guidance for supervisors who will be working closely with new colleagues in this unusual role. The recommendations in this resource are based on our own experiences and perspectives and are also informed by input from Sophia Abbot, post-bac fellow at Trinity University; Leslie Ortquist-Ahrens, director of the Center for Teaching and Learning and director of faculty development at Berea College; and Khadijah Seay, Andrew W. Mellon post-baccalaureate fellow for Student-Faculty Partnerships Program at Berea College.

SITUATING, STRUCTURING, AND SUSTAINING THE PROGRAM | 83

Table 1. A range of institutions that have created post-bac fellow positions

Name of Institution	Trinity University	Berea College	T.A. Marryshow Community College	Massey University	University of Missouri	Lahore University
Kind of institution	Private, liberal arts college	Tuition-free, liberal arts work college	Open access community college	Large, public, pre-professional university	Public, land-grant research university	Private university
Location	San Antonio, Texas, United States	Berea, Kentucky, United States	Grenada, West Indies	Palmerston North, Aotearoa New Zealand	Columbia, Missouri, United States	Lahore, Punjab, Pakistan
Purpose of position	To bring pedagogical partnerships into their existing Collaborative for Learning and Teaching	To support the further development of a partnership program that had been piloted the year before the post-bac fellow arrived	To help design and develop the first Educational Development Unit based on a strong pedagogical partnership approach	To expand upon pedagogical partnership work under way through informal and formal approaches	To help design and develop a pedagogical partnership program as part of the first teaching and learning center	To design a partnership program

As with all partnership work, much will depend on context, purpose, and participants. We encourage program directors to use the backwards design template Melanie created to help people think through what they are looking for in a possible post-bac fellow role and what will be needed to support such a person. We include that template in the "Three Stages of Backward Design for Creating Post-Baccalaureate Pathways to Educational Development" resource.

How do you plan for sustainability?

It can be difficult to think about sustainability when your initial focus is on how to introduce a program that might seem to challenge well-established premises and practices. All your attention may be trained on finding a place and way to get started. However, considering from the outset how the program might be sustained over time and considering how individual partners sustain their work within any given semester will make your program more likely to succeed in the short and the long term.

Sometimes it works well to establish institutional commitments that structure partnership into the institution from the conceptualization and early stages. Linking or situating the program in an established department or center, or gathering it under an umbrella that covers a wider set of programs with similar spirit, can situate—or limit—what you are trying to do with partnership. Other times the most effective way to move toward sustainability is to create enough interest and document enough positive outcomes that others in the community, particularly faculty and administrators, seek to integrate the program into the ongoing work of the institution.

One question for all participants—program directors, student partners, and faculty partners—to think about regarding sustainability is size. It is typically easier for those involved and more impressive for those observing if the program starts small and grows organically and responsively. Kelly Matthews of the University of Queensland, Australia, poses the question this way:

> How many partnerships can be effectively facilitated? This may seem an odd challenge to someone just starting a program, but a highly successful program might have a lot of faculty who want to be involved and then there are the issues of resources. Can the director effectively manage the program? Are there enough financial resources? One may need to develop a hierarchy—junior folks privileged over senior, those who have not done the program previously privileged over those who have. (personal communication)

Steve Volk, founding director of Oberlin College's pedagogical partnership program, takes a different angle, arguing that small numbers can create powerful outcomes (see the "Outcomes of Pedagogical Partnership Work" resource for his full discussion). The size of your program will depend on institutional and individual commitment, resources, and goals.

Linked to considerations such as size are, once again, origins and institutional structures. If your program launches with grant support, how will it be sustained after the grant is finished? It is important to begin planning early for such a transition. As you think about sustainability generally, how can you begin to structure in forward-thinking dimensions, especially those that might help institutions evolve to be more congruent with partnership practices. As Beth Marquis, Associate Director (Research) of the Paul R. MacPherson Institute for Leadership, Innovation and Excellence in Teaching, noted: "We recently modified our project selection criteria, and included 'engaging new people in the program' and 'contributing to key departmental/institutional priorities' as desirable, but not required, features" (personal communication).

There are various ways to think about scale, including: involving a meaningful number of students and faculty in the work each year (i.e., impact measured by numbers of direct participants); having a small number of partnerships focus on informing the teaching and learning of a meaningful number of faculty and students (i.e., impact intentionally focused on a broader scale); or iteratively doing this work over multiple years so that the results accrue over time (see also Cook-Sather 2020, in press).

There are also various considerations for differently positioned participants in pedagogical partnership programs. We discuss these below.

What can program directors do to work toward institutional sustainability?

At Bryn Mawr and Haverford, SaLT started out as a grant-funded pilot project designed to respond to the expressed interest of a handful of faculty members in making their classrooms more inclusive of and responsive to a diversity of students. Because of the benefits that accrued to these faculty members and with additional grant support, the program expanded to support a larger number of faculty focused on a wider range of issues (i.e., not only creating culturally responsive classrooms but also team teaching, integrating technology into teaching, and more). The positive feedback from participating faculty inspired the provosts at both Bryn Mawr and Haverford Colleges to dedicate the resources to support Alison in committing half of her time to running the SaLT program and associated pedagogy seminars and to offer the opportunity of participation in SaLT to every incoming, continuing faculty member at both colleges in exchange for a reduced teaching load in their first year. This is a significant institutional commitment. While not every incoming faculty member chooses or is able (for scheduling reasons) to participate, the institutional commitment sends a strong message to incoming faculty, who regularly comment on how impressed they are with the institutions' dedication to supporting teaching in this way.

Furthermore, since there is an operating budget for SaLT that supports student consultants in working with any faculty member at any point in their career, the program can be responsive to faculty and staff interests and accommodate new needs that arise. For instance, as we mentioned previously, under the leadership of an experienced student partner, the SaLT program piloted a collaboration with the access services offices on both Bryn Mawr's and Haverford's campuses to assist them in thinking about how to support the increasing diversity of students who attend the colleges and their need for academic and other forms of support.

In the "Working toward Programmatic Sustainability" resource, we share approaches that program directors at various institutions have taken to planning for programmatic sustainability.

What can faculty partners do to work toward institutional sustainability?

Within their own institutions, faculty partners can share the outcomes of their pedagogical partnership work with faculty colleagues, department chairs, and administrators, thereby advocating for the continuation or expansion of the partnership program. At Bryn Mawr and Haverford Colleges, faculty enthusiasm and requests for additional opportunities to partner with students and be in dialogue with one another contributed to the expansion and institutionalization of SaLT and the inclusion of SaLT in grant proposals to outside funders.

Faculty partners who have participated in pedagogical partnership and subsequently assume leadership roles, such as chairs of departments, can play a critical role in advocating for other faculty members and ensuring that they have the opportunity to participate in pedagogical partnership. For instance, department chairs can encourage faculty who are on visiting appointments at a college to negotiate for the opportunity to work in a pedagogical partnership as part of their hiring package. It is in the institution's best interest to consider ways of supporting interim faculty members, who have extensive contact with students but little time to learn the culture and practices of the institution.

Extending their reach beyond their institutions, faculty can share their experiences with colleagues through writing about their partnership work. By doing so they contribute to both informal and scholarly conversations about pedagogical partnership work, helping that work not only be sustained but also to spread. Publishing reflective essays in venues such as *Teaching and Learning Together in Higher Education* and the *International Journal for Students as Partners* contributes to the growing conversation about pedagogical partnership within educational development, and publications in journals in faculty members' own fields (e.g.,

Lillehaugen et al. 2014; Rose and Taylor 2016) introduces the notion of partnership into other disciplines.

What can student partners do to work toward institutional sustainability?

Student partners can also play a vital role in sustaining and spreading the spirit and practices of pedagogical partnership work. They can encourage other students to apply and participate as student partners, they can share the powerful impact of their experience with those in positions such as dean, provost, president, and institutional researcher, and they can share their experiences with prospective students.

Students can also take the work of pedagogical partnership beyond the program. With the confidence and eloquence they develop through participating in pedagogical partnership, they can engage more actively in conferences in their own disciplines (see Mathrani 2018, for a discussion of this point), and they can participate in educational development conferences (see Ntem 2017). For instance, with support from an Arthur Vining Davis Foundations grant, four student partners in the SaLT program went to an annual meeting of the Association of American Colleges and Universities, attended multiple sessions, then came back to Bryn Mawr and Haverford Colleges and designed a workshop for faculty members focused on developing more inclusive and responsive practices. During that workshop, faculty not only gathered new ideas and expanded upon existing strategies for their own classrooms and departments, they generated new ideas for extending and expanding pedagogical partnership options at the colleges.

Like faculty partners, student partners can contribute to wider conversations about and scholarship on pedagogical partnership. Presenting at conferences, serving as consultants for other institutions starting up pedagogical partnership programs, and writing reflective essays, scholarly articles, and this book are all examples of student partners taking an active role in sustaining and spreading practices, understandings, and possibilities of pedagogical partnership work.

What helps participants sustain this work as it is unfolding?
For the program directors, faculty partners, and student partners involved in pedagogical partnership work, it is important to think about sustainability as the work is unfolding. We explore in detail in chapter 4 ways of facilitating and supporting partnership, and as we suggest in that chapter how you conceptualize facilitation of pedagogical partnership—how you frame it, why affirmation is so important, and what some useful approaches to conceptualizing feedback might be—will contribute not only to the support but also to the sustaining of the work. Similarly, being clear on and discussing who has what roles and responsibilities in pedagogical partnership can help lay a strong foundation to begin the partnership work as well as help make it sustainable over time. Finally, keeping a focus of partnership work on developing relationships built on listening and deep engagement can help energize participants and ensure ongoing communication.

There are some particular strategies that program directors can use to support faculty and student partners and thereby contribute to sustainability as partnerships are unfolding. As we discuss in detail in chapter 5, program directors can make clear that they are available for consultation, provide guidelines and feedback mechanisms, and make space in the regular meetings of student partners to explore challenging issues as well as celebrate accomplishments. Student partners can also encourage, support, and affirm one another in these meetings and in confidential discussions outside the meetings. Other student partners are the only ones who will understand the work and the only ones with whom program directors can speak, since pedagogical partnership work is confidential.

The final way to think about sustainability is to think about approaching pedagogical partnership work at every stage with clarity and candor. As we discuss in chapter 8, it is important to address head on the logistical and emotional challenges pedagogical partnership can present. Taking an organized but flexible attitude and approach to scheduling, discussing the complexities that can emerge regarding the diversity of identities and roles of participants, and supporting all participants in managing the emotional labor involved in partnership can go a long way toward ensuring sustainability for everyone involved.

YOUR TURN

Thinking about structure:

Might you convene groups of campus stakeholders, including students, and ask them:

How will a pedagogical partnership program fit into the larger institution (e.g., in relation to reporting, other programs, and promotion and tenure)?

Where should it be located?

How should you compensate student and faculty partners' work?

Deciding on terminology:

What you call your program and its participants matters, and it will depend on context. What kinds of campus-wide and more focused discussions might you have in which you invite stakeholders to discuss what you might call what you want to do?

Considering the names of other programs and partners, which terms resonate for you and your campus, which do not, and why?

Planning to launch and to sustain partnership programs:

Given the advice in this chapter, in the "How the SaLT Program Got Started" resource, and the "Steps in Launching Pedagogical Partnership Programs" resource, what set of steps can you generate for yourself for planning a pilot program?

Are there [temporary] positions, such as post-baccalaureate fellow, that you might create to help launch, develop, or sustain a partnership program?

What are the key considerations regarding sustainability in your context?

4 WHAT ARE THE SHARED RESPONSIBILITIES OF FACILITATING PEDAGOGICAL PARTNERSHIPS?

We discussed in chapter 2 that how you conceptualize partnership will help you decide what kind of program you want to develop, and we focused in chapter 3 on how to situate, name, and launch your program. Once you get clear on those kinds of questions and have a plan for your launch, you will want to think about how to frame, facilitate, and support the daily work of pedagogical partnership.

In terms of how you might conceptualize facilitation of pedagogical partnership, we discuss in this chapter what we consider the most productive way to frame pedagogical partnership work, why affirmation is so important to pedagogical partnership, and some useful approaches to thinking about feedback. Next we discuss what we see as the shared roles and responsibilities for all participants in partnership, how all participants can keep in focus that the work of pedagogical partnership is first and foremost about building relationships and learning to listen and engage as pedagogical partners, and how to keep in mind that it's OK if student and faculty partners have different expectations that lead to different outcomes.

We also identify the overarching attitudes and approaches that all participants in partnership might embrace, including: bringing an open mind to everyone's contribution; building trust; co-creating an approach to the work; practicing professional and confidential communication; being present to and mindful of others in pedagogical partnership; and advocating for pedagogical partners and for pedagogical partnership itself. Finally, we note the kinds of things for which student partners are *not* responsible.

What is the most productive way to frame pedagogical partnership work?

We have found that it is most productive to frame pedagogical partnership work as focused on sharing perspectives with the purpose of dialogue, not necessarily critique and change. As Cook-Sather, Bovill, and Felten (2014, 23) have argued, "The goal of student-faculty partnership work is not change for change's sake but rather to achieve a deeper understanding of teaching and learning that comes from shared analysis and revision." We recognize that some faculty may choose to undertake pedagogical partnership because they are seeking to revitalize or revise their pedagogy or curriculum, and change, either of understanding or of practice, may indeed result from the partnership work. However, we recommend that:

- all participants in pedagogical partnership frame partnership as aiming to foster an exchange of perspectives;
- students and faculty begin partnership with a focus on what is already effective in the faculty partners' practices and why; and
- partners then move to explore what, if anything, might be revised.

Program directors can offer this kind of framing when initially contacting or when responding to prospective faculty and student partners. They can also emphasize this kind of framing in the guidelines they develop and share with faculty and student partners. And finally, they can create structures, particularly within the weekly student partner meetings and the opportunities for reflection and assessment discussed in chapter 9, for stepping back and focusing specifically on what is working well and why.

Faculty and student partners can also be intentional about framing partnership in positive terms. If they start by getting a sense of one another's perspectives on what each values and hopes for in teaching and learning, then they can work together to deepen existing commitments and reinforce successful practices as well as explore whatever pedagogical and curricular challenges the faculty member might be experiencing. We emphasize the importance of this kind of framing because, as we discuss in chapter 1, there is a big difference—psychologically and practically—between entering partnership with the assumption that something is "wrong" and needs fixing and entering partnership with the assumption, as Smith College's pedagogical partnership program puts it, "that there are many ways to teach well and that all teaching is improvable" (Smith College Student-Faculty Pedagogical Partnership Program). Our premise is that being cognizant of and acknowledging what works well provides a strong psychological and practical foundation for both affirmation and improvement. The faculty member quoted below articulates the power of positive reinforcement:

> [My student partner] provided plenty of positive reinforcement (which was great, very empowering) and identified a couple of issues to work on/watch out for in the future. It's funny, it is so easy to think that only negative criticism will suggest change . . . but that really isn't true. Having something that works pointed out is just as effective, since it can lead you to think, "Oh, I should do that more!" or, "How can I work that into future classes/discussions?" (Faculty partner quoted in Cook-Sather, Bovill, and Felten 2014, 146)

Why is affirmation so important to pedagogical partnership?
Related to the point above about framing, we want to emphasize in particular the importance of affirmation. By that we do not mean superficial, empty, or false praise. Rather, we mean the genuine recognition of intention and of endeavors to achieve a laudable goal. Such recognition requires finding and focusing on positive and productive effort—it is searching for and supporting the good faith attempts and actual accomplishments of faculty and student partners. Because what it means to be kind or nice versus being constructive and critical varies across cultures, it is important to be in conversation with all involved in partnership about what affirmation means.

The most basic way in which affirmation is important to all participants in partnership—program directors, faculty partners, and student partners—is in recognizing that each participant is taking a risk in embracing pedagogical partnership and warrants recognition of the courage it takes to do so. Because pedagogical partnership runs counter to traditional hierarchical structures and modes of interacting among those in higher education, it is important to affirm that partnership work requires the courage to assert respect, reciprocity, and shared responsibility alongside traditional ways of thinking and being together. It requires bravery and it creates a brave space—a more useful construct, to our minds, than safe space. Alison distinguishes between safe and brave space:

> Safe space implies that danger, risk, or harm will not come to one in that space—that the space as constructed precludes the possibility of those phenomena. . . . Brave space, on the other hand, implies that there is indeed likely be danger or harm—threats that require bravery on the part of those who enter. But those who enter the space have the courage to face that danger and to take risks because they know they will be taken care of—that painful or difficult experiences will be acknowledged and supported, not avoided or eliminated. . . . This alternative to safe space resonated not only with my thinking about classroom practice but also in relation to the spaces created through student-faculty pedagogical partnerships. (Cook-Sather 2016b, 1)

Affirmation is particularly important for faculty because inviting a student partner to observe one's teaching or help redesign one's curriculum requires being vulnerable and trusting, willing to emerge from the standard "pedagogical solitude" (Shulman 2004) in which most faculty labor. As Cook-Sather et al. (2017, 129) argue:

> Student partners' focus on affirmation and re-affirmation builds trust and confidence. It also gives faculty the opportunity to clarify their pedagogical rationales, perhaps for the first time, to themselves, their student partners, and, in turn, to their own students. Finally, it creates a foundation from which faculty can engage in

genuine exploration and productive risk taking in partnership with their student consultants.

Practicing affirmation and working to be authentic in affirming the efforts of faculty partners gives student partners in particular opportunities to develop empathy for those good faith attempts. The practice of affirming and acknowledging the specifics of positive strategies, steps, and approaches builds a perspective that students can take to their other courses and interactions with other faculty. A student partner in the SaLT program and the founder of Ursinus College's partnership program offer thoughts on the importance of affirmation and support:

> "Faculty often come into partnerships with the notion that they will be critiqued, and that's why building a strong foundation of affirmation is key at the beginning of, and throughout, a partnership."
>
> —Natasha Daviduke,
> student partner in the SaLT program
> (personal communication)

> "A few years ago I shared an Atul Gawande (2011) piece on mentoring with the faculty who were working with student consultants. The point was that high-level professionals (his focus was on surgeons) still get observed and 'coached'—this happens in many professions, but it doesn't happen much in teaching. I thought this was valuable, in that it reminded me that professionals with a high level of expertise still need, and deserve, support."
>
> —Meredith Goldsmith, founding director,
> Teaching and Learning Institute,
> Ursinus College, United States
> (personal communication)

Finally, affirmation of student partners is important. Assuming the role of pedagogical or curricular consultant to faculty members is daunting. Almost everything in formal education tells students that they are there to learn, not to teach, to listen to the experts, not to claim their own expertise, to attend to a monologue, not contribute to a dialogue. It is important for program directors, faculty partners, and other student partners to consider ways in which they can affirm students' identities, knowledge, perspectives, questions, and insights. Pedagogical partnership invites student partners to offer their perspectives as part of a thoughtful conversation, not as any kind of prescription for practice. Student partners' experiences and insights meet faculty partners' experiences and insights, and the result is a more informed discussion of what is happening and what is possible in teaching and learning in higher education.

The following are some examples of affirmations we use in the SaLT program. They can be offered by program directors, faculty partners, or student partners:

- "I really appreciate the thought and effort you have put into creating this assignment/activity/approach/set of observation notes."
- "That comment/activity/approach prompts me to think in a whole different way about X. Thank you for that reframing."
- "I am so grateful for the way we are able to disagree and learn from our disagreement about this question/activity/practice."
- "I am really glad that you gave students an in-depth explanation as to what the class will entail so that there is less confusion about what the expectations are."
- "I noticed that for the first half of the class period, students were willingly participating rather than being cold-called on as much. I think the transition [to willingly participate] has a lot to do with the questions starting off small and then leading to a larger thematic question."
- "Love how you reiterated and framed the question so that students can figure out how to answer the question you are specifically targeting as opposed to stating what sounds 'right.'"
- "Nice way to stimulate the metacognitive awareness aspect of the work we are doing. This will guide students to think through making continuous connections."

What all of these affirmations have in common is that they are genuine expressions of appreciation, they specify what the appreciation is for, and they reveal what matters to the person uttering them as well as what that person appreciates about the interlocutor's effort.

What are some useful approaches to conceptualizing feedback?
One of the threshold concepts to pedagogical partnership that we noted in chapter 1 and discussed in detail in the "Threshold Concepts in Pedagogical Partnership" resource is that partnership is not about finding what is wrong and fixing it. Oftentimes faculty partners fear and student partners expect that the student partner's role is to identify problems in their faculty partners' pedagogical and curricular approaches and to remedy them. While faculty partners may want to revise their curricular and pedagogical approaches, this find-problems-and-fix-them frame is not the most productive one with which to approach partnership.

When Sophia Abbot was the post-bac fellow for the Collaborative for Teaching and Learning at Trinity University, she wrote:

> Many students (in my experience) express an anxiety around giving *helpful enough* feedback (a fear I shared when I was a SaLT consultant myself). When framed as perspective sharing and reminding students there's no goal for accomplishing a particular change, I find students feel less of a pressure to always have something constructive and classroom changing to contribute in their reflections with faculty. (Personal communication)

Student partners can have other worries about feedback. They worry that they might not notice important things or that the way they deliver their feedback might upset or offend faculty, and they can feel many other manifestations of uncertainty around their capacity and faculty receptivity. One Berea College student partner describes this concern and also what helped her address it:

> One of the biggest challenges of this partnership was learning how to give appropriate, authentic feedback. In the beginning, my feedback was complimentary and not actually helpful; Amanda was already receiving feedback like this from her peers. I was afraid that my suggestions would stifle conversations, be read in the wrong tone,

or overstep the professional line. I had to become more comfortable with reflective feedback so that I would be fully invested in her teaching goal. I eventually found that it worked best to ask questions about what I saw so that a conversation could stem from that. I did not want my feedback to be only about how I would do things differently because then there would be no room for conversation.

—Ashley Ferrell,
Technology Help Desk Student Supervisor,
Berea College, United States
(personal communication)

It is important to give careful consideration to how to conceptualize and offer feedback that is affirming and productively challenging. In the SaLT program, we talk a lot about starting with a focus on what is working well and why and also on how to make feedback to faculty "hearable." In Berea College's pedagogical partnership program, the work of Douglas Stone and Sheila Heen (2014) on feedback offers a useful springboard for discussion—both in the faculty and the student meetings—about different kinds of feedback and about the triggers that can make it hard to hear feedback. Stone and Heen's advice provides faculty with some guidelines for shaping and receiving feedback, and their analysis sensitizes student consultants to an array of reasons a partner may hear some things more easily than others. Students are at times surprised how vulnerable faculty partners may feel, and such a framework can help them understand why. See the "Ways of Conceptualizing Feedback" resource.

It is useful, when focusing on how to receive as well as offer feedback, to return to the principles that underlie pedagogical partnership: respect, reciprocity, and shared responsibility. The finding-problems-and-fixing-them frame, everyone's sensitivity to receiving feedback, and everyone's need to learn how to offer constructive feedback can, at least initially, work against these principles. If, however, they are intentionally embraced alongside deliberate efforts to offer and receive feedback as described above, the results are at once more affirming and more inspiring. A student partner from Berea College's pedagogical partnership program captures this potential:

> This program helped me to understand how to give and receive helpful feedback. The most important lesson I learned from this is that learning can be bidirectional; the faculty is wanting to develop and learn just the same as the students. Feedback is always welcomed and appreciated if it is delivered the proper way. I think this program has provided me with ways to give feedback as a student and has also prepared me to receive feedback in future professions. (Personal communication)

What are shared roles and responsibilities for all participants in partnership?

The co-creation of pedagogical partnerships unfolds through building relationships based on genuinely listening and engaging and on recognizing that different partners may have different goals that lead to different outcomes, some of which can be known in advance and some of which emerge through the collaboration. As Matthews (2017a, 4) argues: "While the process of engaging in partnership is associated with a range of beneficial and desired outcomes for both students and staff (Mercer-Mapstone et al., 2017), the driving force for engaging in [partnership work] is not achievement of any particular, predetermined outcome." So, given this organic nature of partnership, how might partners approach the work of building relationships, learning to listen and engage, and be OK if student partners and faculty partners have different expectations that lead to different outcomes?

How can all participants keep in focus that the work of pedagogical partnership is first and foremost about building relationships?

While partnerships are highly individual and dialogic, and every partnership will be different, everyone involved in partnerships—program directors, faculty partners, and student partners—can work to create conditions for partnership based on premises of respect, reciprocity, and shared responsibility (Cook-Sather, Bovill, and Felten 2014). Respect is an attitude that entails taking seriously and valuing what someone else brings to an encounter. It demands openness and receptivity; calls for willingness to consider experiences or perspectives that are different from our own; and often requires a withholding of judgment. If respect is an attitude, reciprocity is a way of interacting; it is a process of balanced give-and-take in which there is equity in what is exchanged and how it is exchanged. Responsibility is both required for and inspired by partnership. It is student partners sharing insights based on their own experience and expertise and learning from faculty partners about their pedagogical rationales and goals, and it is faculty partners engaging with—not necessarily enacting—what student partners have to offer.

Building pedagogical partnerships based on these principles entails valuing the other participants involved and taking the time and energy to attend to them in genuine ways. Relationship building begins with the first communication between student and faculty partners, at which it is helpful for them to discuss why they are interested in this work and what hopes they bring to it. Discussing previous teaching and learning experiences, current study or research interests, and generally just slowing down to have these more personal exchanges help participants remember that pedagogical partnership is not just transactional. If faculty and student partners engage one another as whole people, they can build a strong and trusting connection that will enable the part of their work that is focused on analyzing teaching and learning. We return to this discussion in chapter 6 with some specific recommendations for building relationships in classroom-focused partnerships.

How can all participants learn to listen and engage as pedagogical partners?

One of the threshold concepts we noted in chapter 1 and discussed in detail in the "Threshold Concepts in Pedagogical Partnership" resource is that students have knowledge of teaching and learning. This threshold concept can cause student partners to hesitate to speak and faculty partners sometimes to struggle to hear what students have to offer. There are other ways in which all participants need to learn to listen and engage as partners.

Because it is most countercultural, learning to listen to students might be hardest. Program directors will want to give careful thought to how to honor student perspectives without suggesting or implying that students have all the answers or solutions to pedagogical challenges. In other words, they can work to find ways to frame student perspectives as essential and authoritative but not definitive or omniscient. Pedagogical partnership is a co-creational process; therefore, when a program director or a faculty partner invites a student's perspective, it is necessary not only to acknowledge that student's experiences but also to share their own perspectives as well. This way, all partners can map out the possible gaps and loopholes as a way to figure out how best to proceed.

The skill of listening—and the experience of being listened to—must be fostered and supported, not taken for granted. At Berea College, student partners spend time learning about listening and practice strategies together before trying them out with faculty partners, especially early on in the relationship. They begin with a set of guidelines developed by Deandra Little and Michael Palmer, formerly and currently of the University of Virginia, respectively. They map levels and kinds of listening and offer productive approaches to questioning. The conceptual categories include listener-, problem-, and speaker-focused listening, each with explanations, and Little and Palmer provide examples of powerful questions to use when the goal is to clarify the situation, set goals, create possibilities, and measure action. We share these guidelines in the "Ways of Thinking about Listening" resource.

One of the most important kinds of awareness we have noted has to do with the complexity of identities. Both student and faculty partners bring with them to pedagogical partnership multiple identities, and part of listening well is not reducing people to any single aspect of their identities. In particular, given the change of roles pedagogical partnership catalyzes, we recommend that all participants in pedagogical partnership try to avoid the danger Storrs and Mihelich (1998, 7) identify: that "a politics of experience often has the unintended result of reducing one's complex identity into its most visible component"—in this case, student or faculty member. If student and faculty partners are reduced to their studentness and facultyness, you lose all context, personal preferences, and other factors that influence their experience. Therefore, listen for context as well as content; invite expansion and explanation.

Finally, remember that when anyone—program director, faculty member, or student partner—is sharing their perspective, that perspective is one that is personally experienced and so one valid way of perceiving and making sense, but not the only valid way. Student partners need to learn to trust their experiences and interpretations of them, but they must simultaneously become more open to the legitimacy and value of other viewpoints. Education students in particular will sometimes feel inclined to share their knowledge from having studied education in a way that can sound or feel too directive or prescriptive to faculty. Everyone's perspective needs to be valued, but none should be privileged over the others. Instead, all should be explicitly put into dialogue with one another. As former student partner Natasha Daviduke asserts: "Partnership means ideas flow both ways, and each person is valued for the experience they bring to the table" (personal communication).

One of the most important dimensions of listening and engaging as pedagogical partners is asking good questions. In keeping with the premises of partnership we emphasize in this book, good questions are ones that are respectful rather than judgmental, genuine rather than assuming or looking for a particular response, and open and inviting of further exploration rather than closing it down. In the "Questions that Facilitate Productive Talking and Listening" resource, we list some of the questions we have developed through SaLT.

How do we keep in mind that it's OK if student partners and faculty partners have different expectations that lead to different outcomes?
While student and faculty partners are in a co-created pedagogical partnership, just as they contribute different things to the partnership, they may have different expectations that lead to different outcomes for each. Not only is that OK, it is actually very consistent with the premises of pedagogical partnership. Everyone involved—program directors, faculty

partners, and student partners—can remind themselves regularly that these differences are healthy and can be supported.

One way to do this is to recognize, and remind one another to keep in mind, that this work is ongoing, that it is complex and complicated, and that not only are there multiple ways to teach well, there are rarely easy solutions to pedagogical or curricular challenges. Pedagogical partnership work is part of the larger project of striving toward more communicative and balanced relationships in higher education. Stepping back from the daily work and regaining perspective on how it fits into all participants' larger set of experiences, practices, and goals can help.

In chapter 8, we discuss the challenges of pedagogical partnership, some of which emerge from and contribute to differences in expectations and outcomes. In the "Outcomes of Pedagogical Partnership Work" resource, we present the most common outcomes of pedagogical partnership for students, faculty, program directors, and institutions, some of which are shared and some of which are different.

What overarching attitudes and approaches might all participants in partnership embrace?

To engage in the work of building relationships, listening, and supporting the pursuit of shared and respective goals, it is helpful if all participants in pedagogical partnership embrace a set of attitudes and approaches that facilitate productive engagement. In this section we describe what this looks like for program directors, faculty partners, and student partners.

How do you ensure that you bring an open mind to everyone's contribution?

Pedagogical partnership work is likely to be most effective if all participants enter into this work with the mindset that everyone brings valuable experiences and perspectives. Program directors and faculty partners can remind themselves that students might not be experts in facilitation or have the level of disciplinary expertise that faculty have, but they bring experience and expertise as students and as knowers more generally (Sorenson 2001; Cook-Sather, Bovill, and Felten 2014; de Bie et al. 2019). Reconceptualizing students as partners in pedagogical exploration requires challenging assumptions that are inscribed in the hierarchical structures and clearly delineated roles of higher education, but it does not require invalidating program director or faculty expertise. The most productive mindset for program directors and faculty partners to develop, therefore, is one of openness and receptivity to what students have to offer that can inform and extend the expertise those program directors and faculty partners already have, as well as open up experiences, perspectives, and possible approaches that they may not have considered.

Program directors and student partners can enter into pedagogical partnership work with the mindset that faculty are accustomed to working from their disciplinary expertise but they may or may not have had the opportunity to delve deeply into explorations of pedagogical and curricular development. Whether faculty are coming straight from graduate school or have been teaching for a while, they likely have absorbed—and had little time or opportunity to question—the pedagogical and curricular approaches that are the norms within their disciplines. Questioning those can feel destabilizing, and so program directors and student partners need to be empathetic to the challenge of engaging in the ongoing process of "'self-authoring' a professional identity as an educator" (Gunersel, Barnett, and Etienne 2013, 35; see also Cook-Sather 2016a). The particular intersection of disciplinary and pedagogical orientations and individual identities that each faculty member brings requires that program directors and student partners learn from faculty partners about their previous experiences, their commitments, and their hopes and goals for their pedagogical and curricular development. Being inquisitive and receptive helps to keep an open mind to what faculty bring to pedagogical partnership.

And finally, faculty and student partners can focus on how program directors have as their main goal the support and facilitation of dialogue about pedagogical and curricular co-creation and embrace their efforts and recommendations within that frame. Because program directors occupy the most administrative role in the trio, faculty can worry that program directors are part of the evaluative machinery of the institution, and depending on how the program is designed in terms of student compensation for their work, students may experience program directors as their bosses. Like the shifts of mindset articulated above, faculty and student partners may need to step back from assumptions and expectations of those in administrative roles and be receptive to the effort program directors are making to create liminal spaces—outside of regular, more evaluative structures, roles, and relationships—within which faculty and student partners can explore, experiment, (re)affirm, and revise as needed. Equally, they can strive to have an open mind regarding how what they try out in the "as-if" spaces of pedagogical partnership might inform their work beyond the pedagogical partnership itself (Cook-Sather and Felten 2017a).

How can you build trust?

As Goldsmith, Hanscom, Throop, and Young (2017, 7) assert: "At the very heart of partnership is . . . trust. Trust enables collaboration and dialogue, growth and reflection, for persons, programs, and institutions. The need for trust should not seem unduly daunting. . . . Trust is built one question, one conversation, at a time." We suggest that program directors need to be thoughtful and intentional about building trust with both faculty partners and student partners. The main areas in which trust needs to be built with faculty partners are in relation to the threshold concepts we identified in chapter 1: faculty fears of surveillance, that the program aims to "fix" their teaching by imposing particular pedagogical practices, and that program directors and student partners expect faculty to do what their student partners say.

Trust building can entail reminding faculty that all the work they do is confidential and that the program director does not see student partners' observation notes or participate directly in the curriculum design or redesign process. It can entail regularly inviting and responding to faculty members' own commitments and interests, thereby reinforcing the idea that program directors aim to meet faculty where they are rather than to impose any particular theory or approach or to expose faculty in any way. Likewise, it can include regular reiteration of the goals of the program: that the purpose is dialogue not imposition, and that student partners have a perspective on, not a prescription for, pedagogical and curricular approaches. It can also encompass adjusting program structures and practices, such as the classroom observation component of classroom-focused pedagogical partnerships, so that the faculty partners still benefit from dialogue with a student partner but need not have the student partner in their classrooms if that makes them feel too vulnerable or if the content of their courses is too sensitive (as in many social work courses). All of these approaches contribute to building faculty trust because they are responsive to needs and goals that faculty identify, and they directly address and aim to dispel the particular worries some faculty bring to pedagogical partnership.

Program directors' efforts to build trust with student partners also focus on addressing the threshold concepts identified in chapter 1. The self-doubt that many student partners bring regarding their capacities to be pedagogical partners and the misperception with which they embark upon pedagogical partnership—that their job is to find problems and fix them—are both challenging to address. Program directors can build trust in relation to the first issue, concerning student self-doubt, by creating spaces and opportunities through which students can articulate and come to see their capacities. For instance, as discussed in detail in chapter 5, program directors can invite student partners to reflect in writing on the strengths and skills they bring to pedagogical partnership work and then ask them to share and affirm those with other student partners, reinforcing the ways in which these contributions can inform pedagogical partnership work.

Building trust in relation to the misperception that the student partner's job is to find problems with their faculty partners' curricular and pedagogical approaches and fix them entails regularly repeating that this is not their job. Many student partners have stated that it takes them several weeks to come to believe this, but the repetition, which is a form of permission to let go of that notion of the work, helps build this trust. Linked to the practices of relationship building, affirmation, listening, and accepting differences of goal and outcome, as discussed in earlier sections of this chapter, contribute to building trust.

Faculty partners' efforts to build trust focus primarily on their work with their student partners. Student partners often describe the necessary foundation for trust in terms of the respect on which it is premised and the time it takes to build. As one student partner explained: "Partnerships that place undergraduates in the role of consultants to faculty members create processes that inherently require reciprocal respect and shared responsibility." She continued: "Fostering this mutual respect and responsibility takes time because it is rare for student voice to be legitimized in such a formal manner." What helped this student build trust in her faculty partner was, in part, the fact that "we both knew he was interested in developing his skills as a professor. Because of this, we were able to proceed and take each other seriously and engage in a relationship of mutual and generative respect" (Kahler 2014, 1).

This mutuality is noted by many student partners. As Ann, a student ambassador in a partnership program in Australia, put it: "Learning is not one sided; it's teachers and students engaging in dialogue. It's not like you just learn from teachers. They can learn from you and it doesn't have to be limited to what a syllabus says" (Bell et al. 2017, 5). Faculty members can build trust with their student partners by demonstrating that they are open to engaging in respectful dialogue, willing, where possible, to experiment with the curricular and pedagogical approaches they co-create with their student partners, and ready to offer a rationale for why they are or are not open to acting on the perspectives and suggestions of their student partners.

Student partners' efforts to build trust focus primarily on their work with their faculty partners. In the SaLT program, we have found that such trust building works best if student partners focus first on what is working well and why in their faculty partners' practice, affirming existing strengths and capacities they discern. "The Pedagogical Benefits of Enacting Positive Psychology Practices through a Student-Faculty Partnership Approach to Academic Development," co-authored by Alison and faculty and student partners (Cook-Sather et al. 2017), describes how, when student partners practice affirmation and encouragement of strengths-based growth, they help accelerate processes of faculty acclimation and self-authoring and sustain energy for continued development. Faculty typically work alone or in collaboration with other faculty; it is unusual to collaborate with students in this way, and so they need to know that they can trust student partners.

Particularly when student partners encounter what might feel like resistance in their faculty partners, it is important to redouble trust-building efforts. As one student partner explained when she encountered what she perceived as resistance from her faculty partner:

> I jump back to building a community and trust. People need positive reinforcement to carry out change. I have had more personal check-ins when faced with resistance because I always think there is something more past the surface. I try to build a space for this multiplicity. (Student partner quoted in Ntem and Cook-Sather 2018, 89)

While trust is essential to functional and meaningful pedagogical partnerships, trust is also a tricky phenomenon. As Alise de Bie notes, "there may be very good reasons why an ethic of distrust is crucial to partnerships across difference and status." As she argues: "The 'pain' of partnership is one moment where distrust seems especially significant—where it's a good idea to be skeptical, uncertain, to distrust partnership discourse that often presents partnerships as (only) a good thing" (de Bie and Raaper 2019). While we have found trust to be essential to our work through pedagogical partnership, we agree with de Bie that totalizing narratives or single "right ways" are problematic.

How might you co-create an approach to the pedagogical partnership work?

Co-creation is the premise of pedagogical partnership, but how do you do it? In their more administrative role, program directors can at once offer a basic structure for the partnership work and be open to reimagining and revising it in response to input from faculty and student partners. The guidelines for working in partnership offered in chapters 6 and 7 and in the "Guidelines for Student and Faculty Partners in Classroom-focused Pedagogical Partnerships" resource, for instance, are informed by both Alison as the SaLT program director and many student and faculty partners. Furthermore, program directors can share the responsibility for facilitating components of the pedagogical partnership work, such as orientations and the weekly meetings of student partners. Experienced student partners and post-bac fellows can co-facilitate or facilitate on their own the orientations for student partners described in the "Sample Outlines for Student Partner Orientations" resource. The particular questions student partners bring to the weekly meetings, their requests for feedback on ideas they have or frustrations they are experiencing, and their proposals that the group delve into particular challenges within partnership (e.g., resistances, which led to Anita and Alison publishing an article on that topic [Ntem and Cook-Sather 2018]) are all opportunities for student partners to co-create approaches to the work of pedagogical partnership.

Faculty partners can contribute to a co-creation approach by formulating and sharing with student partners their pedagogical commitments and rationales as well as their hopes, questions, and concerns toward the goal of identifying an initial focus for the pedagogical partnership work. This focus may be vague or only partially formed at first, and it is likely to evolve over the course of the partnership, but having a sense up front of what matters to a faculty partner and what they want to explore helps student partners focus their attention and energy most productively. Part of the work of being a faculty partner is developing language to use in dialogue with student partners; it can be in part through partnership that faculty develop language for identifying underlying and perhaps unconscious pedagogical commitments and for refining articulations of pedagogical rationales.

Student partners in SaLT have indicated that they feel least able to develop productive pedagogical partnerships when their faculty partners are not forthcoming or open. As one student partner described this: her faculty partner was "resistant to let me into her pedagogical thinking space'" (student partner quoted in Ntem and Cook-Sather 2018, 87). When faculty partners let their student partners into their pedagogical thinking space in relation to classroom-focused pedagogical work, "the instructor and consultant review the proceedings of each class together, noting anything from how each class fit into a broader pedagogical arc to an interesting comment a certain student made." Ideally, as these student and faculty partners continue, "the partnership works not as a one-way critique, but as a way to reflect and grow together, offering each other feedback and solving the puzzles of the class as a team" (Abbott and Been 2017, 1). Even when such co-creation is challenging, "dealing with the uncomfortable places real conversations can take you allows you to reconstruct more productive approaches to the classroom" (Faculty partner quoted in Cook-Sather 2015).

For student partners, a co-creation approach entails attending closely to faculty members' existing pedagogical commitments and those that may still be developing, as well as sharing thoughts and insights that their faculty partners might not have previously considered or worked through. The balance between being receptive to faculty interest and focus on the one hand and sharing their own experiences and ideas on the other contributes to a co-creation approach. Learning to achieve this balance is a unique process for each partnership—dependent on the individual faculty and student partner—and it is partly a process of developing language to use in dialogue with faculty partners. This includes using the kinds of affirmations and questions we mentioned in previous sections in this chapter and in the "Questions that Facilitate Talking and Listening" resource, and learning to explain the "why" behind those affirmations and questions, respectfully but confidently.

Student partners bring particular contributions to pedagogical partnership. In the "Student Partners' Particular Contributions to Pedagogical Partnership" resource, we expand on these points about what students bring in particular to pedagogical partnership by addressing these questions:

- What contributes to the quality of attention that supports reflection?
- What is important about the student perspective . . . and gathering other students' perspectives?
- Why is it useful to have a student perspective from outside the discipline?
- How do student partners affirm multiple forms of knowledge?

How do you practice professional and confidential communication?

Pedagogical partnerships require professional communication across positions and roles, all of which needs to respect and keep confidential the pedagogical partnership work upon which they focus. Much of the planning and organizing work that program directors do takes place over email, and so it is worth being cognizant of what you include in email messages. For instance, when Alison writes about the SaLT program to faculty members who are joining Bryn Mawr or Haverford College, she introduces herself, describes her history at the institutions, and explains the philosophy and approach of the program. This gives prospective faculty partners time to process what they will be signing on to if they choose to participate.

Faculty partners also need to consider the nature of their communications. Because students and faculty enter into pedagogical partnership from their respective institutional roles, faculty can facilitate the transition into a different kind of working relationship through being intentional about how they address and communicate with student partners. As the student reflection below illustrates, communication is linked to trust and the building of a productive professional relationship:

> The confidence I had developed in my first partnership helped to reassure me that my perspective matters; I just had to find a way to express it so my faculty partners could hear it. During my final partnership, I struggled due to differences in communication styles between me and my faculty partner. In one instance, my partner and I had—as trivial as it may sound—very different ways of expressing ourselves in writing, so our email exchanges often times led to misunderstandings and thus a lack of trust. I made a focused effort to make my email messages sound more like hers, both to try to make them more accessible to her and also to build a new kind of strength for myself. This was a different way of finding a place of belonging for myself. While I didn't feel as fully welcomed for my whole self as I had in my first partnership, I did feel that my partner respected my perspective, and I also felt strengthened by making a place for myself through my efforts. (Colón García 2017, 3)

Student partners have some of the greatest challenges in practicing professional and confidential communication because of the multiple relationships in which they function. Like program directors and faculty partners, student partners need to consider the kinds of email messages they send, both as initial contacts and throughout the partnership. In SaLT, student partners are the first to make contact with their faculty partners, so they set the tone of the partnership. Opening these with professional greetings (e.g., "Dear Professor Smith") and including the appropriate level of detail (see the "Sample Message to Student Partners from the SaLT Program Director" resource) constitute professional communication.

A more complicated challenge for student partners is managing peers and friends who are enrolled in the class on which the student partner is working. In the SaLT program, we emphasize the importance of student partners listening to peer and friend input but not sharing their own perspectives or interpretations of their faculty partners' goals. They can offer to share their peers' and friends' perspectives anonymously with faculty partners, but they should not endeavor to address the perspectives on their own. It is important that student partners avoid sharing what faculty partners discuss or trying to explain what they think their faculty partners are trying to achieve. Sharing that kind of information constitutes a violation of the confidentiality of the partnership.

It is essential that student and faculty partners communicate with one another and with program directors if they are not able to fulfill their responsibilities or if they have a concern of any kind about their partnership. Early and ongoing communication about any problems or issues—as well as about what is working well!—supports realizing the potential of pedagogical partnership and helps prevent miscommunication from escalating into tension and distrust.

How can you be present to and mindful of others in pedagogical partnership?

Pedagogical partnership programs like SaLT require lots of meetings. Program directors regularly meet with student partners, and faculty and student partners have weekly or biweekly meetings. Given how busy everyone is (one of the main logistical challenges of pedagogical partnership that we discuss in chapter 8), it is important that all participants schedule regular meeting times, stick to those as faithfully as possible, and contact those with whom they were scheduled to meet if they have to cancel. These are standard practices of common courtesy, but failing to adhere to them has a particularly detrimental effect on pedagogical partnership, striving as it does to build relationships premised on trust, respect, and co-creation.

Pedagogical partnership demands real and deep commitment and requires time and work to succeed. Reading the messages and guidelines that program directors provide can help both faculty and student partners be prepared for the practical and emotional intensity of pedagogical partnership work (and also the challenges that we discuss in chapter 8). Similarly, engaging fully in the orientation sessions offered to student partners, as described in chapter 5 and the "Sample Outlines for Student Partner Orientations" resource, can help ground and make real the ideas and approaches described in the guidelines and afford student partners an opportunity to learn from one another about pedagogical partnership work.

For all participants, the most regular and ongoing way to be present is to participate actively and thoughtfully in weekly meetings. These meetings are spaces for actively sharing experiences, questions, insights, celebrations, struggles, and every other aspect of partnership work. It is essential that everything that is said in these meetings stays in these meetings; they must remain confidential. A useful guiding principle for these spaces is: Leave what is said; take what is learned.

In the weekly meetings of the student partners and program director, it is beneficial to both experienced student partners and the students who are just starting out in the partner role if the experienced student partners share previous experiences, strategies, and approaches they have developed, as well as the insights they have gained from their work. It is also important that experienced partners are conscious of the fact that every partnership is different and so for themselves and for others, there should be no "one right way." Indeed, as we note in chapter 1, sometimes a second partnership is hardest because student partners expect it to be like the first. So, the most productive role experienced student partners can play—for themselves and for new student partners—is to describe their approaches, their evolution, and their ever-deepening understanding of their work (see Eze 2019 for an example of such a description).

How might you advocate for pedagogical partners and for pedagogical partnership itself?

Because the work of pedagogical partnership is unfamiliar to many, radical to some, and challenging to all, it is essential that participants in pedagogical partnership advocate for the work and for one another in the work. The various attitudes and approaches we have outlined here can inform efforts that program directors, faculty partners, and student partners make to advocate for all participants involved. All participants can promote the ideals of partnership beyond the institution as well—through publications, presentations, and informal conversations. The "Partial List of Themed Issues of *Teaching and Learning Together in Higher Education*" resource provides one set of examples.

For what kinds of things are student partners not responsible?

Pedagogical partnerships focused on classrooms and curriculum concentrate on teaching practices and course design and redesign. In the SaLT program, responsibilities that student partners should not assume include clerical kinds of work, such as photocopying.

The student partners in classroom-focused partnerships are there to observe and offer feedback. They are not there to participate, unless their not doing so would be too awkward. For instance, one student partner worked with a professor who started all her class sessions with physical activities meant to build trust and create certain kinds of embodied experiences. The faculty partner felt that it was essential that her student partner do these activities as well, lest the students enrolled in the course and she herself were made to feel self-conscious. Sometimes, especially in small classes, it can also be beneficial for the student partner to participate occasionally. As former SaLT student partner Sasha Mathrani suggests, "The faculty partner and student partner should be on the same page about how much participation they feel makes sense, and if they want a make a change they should be in communication about it" (personal communication). In chapter 6, we discuss in detail the importance of setting expectations at the beginning of the semester in which a faculty and student work in classroom-focused pedagogical partnership.

Unless the student partners are enrolled in the course or the partnership is between the professor and the entire class, they should not be expected to do the readings or assignments for the course. They are compensated for the pedagogical support they are offering, and if a faculty member wants student partners to do additional academic work, that needs to be negotiated with the student partner and be part of what they are compensated for.

Finally, student partners should not be in the role of attempting to explain to students enrolled in a course what their faculty partner's pedagogical goals are. The student partner's role is to observe classroom practice and to gather and share student perspectives if their faculty partners are open to that, but it is not to mediate in this sense.

YOUR TURN

Conceptualizing facilitation:

Everyone has different ideas about what facilitation entails, and people on your campus may have different notions of the facilitation roles in pedagogical partnership.

What is the range of forms of facilitation already enacted on your campus?

How do you see facilitation of pedagogical partnership as described in this chapter being similar to those forms or constituting a new form of facilitation?

What particular challenges, if any, do you anticipate with the forms of facilitation partnership requires?

How can you convey to potential participants in pedagogical partnership programs the importance of affirmation?

What approaches to building trust have been successful on your campus and how might they be integrated into your pedagogical partnership work?

Clarifying roles and responsibilities:

What is your understanding of the shared roles and responsibilities of all participants in partnership? What are the distinctions or differences among the roles and how can you support participants in clarifying those for themselves and for one another?

In what contexts and in what ways are feedback offered on your campus? How are those similar to and different from the feedback in and about pedagogical partnership discussed in this chapter and in the "Ways of Conceptualizing Feedback" resource?

Fostering productive attitudes and approaches:

What kinds of trust-building activities might you explore and create as part of developing pedagogical partnerships on your campus?

Considering the discussion of overarching attitudes and approaches we offer, which might already exist on your campus, which might need to be developed, and how will you support both?

What challenges of communication (e.g., writing professional emails, being cognizant of others' investment in partnership and other commitments) do you anticipate within your partnership program and also between participants and those not involved? How will you prepare partners to manage these?

What will student partners **not** be responsible for in your partnership program? How can you keep in mind and convey those boundaries to others?

5 WHAT APPROACHES MIGHT PROGRAM DIRECTORS TAKE TO PLAN FOR AND SUPPORT PEDAGOGICAL PARTNERSHIPS?

Particular to the role of program director are the administrative duties of a pedagogical partnership program, in addition to the pedagogical and facilitative responsibilities shared by all participants. Typically, the program director is responsible for positioning, managing, and troubleshooting the pedagogical partnership program, communicating with those in other offices, such as student payroll and administration, and managing the overall logistics of the program. The most basic responsibilities of the program director are to:

- **Manage:** Situate and oversee the program, handle its budget and hiring procedures, and ensure that there is communication within and beyond the program.
- **Organize:** Invite and match student and faculty partners.
- **Prepare:** Provide initial guidance and structures within which student-faculty pairs embark upon their work.
- **Facilitate**: Host and engage in the regular meetings of student partners and, in some cases, faculty partners.

In this chapter, we detail approaches that program directors can take to these four sets of responsibilities in relation to classroom- and curriculum-focused pedagogical partnerships.

How can program directors invite and respond to prospective participants in pedagogical partnership?

After considering all of the larger framing issues we have discussed in chapters 1, 2, 3, and 4, program directors will want to consider the daily work of organizing and managing pedagogical partnerships. We focus in this chapter on questions that program directors will want to address, sometimes on their own and sometimes in collaboration with others involved in the partnership program. For both classroom- and curriculum-focused partnership, program directors will want to invite or respond to prospective faculty and student partners and support them in general ways as their work unfolds. There are also specific ways that program directors may want to support these different kinds of pedagogical partnerships as they unfold.

How do you invite or respond to prospective faculty partners?

Different programs take different approaches to identifying and inviting prospective faculty members to participate in pedagogical partnership. At Bryn Mawr and Haverford Colleges, in exchange for a reduced teaching load in their first year, all incoming faculty members have the option of applying to participate in a semester-long pedagogy seminar that meets weekly and is linked to a semester-long pedagogical partnership with an undergraduate student (Cook-Sather 2016a). This invitation is issued by the provost when the faculty member visits campus and explained and discussed further with the provost during hiring negotiations. If faculty choose to participate in this option, they are assured a pedagogical partnership with a student. In addition, at Bryn Mawr and Haverford, any faculty member at any point in their career, no matter what the nature of their appointment (tenure track, continuing non-tenure track, visiting, full-time, part-time, etc.) may request to work with a student partner through the SaLT program. This information is posted on our website. Aside from the incoming faculty, we do not directly invite faculty members to participate in the program; they choose to participate and contact Alison.

At other institutions, program directors take different approaches. For instance, at Berea College, the program director invites experienced faculty and student partners to make a presentation at a faculty meeting and shares a one-page overview that includes comments from both faculty and student participants about their experience. At Smith College, they hold a teaching arts luncheon once a year, usually in the spring, to explain pedagogical partnership, and they feature two pairs of student and faculty partners, who share their experiences. Each May, the director of the pedagogical partnership program at Smith runs a two-day institute for interested colleagues (see the "Summer Institute for Faculty Participants in Pedagogical Partnership" resource, and about 90% of participants go on to participate in the program. At Lewis & Clark College, faculty hear about the program through word of mouth, an announcement at a faculty meeting (by a faculty member who has already participated), email, and the teaching and learning center website. The Ursinus College program director targets faculty who are in their first year with emails sent specifically to them and by attending one or two of their dean's colloquium meetings and talking about the benefits of working with a student partner. Staff of their Teaching and Learning Institute also talk about the program at their open house and any events that they host. At the beginning of every semester, the director sends out an advertisement with a link to a form to request a partner. Her sense is that many faculty sign up either because of positive word of mouth from their colleagues or encouragement from their department chairs if their teaching evaluations haven't been as strong as they would like.

The "Inviting Faculty and Students to Participate in Pedagogical Partnership" resource includes examples of messages to send to prospective student and faculty participants. Examples include those messages developed by Sophia Abbot, former student partner in SaLT and subsequently fellow for collaborative programs in the Collaborative for Learning and Teaching at Trinity University; Kathy Oleson and Libby Drumm, the first two directors of Reed College's Student Consultants for Teaching and Learning program; and Diane Skorina, staff co-director of Ursinus College's pedagogical partnership program, and Susanna Throop, former director of Ursinus' pedagogical partnership program.

We recommend that program directors develop an approach that is in keeping with their institution's norms of communicating opportunities and, as the examples above suggest, that uses multiple venues and modes. As we discussed in the previous chapters of this book, the ways you conceptualize, situate, and name your pedagogical partnership work should resonate and, where appropriate, productively challenge norms in your context.

How do you identify prospective student partners or respond to their requests to participate?

In chapter 2, the "History and Structure of the SaLT Program" resource, and the "How the SaLT Program Got Started" resource, we discuss in detail the origin and development of the SaLT program. As we explain, it was piloted by a group of five faculty members from different departments who wanted to make their classrooms more welcoming and responsive to a diversity of students. At the recommendation of student focus groups, a group of student consultants who identified as people of color worked with these faculty members (Cook-Sather 2018a; 2019a). That beginning established for SaLT a reputation as a "counter space," which Solórzano et al. (2000, 70) define as academic and social spaces on and off campus "where deficit notions of people of color can be challenged and where a positive collegiate racial climate can be established and maintained." Because of that reputation, students of color have continued to apply to participate, and they are overrepresented as student partners (relative to their overall representation at the colleges).

Therefore, the first answer to the question of how program directors identify or respond to prospective student partners is to consider what message the advent of your program sends and to be intentional about that, since it will contribute to the reputation the program develops on campus. Relatedly, it will affect which students will hear about the program from their friends and be encouraged to apply. The explicit and implicit goals of the program, as we discussed in chapter 1, will affect which students are compelled by the program. As Matthews (2017a, 3) argues:

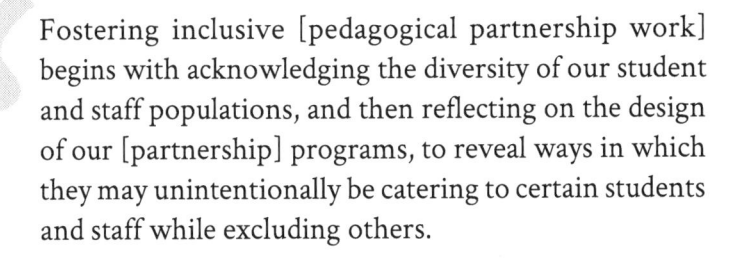

> Fostering inclusive [pedagogical partnership work] begins with acknowledging the diversity of our student and staff populations, and then reflecting on the design of our [partnership] programs, to reveal ways in which they may unintentionally be catering to certain students and staff while excluding others.

A second answer to the question of how you identify prospective student partners is to invite current student partners to make recommendations. Clearly, this is only possible after you have run the program for a semester or more, but program directors can also invite students to participate in focus groups, as we did to conceptualize the SaLT program, prior to launching the program and get a sense from students about who among them might be well positioned to participate in the program and be interested in doing so. Student recommendation is our preferred approach in the SaLT program because student partners know best what the role requires and entails. They can convey those requirements and expectations to their peers in ways that a program director or faculty member cannot. This is another way, then, that student expertise can have a role in shaping who participates in the program and what kinds of issues will get foregrounded as a result.

A third way to identify student partners is to ask faculty for recommendations. It is important that faculty and staff understand the explicit and implicit goals of the program so that they think about a diversity of students to recommend. If faculty and staff do not have a clear understanding of the goals of the program, they might make assumptions about who the "best" student partners might be. Students designated "best" often hold leadership positions on campus, earn high grades, and fit a fairly standard profile of "the successful student." We use all these quotation marks here to signal our perspective that such narrow definitions of success can be problematic in and of themselves, and they can also exclude students who have essential experiences and perspectives to share.

Sophia Abbot, former student partner in SaLT and subsequently fellow for collaborative programs at the Collaborative for Learning and Teaching at Trinity University in Texas, also seeks faculty recommendations for student partners in the Tigers as Partners program. Her invitation is reproduced here:

> Hi All,
>
> Thank you so much for agreeing to participate in this first iteration of Tigers as Partners! My first step for getting this started is

> collecting applications from students who are interested in participating. For that, I need your help!
>
> If you have any students (sophomores and above) whom you feel would make good partners to faculty, I would appreciate you recommending they apply. Great student partners are thoughtful, empathetic, organized, and strong communicators. There is no minimum GPA required, nor do the students you recommend need be your strongest students -- indeed, often students who have had to struggle somewhat in a class before succeeding, or who don't necessarily identify as future PhDs, make the best partners to faculty. The student job posting can be found here: [link to jobs website]
>
> Student applications are due December 5th.
>
> I will be reviewing applications and personally interviewing all potential students, so also feel free to be liberal with your recommendations. Thanks, in advance, for your help!
>
> Sincerely,
> Sophia

It is likely that you will combine these approaches, as Floyd Cheung, founding director of the Student-Faculty Pedagogical Partnership Program at Smith College, does:

> At the end of the May institute for faculty partners and before I make assignments for the coming year, I ask colleagues to suggest students that they believe will be good at being partners. Before student partners finish their stint at the end of a semester, I ask them to suggest peers that they believe can do their job. I send to all recommended students a letter of invitation to apply to serve as a pedagogical partner in the Smith College program. (Personal communication)

We mention above that numerous students of color seek out the SaLT program for the counter space it provides. Many of these students may fit the standard profile of "the successful student," problematic as it is, but experience a wide range of challenges because of the overall unwelcoming nature of the institutions to underrepresented students. One of the research projects in which Alison and several student partners, including Anita, have been engaged focuses on the experiences of underrepresented and underserved students who participate as student partners (Cook-Sather et al. 2019), and Alison has drawn on their perspectives to argue for an expanded definition of "success" (Cook-Sather 2018b). When we recognize underrepresented and underserved students, such as students of color, for instance, as "holders and creators of knowledge" (Delgado-Bernal 2002, 106) essential to developing inclusive and responsive approaches to classroom practice (Cook-Sather and Agu 2013; Cook-Sather et al. 2017), we take steps to counter epistemic injustice by positioning these students as having expertise and value as knowers and producers of knowledge (de Bie et al. 2019; Marquis et al., under review).

A final way to invite and respond to prospective student partners is to have a public web presence or a physical display with information about the role and an open invitation to apply. We have this information on the SaLT program web page, and all students are welcome to apply. There are no GPA or other requirements, and while there is an application form, it is not intended to exclude students but rather to initiate the reflective process that will be essential to productive participation in pedagogical partnership. (See the "SaLT Program Student Consultant Application Form" resource.)

Across all of these approaches, program directors will want to keep in mind that any invitation and selection will send a message and have implications both for those involved and those not involved. We end this section with a quote taken from *Engaging Students as Partners in Learning and Teaching: A Guide for Faculty*:

> Think carefully about the implications of choosing, and by implication not choosing, particular groups of students, and expect to be surprised as you learn more

about your partners and yourself in this work. If you are not working with an entire class of students, you will need to consider carefully what criteria you will use to select students and be transparent about this. (Cook-Sather, Bovill, and Felten 2014, 150)

How can program directors support participants as their partnerships unfold?

It is essential that faculty and students see that program directors have thought about how to support them and are responsive to their experiences and suggestions. If they know they can offer real feedback and that program directors will make changes, that inspires trust and confidence.

How do you make clear to faculty and student partners that they can seek your support or mediation?

It is especially important that program directors provide support if there are differences of expectation, style, approach, etc. between student and faculty partners. Program directors may need to mediate conversations in which each participant in the partnership restates their hopes and goals and through which the program director helps to reinforce the premises established for the partnership program. Program directors may also need to support an individual faculty partner or student partner if one or the other of the participants in a partnership feels particularly vulnerable or poses particular challenges. It is helpful if program directors convey to participants their willingness to take on these roles at the outset and regularly as partnerships unfold, and if they discern any tensions or issues. Depending on the size of your program, this can be challenging, so it is helpful to think through what is manageable in terms of offering support.

For faculty partners, it can be especially helpful for program directors to clarify goals, reaffirm that this work should be driven by faculty priorities, and reiterate that it is intended to support faculty in analyzing their practice. For student partners, it can be especially helpful for program directors to emphasize that everything that happens is a learning experience—part of building insight, vocabulary, and capacity for working across differences of perspective and position/power. In general, being transparent that the spaces program directors create to share vulnerabilities and concerns are confidential helps to build trust. Are there fears? What are participants nervous about? What are their thoughts? Letting them know that this is an emotionally intensive experience that develops in them life skills can help put tensions in perspective. (We return to this point in chapter 8.)

What kinds of informal and formal feedback mechanisms should you develop?

We discuss this question in detail in chapter 9, but here we mention several ways in which we recommend gathering feedback.

1. **Offer occasional, reflective prompts** to invite participants to gather their thoughts just for themselves about how things are going. Both student and faculty partners have indicated that such moments of stepping back have afforded them much-needed pauses in what otherwise ends up being a quickly unfolding process in which they are deeply engaged and on which they do not have the opportunity to gain perspective.
2. **Have semi-formal, midterm feedback.** As with such approaches faculty might use in their courses (described in detail in chapter 6 and in the "Gathering Feedback" resource), these can be a way not only for individuals to reflect on their experiences and offer feedback but also for everyone involved to see how others are experiencing their partnership work.
3. **Gather end-of-of-term feedback** to offer participants another opportunity to step back from the work, this time to get a long view of how it unfolded over the course of the semester.

For all feedback, we recommend that program directors frame questions in terms of what is contributing to and what is detracting from the partnership work (not what students or faculty like or don't like). We also recommend being explicit about the purposes for gathering feedback. In the SaLT program, we explain that the purposes are: to give participants the opportunity to step back and look over the semester and their experience, get some perspective on both, and capture some of their thoughts for their own ongoing learning; to consider what they might want to continue and what they might want to revise within the partnership approach; and to gather their perspectives to share with administrators and in reports (all anonymously).

How regularly do you need to communicate with administrators?
While it is essential that pedagogical partnership work unfolds in a brave space (Cook-Sather 2016b; Arao and Clemens 2013) separate from review for reappointment or promotion, it is also important that program directors keep clear lines of communication open with provosts, deans, and other administrators. Part of this communication is reiterating that the relationship between this program and review processes needs to be explicit and transparent. The way in which the program director fits within the overall leadership of the institution likewise needs to be explicit and transparent. For instance, Alison has made clear that she can never sit on the Committee on Appointments at Bryn Mawr College, which reviews all faculty for reappointment and promotion. If these things are not clear ahead of time, when worst case scenarios arise, decisions will have to be made on the fly, and it could be complicated. There are many different ways for such programs to be fit into an institutional structure and for program directors to work with administrators; there is no one right answer. The point is that it is important for those relationships to be thought through.

What can program directors do to plan for and support classroom-focused pedagogical partnerships?
For the most part, faculty and student partners do not come as pairs or teams to participate in classroom-focused pedagogical partnership, as they often do for curriculum-focused pedagogical partnership. Typically, they express their interest separately, and then one of the roles of the director is to link them up and provide ongoing support.

For all pedagogical partnerships, program directors will want to consider how to compensate student and faculty partners. The three most common ways to compensate student time and expertise are to situate the position as a campus job, compensated with hourly pay through departmental, curriculum development, or provost's office budgets; to enroll the student in a quarter-credit or a half-credit course; or to create a scholarship. The most common ways to compensate faculty partners, if the institution does so, is through course development grants and fellowship positions. (We discuss compensation in detail in chapter 3.)

How do you assign student and faculty pairs?
In the SaLT program, assignment of student-faculty pairs for classroom-focused pedagogical partnerships is almost entirely random, based on student and faculty schedules. This is intentional, although there are some exceptions. There are several reasons behind the intentionality: participants' busy schedules, the question of whether the student partner needs to be in the discipline of the faculty partner, and power dynamics. We address each of these below.

How might you manage participants' busy schedules?
Both student and faculty schedules are such that pairing within a cohort of participants is extremely challenging. In SaLT, the majority of student and faculty participants in any given semester apply the semester prior to participating in the program, and so the director's role is to match up pairs over the summer or during winter break. Once Alison has a list of all participating faculty, the courses they wish to focus on, and the meeting times of those courses, she sends student partners this list in the form of a table and asks all student partners to write their names next to each course time they are available. She also asks student partners to indicate if they have background experiences that might make them particularly well suited or less well suited to any given partnership, in case there is flexibility in terms of scheduling.

In the Tigers as Partners program at Trinity University, Sophia Abbot took a slightly different approach. She started by listing all the student partners whose schedules would allow them to pair with a particular faculty member, and then (because she had the privilege of getting to know faculty through new faculty orientation and other programs, and because she interviewed all the student partners), she thought about which students might pair best with a particular professor based on personality. For example, she avoided pairing a confident and vocal male student with some new and more uncertain female faculty members to avoid reproducing problematic interactions that such female faculty have learned to be especially wary of. Alternatively, she paired some really enthusiastic and outgoing faculty with more stoic students to balance the energy in the partnerships and offer the faculty and students some alternative perspective on how to be. Finally, in one case of a white male professor who wanted to work with a student partner to think through authentically facilitating a class on diversity in the classical world, Sophia talked one-on-one with a black female student partner whom she knew was interested in these topics before pairing her to re-check whether she was willing to do this work; Sophia's intention was to avoid placing the student partner in a position of acting as a token student of color. And through all of this, Sophia paired students and faculty cross-disciplinarily.

The process Sophia used is more time-consuming than a more random one, but it helped her to facilitate some deep and fruitful relationships—several of which sustained in future semesters into deeper co-mentoring relationships. Interestingly, the more random pairing approach Alison uses has also proven successful in almost all cases and has also led to long-term, co-mentoring relationships. So, the particular approach to pairing may be less important than the support provided to participants that fosters deep and fruitful relationships.

Should student partners be in the discipline of their faculty partners?
In our experience in the classroom-focused partnerships through the SaLT program, it is typically more beneficial to faculty and student partners if the student partners do not have knowledge of the subject matter, although, as indicated above, some student partners might feel better or worse suited to a partnership based on previous experiences, and some faculty have specified that they need to work with a student partner who has some disciplinary knowledge. Almost all faculty members start out thinking it would be more helpful to have a student partner who knows the subject matter, but as the partnership unfolds, they come to see the benefits of having a student partner who does not make assumptions and can pose "naive" questions that would not likely occur to a faculty expert or a student with disciplinary knowledge. A former student

partner captures the power of having a perspective from outside the discipline in this way:

> While at first I felt out of my element, I discovered that observing teaching techniques, understanding student reactions and needs, and offering constructive feedback did not require an understanding of the discipline. In fact, my lack of familiarity with the subjects allowed me to consider the clarity of my partners' instructional styles and highlight disciplinary norms that may have been challenging to new students. (Daviduke 2018, 156)

The exception to the typical, cross-disciplinary pairings in the classroom-focused strand of the SaLT program is when a faculty member wishes to focus on an advanced course on which they want curricular as well as pedagogical input. In this case, the student partner's knowledge of content is necessary to achieve the goals of the partnership.

The curriculum-focused strand of the SaLT program typically has students with deep content knowledge, or at least who have taken the course, working with faculty. Because the focus of the work in this strand is how to best engage students around particular subject matter, faculty find it more productive to work with students inside the discipline. The course design/delivery consultants branch of McMaster University's Student Partners Program started out with random pairings like SaLT, but they found that many faculty members preferred having student partners with disciplinary knowledge, so they shifted to offering faculty members a choice.

As with many aspects of pedagogical partnership, there is no one right way to do this work, but it is worth thinking through the benefits and drawbacks of, and developing a rationale for, whichever approach you decide to take.

What about power dynamics?

There are always power dynamics between faculty and students because they are structured into our institutions of higher education. It is essential to keep in mind that these are always at play, and while pedagogical partnership aims to disrupt them, partnership work nevertheless unfolds within their influence. Numerous scholars have addressed this issue as partnership approaches have emerged, as the quotes below capture:

> "The professor who acknowledges their fallibility helps to break down the established power dynamic between student and faculty and allows the teacher to become a learner as well."
>
> —Kehler, Verwoord, and Smith 2017, 8
>
> "Engaging with Mariah, Rhiannon, and the many students with whom I have shared learning experiences has stretched me in ways I couldn't have predicted, challenging me to practice my politics, to engage my feminist praxis, and to be accountable for my power."
>
> —Vicki, faculty partner
> (quoted in Cates, Madigan, and Reitenauer 2018, 39)

Within the larger realities of power dynamics, there can be particular power dynamics within departments that are established in existing relationships between faculty and students. Sometimes faculty and students who have an existing relationship have a hard time shifting into this kind of pedagogical partnership, especially if the student is or could in future be enrolled in the faculty member's courses. Some students have felt constrained by power dynamics, departmental politics, and already established roles, and so the partnerships have not afforded either participant an opportunity to maximize the potential of this relationship. So, if faculty and students from the same department want to work in pedagogical partnership, think with them about how they will transition from the more traditional power dynamic into a dynamic of shared responsibility.

How do you achieve the best balance between offering support and affording participants flexibility and freedom?

Both faculty and students appreciate knowing program directors have thought through how to structure classroom-focused pedagogical partnership. They feel safer and more confident in what is, by definition, a vulnerable-making experience. A faculty-student pair described the way in which the SaLT program "allowed us to 'hold a space' where we could develop practical wisdom about teaching and learning together while increasing effectiveness during the very semesters during which we collaborated." They explained that the program "sustained tension between structure and freedom, providing guidelines to support our interactions but also the flexibility to experiment and learn from our mistakes and innovations" (Schlosser and Sweeney 2015, 1). This is what we aim for in the SaLT program, and while that balance will be different for different individuals and partners, having it as a goal is what allows us to both provide support structures and be responsive in changing them. We pose below some questions that we have received and that allow us to address how we strive to balance offering structured support with affording participants flexibility and freedom.

What kind of parameters or guidelines do student and faculty participants find helpful?
The majority of participants in the classroom-focused partnerships in the SaLT program have indicated that they find the set of guidelines we provide a very helpful starting point for establishing and building pedagogical partnerships. Those guidelines, scattered and elaborated upon throughout this book (and also included in short form in the "Guidelines for Student and Faculty Partners in Classroom-focused Pedagogical Partnerships" resource, provide recommendations, not requirements, for how to establish rapport, develop a focus for partnership, revise approaches as the partnership unfolds, and conclude partnerships. They also include advice from experienced partners and sample observation notes. Below is the table of contents:

Table of Contents	
Introduction	2
Basic expectations for student consultants	3
Laying the foundation for productive pedagogical partnership work	4

- Reading the guidelines
- Making early contact
- Building rapport
- Establishing a focus for your work

Introducing student partners to the faculty member's class — 8

Agreeing on the student partner's role and responsibilities — 8

Deciding when to meet and structuring meetings — 9

Techniques that student and faculty partners can use — 10
- Taking observation notes
- Writing up observation notes
- Mapping classroom interactions
- Gathering feedback

Revising the approach or focus of your partnership as the term progresses — 20

Capturing all the work you have done over the course of your partnership — 20

Concluding partnership — 23

Making the most of your partnership from start to finish — 24

Advice from experienced student consultants — 25

Students' responses to the question: "What have you gotten out of the experience of working as a student consultant?" — 27

Faculty feedback on working with a student consultant — 30

In the SaLT program, all student partners have the opportunity to discuss the guidelines during orientation. Faculty participants have the opportunity to discuss the guidelines if, for instance, they are enrolled in the pedagogy seminar linked to pedagogical partnerships, or if they contact Alison with any questions (although most find the guidelines sufficiently clear). We recommend that you provide an opportunity to discuss guidelines for partnership early in the semester when partnerships begin (or in the previous semester).

Regarding curriculum-focused partnerships in the SaLT program, faculty and student partners have typically developed their own approaches (see examples in chapter 7). Many have found the template for backward design in *Understanding by Design* (Wiggins and McTighe 2005) or the guidelines offered by L. Dee Fink (2013) in *Creating Significant Learning Experiences* useful.

What are useful approaches to orienting faculty and student partners who are embarking on a classroom-focused partnership?

Because pedagogical partnership is a new experience for virtually everyone, it is helpful to create opportunities for all participants to share hopes, expectations, concerns, questions, and aspirations regarding pedagogical partnership. We recommend, if possible, creating an orientation session that includes both student and faculty partners, with part of the time devoted to each constituency and part of the time devoted to cross-constituency dialogue.

The "Plans to Orient New Faculty and Student Partners" resource includes plans for orientation that Alison has used to support multiple institutions in launching pedagogical partnership programs. It includes as well a plan that Leslie Ortquist-Ahrens, director of the Center for Teaching and Learning and director of faculty development at Berea College, uses to invite faculty partners to identify and articulate what they expect the partnership experience will be like, what the most pressing questions that they bring to this work might be, what hopes they have for the experience, and what fears they might bring.

Do you need to train student partners before they embark on classroom-focused pedagogical partnerships?

Different programs take different approaches to the question of preparation for the role of student partner, depending on philosophy, student availability, and funding options. The SaLT program and the Tigers as Partners program at Trinity University, for instance, hold orientations prior to the start of the partnerships each semester, whereas the

Student Consultant Program at Ursinus College focuses on supporting students on the job. Orientations typically include opportunities to identify strengths and capacities student partners bring to the role, share hopes and concerns about embarking on a pedagogical partnership, consider possible scenarios and practice skills (e.g., analyzing a syllabus), and identify aspirations. They might be organized like this:

> **Student Partner Orientation Schedule**
> Introductions (10 mins)
> Carousel and discussion (25 mins)
> Sharing scenarios (25 mins)
> Break (10 mins)
> Specific questions (30 mins)
> Check in about logistics (10 mins)
> Aspirations (10 mins)

Or like this:

> **Student Partner Orientation Schedule**
> Community building (15 mins)
> Introductions (10 mins)
> Establishment of expertise (20 mins)
> Skill building: Reading a syllabus (30 mins)
> Break (15 mins)
> Skill building: Taking observation notes (15 mins)
> Logistical organizing (10 mins)
> Written reflections (10 mins)
> Affirmations (5 mins)
> Final thoughts/questions (10 mins)

We offer detailed expansions of both of these plans in the "Sample Outlines for Student Partners Orientations" resource.

Program directors have also developed additional approaches to orienting faculty and student partners to this work in early meetings. For instance, Leslie Ortquist-Ahrens, director of the Center for Teaching and Learning and director of faculty development at Berea College, has developed a "Gets and Gives" grid that asks participants to imagine what each will "get" from and "give" to the partnership. The grid included in the "Plans to Orient New Faculty and Student Partners" resource is an example from one semester during which faculty and student partners completed the grid separately at the outset of their partnerships at Berea, then compared them to one another's grids in their cohort meetings. Returning these completed grids to participants at the end of the semester can be a useful form of reflection and informal assessment.

These approaches to orienting participants focus on prompting reflection, accessing and making explicit assumptions, raising awareness, and encouraging intentionality. They constitute a very different approach to preparing participants than would more formal, structured training. Each year, toward the end of the semester, Alison asks student partners in SaLT whether they would have benefited from a training prior to embarking on partnerships, beyond the orientation, and they say no. Sophia Abbot has asked the same question of the students in Tigers as Partners at Trinity University and received the same universal response. These students indicate that, as we discussed in chapter 4 regarding the primacy of building relationships, being in pedagogical partnership is about learning who their faculty partners are, what their pedagogical goals are, and how to support their faculty partners in making their particular classrooms and curriculum as inclusive and responsive as they can be. Training, the students suggest, would run the risk of seeming to impose a single approach, and what they find both most productive, if sometimes profoundly challenging, is learning how to build a generative working relationship with their individual faculty partners.

What forums for support do student partners in classroom-focused pedagogical partnerships need and how might these be structured?

In consulting with institutions about developing pedagogical partnership programs, Alison always tells potential program directors and participants that the single most important component of such programs is regular opportunities for student partners to meet and be in dialogue with one another and with the program director. Here we discuss that forum and others to support student partners.

Should you facilitate a regular (weekly or biweekly) forum for reflection, dialogue, and support?

These meetings are the most important structural feature of a classroom-focused pedagogical partnership program because it is in these weekly meetings that student partners recognize and further their capacities, develop a language for talking about teaching and learning, build confidence, and gather insights and ideas from other student partners. How these meetings are facilitated will inform student partners' sense of their capacity and agency.

One of the most important skills student partners develop in this forum is how to speak with those in positions of greater institutional power about pedagogical issues. In SaLT, we discuss how to frame feedback and input with sentences like this:

- "If I were a student in this class and was asked to do that activity, I might feel . . ."
- "I once took a class where the professor did [X] and it really helped me understand the concept because . . ."
- "I notice that you . . . ; I am interested in what inspired you to take that approach . . ."

Such statements locate the perception with the student partner, rather than formulate assertions that might sound like critiques or judgments. These formulations require that student partners develop mindsets that are inquisitive rather than judgmental, and they make what student partners have to say more "hearable" to their faculty partners. (See discussion in chapter 4.)

These kinds of statement do not come naturally, as one student partner explains:

> [We have] an incredible support system in our weekly meetings [where] I feel I can raise an issue I'm having and have it addressed, I feel that my opinion matters and is respected . . . [and we can] find ways to frame

ideas and concepts so we can think about them in new and deeper ways. (Student partner in the SaLT program, survey response)

What approaches to facilitation of weekly meetings with student partners have been successful?
Developing a structure that supports reflection and dialogue is among the most important roles of the director of pedagogical partnership programs in collaboration with the student partners. In the "General Guiding Principles for Weekly Reflective Meetings of Student Partners" resource we detail three general guiding principles for reflective meetings that Alison has developed since the first years of SaLT. These are particularly important, from Alison's perspective, in helping student partners develop a mindset that will make them most able to support, in turn, their faculty partners' reflections. We also offer two sets of general guidelines generated by two former student partners, Melanie and one of her contemporaries, Natasha Daviduke, who, in anticipation of our writing this book, spent one semester observing the student partner meetings in the SaLT program to identify useful practices. These lists offer student partners' perspectives on what makes these reflective meetings productive. Below we provide an overview of these guiding principles and offer a glimpse into what an exchange in a weekly student partner meeting of SaLT looks like, drawn from Natasha's notes.

These are the three general guiding principles for reflective meetings that Alison has developed since the first years of SaLT:
1. Focus early on what strengths and capacities student partners bring and how they are putting those to work or further developing them.
2. Regularly remind student partners that faculty partners are vulnerable and not necessarily accustomed to constant reflection and change.
3. Invite and explicitly name the links between classroom and life lessons.

Below are general guidelines generated by Melanie and Natasha, all of which are discussed in more detail in the "General Guiding Principles for Weekly Reflective Meetings of Student Partners" resource:

- Use regular introductions and check-ins to bring people into the space.
- Give students quiet writing time to consider a question or focusing idea of the session.
- Consider how you respond when student partners share from their writing.
- Bring in topics from conversations with faculty so that student partners have a better idea of what their partners might be exploring in other contexts.
- Ask student partners directly if they want to share something in order to bring the conversation back from diversions.
- Try to parse out the causality behind observations that student partners make.
- Pick up on particular experiences that student partners share and ask the group to consider if they have ever done or observed something similar.
- Suggest and invite readings on pedagogy that might be relevant to everyone's partnerships.
- Offer concluding thoughts on a topic before switching gears to a new question.
- Give a lot of space to student partners to comment on each other's work and ask questions.
- Make space for student partners to express their experience as students in context.
- Ask student partners to write up something about their experiences if they find them to be especially salient.
- Consistently offer affirmation.

When program directors employ techniques like those listed above, the weekly meetings can unfold in ways that both affirm and challenge student partners, nurturing their development as consultants able to listen deeply, brainstorm solutions to pedagogical challenges, and celebrate inclusive and responsive teaching.

Example of an exchange in a reflective meeting

We offer here a glimpse into a meeting of student partners and Alison in SaLT. The following is an example of an exchange in which student partners offer their perspectives on a question a faculty member in the natural sciences posed to his student partner:

> **Alison:** Is there anything going on in your partnerships that you want to discuss? Anything that is challenging or worrying you?
>
> **Student Partner 1:** My partner asked me a really interesting question during our last meeting. He asked how he can properly assess a student on material that he knows he didn't fully grasp until he had studied it for several years. He was feeling that asking his intro students to show understanding of concepts that he didn't fully understand at their level was unreasonable.
>
> **Alison:** That's a great question. Does anyone have thoughts about that?
>
> **Student Partner 2:** A question I think it's important to ask is, "How do you know when you've learned something?" In my organic chemistry class, my professor asked us to explain concepts by drawing out pictures and explaining them in no more than 10 words, and it wasn't until I was able to do that that I felt I had learned the concept.
>
> **Student Partner 3:** When I took physics, our professor tried to understand our thought processes by asking us to write out every step when we solved problems. We had to write why we were stuck, so that even if we came to the wrong answer, our professor could see how we had arrived there.
>
> **Student Partner 4:** One thing my partner and I have discussed a lot is having learning goals and making them explicit to the students. It's a helpful way of organizing what you want students to learn and helping them focus their learning.
>
> **Student Partner 5:** My partner uses images for everything. He projects from his iPad and writes next to the pictures so that the concepts are always accompanied by the visual.
>
> **Student Partner 4:** I would also say that it's important for him to tell students that he has also struggled with this material.

> **Student Partner 2**: I agree. I think it's humanizing for the professor and it helps the students to be less hard on themselves if they know that the person teaching them also didn't get everything at their level.
>
> **Student Partner 6**: I think it's also helpful to tell students that this may be the first time they're encountering something and it's ok if they don't understand it because they may have more time to expand their learning in that area.

The student partner who brought the question from her faculty partner to the group was able to take back to him the wide variety of insights student partners offer. All the other student partners benefited as well from this exchange by thinking of and finding language for pedagogical practices that have been successful for them and other faculty, and they also could apply the advice to their work with their respective faculty partners.

In terms of facilitation, note that Alison posed a question, affirmed a response that was offered by one student partner, turned the question back to the group, and then remained quiet as the student partners in the room shared ideas. There are times when a program director will want to share insights and recommendations, but just as often a far richer set of insights and recommendations will emerge from what student partners have to offer.

What kind of structure might weekly meetings of student partners follow?

In our experience, the processes of identifying, exploring, analyzing, celebrating, and problem-solving that the weekly meetings provide are best supported by a loose structure. Because each partnership presents its own opportunities and challenges, it is helpful to make space within the weekly meetings for both individual reflections and open dialogue. Sasha Mathrani, a former SaLT student partner, captures this experience:

> Reflecting on my varied partnerships has helped me identify some of the moments of growth and explicitly

understand the impact of the SaLT program in all my ways of being. I can see how my ability to build relationships and navigate uncertainty has developed over the course of my partnerships, and I realize how learning how to navigate those unfamiliar situations has given me the confidence to speak up in situations outside my partnerships. (Mathrani 2018, 6)

We recommend that you develop a set of prompts that will afford each student partner the opportunity to capture individual experiences in informal writing. This ensures time for thoughtful reflection, as well as supplying records of experiences that can be returned to later and shared in subsequent discussions. Student partners suggest that it is helpful to keep their freewrites or reflections in one place so that toward the end of the semester they can easily return to some of the prompts from the beginning of the semester to track progress.

In the "Sample Outline of Topics for Weekly Meetings of Student Partners" resource we offer a version of the prompts we have used in SaLT and that directors of pedagogical partnership programs at other institutions have adapted for their contexts (see also the syllabus for the for-credit course in the "Sample Student Partners Course Syllabus" resource).

What kind of leadership can experienced student partners take in facilitation?
While the program director might facilitate the majority of the weekly meetings of student partners, it is in keeping with the spirit of partnership to consider ways in which these meetings can be co-facilitated by student partners. Student partners can share their experiences and offer analyses of how they make sense of and act upon the challenges and tensions they have experienced and the links between classroom and life lessons.

Beyond that, a student partner might bring a particular issue or question to the group and lead the discussion around that. This co-facilitation helps student partners deepen capacities to identify and articulate pedagogical challenges, develop language to name and analyze them, and build confidence to address them with faculty partners and others (e.g., other students, faculty who teach courses in which they are enrolled, current and prospective employers). As Natasha Daviduke, former SaLT student partner, argues: "Other student consultants can direct discussion and support their fellow consultants in these meetings. Their individual experiences in their partnerships can provide a trove of valuable techniques for problem-solving within this work" (personal communication). And as Beth Marquis explains: "At McMaster University, we have sometimes had staff and students co-facilitate and support program streams in partnership" (personal communication).

Once student partners have worked in several partnerships, they can assume greater responsibility for mentoring newer student partners, facilitating or co-facilitating student partner orientations, and facilitating weekly meetings when the director of the program is away from campus or on leave, as Anita and other former SaLT student partners have done. These expanded facilitation roles allow student partners to draw on the expertise they have developed and prepare for subsequent, larger leadership roles, such as in post-bac fellow positions (discussed in detail in the last section of chapter 3, in the "Creating Post-Bac Fellow Positions to Support the Development of Pedagogical Partnership Programs" resource, and in the "Three Stages of Backward Design to Support the Development of Post-Bac Fellow Positions" resource. Such increased responsibility can emerge in organic ways, or it can be structured into the program, as the directors of the program at Ursinus College have done (see chapter 3).

What can program directors do to support curriculum-focused pedagogical partnerships?

Cook-Sather, Matthews, and Bell (2019, in press) argue that academic developers are uniquely positioned to reimagine and support curriculum transformation as a relational and reciprocal process in which students have a fundamental right to have a voice and to take an active role. As we discuss in detail in chapter 7, in the SaLT program, there are typically four kinds of curriculum-focused partnerships in which faculty and student partners engage: co-planning a course before it is taught; revising while a course is unfolding; redesigning a course after it is taught; and making explicit and challenging the hidden curriculum of a course. The program director's role is a bit different in each case. We recommend that program directors read those discussions in chapter 7, written primarily for faculty and student partners, and consider how, in any given context, such work might be best supported.

Across all forms of curriculum-focused pedagogical partnership, program directors will want to consider how to compensate the student partner. In most cases—unless the curriculum is being designed or redesigned through collaboration between the instructor and the students enrolled in the course—it will be important to confer with the faculty-student team about which approach would be best. The three most common ways to compensate student time and expertise are to situate the role as a campus job, compensated with hourly pay through departmental, curriculum development, or provost's office budgets; to enroll the student in a half-credit or a full-credit course; or to create a scholarship. (See chapter 3 for an expanded discussion of this point. Options for compensating faculty partners are also addressed there.) Here we note some general considerations for each type of curriculum-focused partnership and provide examples of publications that detail approaches different student and faculty partners have taken.

How can you support pedagogical partnerships focused on co-planning a course before it is taught?

In co-planning a course before it is taught, faculty and students may be starting from scratch or they may be bringing concepts, outlines, general or vague ideas, or clear commitments they want to enact. The program director's role in this case is to support both the impulse and the process. Because pedagogical partnership is countercultural both in the arena of pedagogical practice and in the arena of curriculum design, faculty and students appreciate the encouragement that program directors can offer as well as any support structures that might be put into place.

So, program directors might first affirm that the impulse to co-plan a course is inspiring, and perhaps offer examples of faculty at their own or other institutions who have taken this approach. Here are a few examples toward which program directors can point faculty and student partners:

- Student author Yi Wang and faculty author Younglin Jiang (2012), in the context of a pedagogy seminar in which they both enrolled, spent a full semester co-creating "Cultural History of Chinese Astronomy," a course that they chose to design drawing on Jiang's expertise as a professor of East Asian Studies and Wang's knowledge from her hobby, astronomy;
- Elliott Shore (2012, 1-2) and a group of students co-designed his course on the history of women's higher education, meeting over lunch to talk about "the readings, the assignments, the ways in which the class would operate, the speakers we would invite, the places we would visit and the students who would be invited to take the class";
- Cherie Woolmer and her co-authors (2016) describe the development of a multidisciplinary lesson plan aimed at developing science skills for physics and astronomy, geographical and Earth sciences, and chemistry students at a research-intensive Scottish university;
- Alison Cook-Sather and Crystal Des-Ogugua (2017) spent a full semester, meeting once a week or so, to co-design all the assignments, assessments, and activities for an undergraduate education course at Bryn Mawr College;
- Tanya Michelle Lubicz-Nawrocka (2018) analyzes participants' perceptions of co-creation of the curriculum in the Scottish higher-education sector; and
- Lori Goff and Kris Knorr (2018) describe an applied curriculum design in science course at McMaster University through which upper-level students form partnerships with faculty and educational developers and work in groups to co-create learning modules that become key components of a foundational science course offered to first-year students.

We recommend that program directors offer these as examples and inspirations, not prescriptions, for how student and faculty partners might go about co-creating a course or a module within a course.

Program directors can encourage faculty and student partners to take their time in the design process. It may be that other commitments preclude weekly meetings, but encourage partners to set up a schedule and create forums for dialogue and idea exchange, even if those forums need to be virtual. Using a template such as Wiggins and McTighe's (2005) backward design template or L. Dee Fink's (2013) *Creating Significant Learning Experiences* can structure and capture the planning in which the student and faculty partners engage.

How can you support pedagogical partnerships focused on revising while a course is unfolding?

This form of curriculum-focused pedagogical partnership might well resemble classroom-focused partnerships through which a single student partner works for the duration of a semester to analyze and adjust the course as it unfolds. Alternatively, it might look like a faculty member and all students enrolled in a given course revising it as they go.

If faculty and student partners take the former approach, with the student partners visiting the faculty partner's classroom weekly or biweekly and meeting regularly to revise the course as it unfolds, then program directors can draw on and adapt the approaches to supporting classroom-focused pedagogical partnership work described in earlier portions of this chapter and in chapter 6.

If faculty members choose to undertake curricular co-creation and revision in collaboration with all students enrolled in their courses, then the focus of the program director's support will be more on how to help faculty balance the complicated role of being co-creator and evaluator and help students balance the complicated role of being co-creator and evaluated (unless they include co-creation of assessment, such as Susan Deeley has done in her courses at the University of Glasgow in Scotland—see Deeley and Bovill 2017; Deeley and Brown 2014).

As with supporting faculty and students in co-planning a course before it is taught, in the case of supporting faculty and students in revising while a course is unfolding, program directors may want to offer some examples, not prescriptive models to be replicated but as inspirations, such as these:

- Mary Sunderland (2013) describes how she regularly conferred with students enrolled in her engineering course at the University of California, Berkeley, and revised it according to their feedback;

- Sarah Bunnell and Dan Bernstein (2014, 1) describe how the two of them, a graduate student and a professor at the University of Kansas, also worked with an undergraduate enrolled in the course they co-taught to discuss "the goals that we had for student learning for each section of the course, what was working well (and not as well as we would like), and ways in which we could maximize student learning and engagement with the material";
- Ulrika Bergmark and Susanne Westman (2016) describe a teacher education course that was co-designed by the instructor and the students as the course unfolded in a university in Sweden; and
- Alison Cook-Sather, Crystal Des-Ogugua, and Melanie Bahti (2018) discuss one course assignment that was not only created by the instructor and a student partner for an undergraduate education course at Bryn Mawr College (Cook-Sather and Des-Ogugua 2017) but was also co-created by the instructor and students enrolled as the course unfolded.

How can you support pedagogical partnerships focused on redesigning a course after it is taught?

In the SaLT program, most such partnerships emerge after faculty members have participated in a classroom-focused pedagogical partnership. The faculty partners are therefore familiar with pedagogical partnership principles and practices and carry those into their curriculum-focused redesign process. In these cases, faculty partners tend to be very independent and set up schedules and processes that they know will work for them. Whether faculty and student partners are independent or looking for more guidance and support, program directors may want to point them to some examples of curriculum redesign, such as:

- Richard Mihans and his faculty, staff, and student co-authors (2008) describe the process of redesigning an education course at Elon University through a course design team (CDT). At Elon, each team's process varies, but typically a CDT includes one or two faculty members, between two and six undergraduate students, and one academic developer;

- Louise Charkoudian and her student co-authors (2015) describe how a faculty member and three undergraduate students engaged in a semester-long redesign process through which they revised course content, assignments, and methods of assessment for Charkoudian's first-semester organic chemistry course at Haverford College; and
- Gintaras Kazimieras Duda and Mary Ann Danielson (2018) describe the Collaborative Curricular (re)Construction, or C^3, that was an initiative at Creighton University in Nebraska that paired faculty and students in a process of backward course design. Two cohorts (one in the 2013-14 and one in 2014-15) of faculty-student pairs worked over the span of a year to redesign a theory-, skill-, and laboratory-based course within their discipline.

Program directors might also want to develop examples of structures faculty partners could adapt. In chapter 7, we include the structure that Charkoudian et al. (2015) used.

How can you support pedagogical partnerships focused on making explicit and challenging the hidden curriculum?

This form of curriculum-focused pedagogical partnership might also closely resemble the classroom-focused partnerships discussed above and that are the focus of chapter 6. A term coined by Jackson (1968), the hidden curriculum encompasses the unintentional lesson or lessons taught that reinforce inequities. It resides in the "gaps or disconnects between what faculty intend to deliver (the formal curriculum) and what learners take away from those formal lessons" (Hafferty, Gaufberg, and DiCroce 2015, 35). And, most commonly, what learners take away is a sense that they are not reflected in and may not have the capacity to master the course content.

Keeping in mind that any curriculum, including the hidden curriculum, "always represent[s] an introduction to, preparation for, and legitimation of a particular form of life" (McLaren 1989, 160), faculty and student partners who wish to make explicit and challenge the hidden curriculum need courage, clarity, and intentionality to do so. They will need moral as well as practical support in finding ways to identify, name, and address the hidden curriculum in any given course. It might be useful to encourage them to use sets of principles that strive to counter hegemonic or discriminatory curriculum, such as the eight core feminist principles Chin and Russo (1997) identified—diversity, egalitarianism and empowerment, self-determination, connection, social action, self-reflection, and integrative perspectives—or the New Zealand government's tertiary education strategy that has as one of its priorities to enable Māori to achieve education success as Māori (see also Berryman and Eley 2017).

Examples of faculty and students addressing the hidden curriculum in a variety of ways include:

- Kerstin Perez (2016), in "Striving Toward a Space for Equity and Inclusion in Physics Classrooms," describes how she worked with her student partner at Haverford College to reflect on how her teaching was matching, or missing, her goals and to question the traditional boundaries of what is discussed in an undergraduate physics class, including how those traditionally underrepresented can address difficult and problematic issues in the field;
- Mary Brunson (2018, 2) explores how, through building trust and developing greater comfort with unfinishedness and the "unknowability" of many phenomena, she worked with her faculty partner at Bryn Mawr College to "create a curriculum that would make him more 'in touch' with" his students;
- Lillian Nave and student partners (2018) entirely shifted the focus of Nave's course on international movements in the visual and performing arts at Appalachian State University, North Carolina, United States, to be responsive to what mattered to the students as they were setting foot on campus for the first time after several incidents involving white nationalist activity; and
- Amarachi Chukwu and Kim Jones (forthcoming) at McMaster University in Hamilton, Ontario, Canada, redesigned the course Inclusion in the Engineering Workplace, focusing, as the title of their chapter suggests, on "Feminist Interventions in Engineering: Co-creating across Disciplines and Identities."

Faculty and student partners doing this work appreciate program directors sharing resources on how to develop more inclusive and responsive curriculum and offering moral support for the challenging and wearing work of countering injustice. Student partners in particular appreciate support for the emotional labor they invest in supporting their faculty partners. We discuss this last issue in chapter 8.

Who might participate in the curriculum design or redesign process?

While faculty might typically initiate the course design or redesign process, program directors can suggest a variety of participants, including but not limited to students. For instance, Alison and some of her colleagues designed an opportunity for teams of four—a faculty member, a librarian, an instructional technologist, and a student—to redesign a course in ways that meaningfully integrated technology during a week-long summer workshop (Cook-Sather 2001).

The best way to help faculty decide whom to invite to work with them is to pose some basic questions about purpose and goals, such as:

- What do you want students to know and be able to do by the end of the course?
- What learning experiences during the course do you want students to have?
- What forms of assessment can you develop that are congruent with the goals you have and the learning experiences you aim to foster?
- In what ways are all components of your course inclusive of and responsive to a diversity of students?

Then, ask faculty to consider who can offer helpful insights on these questions, and who might become partners not only in conceptualizing but also in enacting the newly designed or redesigned course.

In the case of co-planning a course before it is taught, faculty may invite a group of students who have taken similar courses, a group of students who might be the intended population to enroll in the course, and librarians, instructional technologists, and others who could bring expertise and insight regarding how to create resources and structures. Many faculty are tempted to invite the "best" students, usually meaning those who are visible, are a fit for the norms of learning in higher education, and therefore do well. We encourage you to urge faculty to think more broadly about who might be productive student partners in planning a course. Students who have traditionally been underserved by, felt unwelcome in, and struggled through standard curriculum might offer very different perspectives and recommendations from those who have found higher education welcoming, supportive, and easily navigable.

These same considerations hold true for faculty who decide to redesign a course after it has been taught or work to make explicit and challenge the hidden curriculum. In addition to drawing on the insights of traditionally successful students, faculty can benefit from seeking to understand and redesign in response to a wider range of notions of what might constitute success (Cook-Sather 2018b; O'Shea and Delahunty 2018). As with the case of course design, the experiences and perspectives of students who have traditionally been underserved by, felt unwelcome in, and struggled through standard curriculum can not only inform a given course but also begin to change the culture of higher education.

YOUR TURN

Inviting and responding to prospective participants in pedagogical partnership programs:

As you are planning to launch or further develop pedagogical partnership opportunities on your campus, what approaches might you take to inviting and responding to prospective participants?

Are these approaches similar to or different from the ways people are invited or responded to regarding other opportunities on campus?

What messages are you sending to prospective participants and to others on campus and beyond regarding who participates and why?

What criteria will you use to match student and faculty partners? When might it make sense for student and faculty partners to be in different disciplines and when in the same discipline?

Supporting participants as their partnerships unfold:

What structures and processes will you develop to support partners in naming and navigating power dynamics?

How will you achieve the best balance between offering support and affording participants flexibility and freedom in classroom-focused partnerships?

- What kind of parameters or guidelines for student and faculty participants will you develop?
- How will you orient faculty and student partners to classroom-focused partnership?
- With what frequency and forms of facilitation will you support reflection and dialogue among participants?

How can you as a program director support curriculum-focused pedagogical partnerships focused on:

- co-planning a course before it is taught?
- co-creating a course while it is unfolding?
- redesigning a course after it is taught?
- making explicit and challenging the hidden curriculum?

6
WHAT APPROACHES MIGHT STUDENT AND FACULTY PARTNERS USE IN CLASSROOM-FOCUSED PARTNERSHIPS?

We discussed in chapter 4 the shared responsibilities for facilitating pedagogical partnership as conceptualized in SaLT and programs like it. In this chapter, we focus on classroom-focused pedagogical partnerships, in which faculty and student pairs work together in long-term (typically semester-long or sometimes yearlong) partnerships to analyze, affirm, and, where appropriate, revise pedagogical approaches as the faculty member teaches the focal course. We discuss foundational steps partners can take to encourage the long-term success of partnerships, how student and faculty partners can establish a focus for their work, and the approaches student and faculty partners engaged in these partnerships can take.

What are the steps in establishing, sustaining, and concluding classroom-focused pedagogical partnerships?

There are different forms of classroom-focused student-faculty partnerships. For instance, Hayward, Venture, Schuldt, and Donlan (2018, 39) describe "student pedagogical teams," which they define as "teams of student 'consultants' who become active and engaged as partners in the teaching and learning process by providing feedback to the professor on course content, assignments, and delivery of material" (Nuhfer, 1995). These students are enrolled in the focal course.

Our focus in this chapter is on pedagogical partnerships between faculty and students when students are not enrolled in the focal course. We offer an overview of how to establish, maintain, and conclude classroom-focused pedagogical partnerships.

How do student and faculty partners lay the foundation for a productive classroom-focused partnership?

Below we outline a series of steps that student and faculty partners can take to lay the foundation for developing a strong and productive partnership. These include:

- reading the guidelines provided by program directors so that you have a clear understanding and shared starting point for embarking on your partnership work;
- making early contact with your partner to ensure that you have time to prepare and plan to begin your partnership; and
- establishing rapport before launching into your work so that you have a human connection that can serve as a foundation for this demanding collaborative work.

Read the guidelines

In the SaLT program, Alison sends a set of guidelines (expanded upon here and included in short form in the "Guidelines for Student and Faculty Partners in Classroom-focused Pedagogical Partnership" resource) to both student and faculty partners. In preparation for embarking upon a partnership, it is helpful if student and faculty partners read these carefully. These are intended to serve as a starting point, not a set of prescriptions, but faculty and student partners have found that they contribute to partners "being on the same page" as they embark upon their work together.

Make early contact

After faculty and student partners have familiarized themselves with the program guidelines, the next step in laying the foundation for a productive classroom-focused pedagogical partnership is making early contact with one another. In chapter 4 we discussed the importance of professional communication for all participants in pedagogical partnership. In the SaLT program, it is typically the student partner who contacts the faculty partner to launch the partnership by asking for an initial meeting. Here is a sample message that Alison offers the student partners to personalize and send:

> Dear Professor [Fill in Last Name],
>
> I hope you are well. I am a [sophomore/junior/senior] majoring in [fill in major] at [fill in name of college], and I will be working as your Student Consultant during the [fill in semester and year] semester through the [name of pedagogical partnership program]. I would like to schedule a meeting with you during or before the first week of classes so that we can establish an initial focus for our work together, discuss my role, and talk about how I will be introduced to your class. I will be available [fill in days and times]. Please let me know which of these times might work for us to meet.
>
> I very much look forward to working with you this coming semester.
>
> Sincerely,
>
> [Your name]

Faculty partners typically receive these messages prior to the start of the semester, and to ensure that they and their student partners can embark upon their pedagogical partnership at the start of the following semester, it is best if they respond promptly and arrange an initial meeting time with their student partners. They might also want to give a preliminary indication of what they are interested in focusing on in the partnership work so that student partners can be thinking about that.

Establish rapport

The next step in laying the foundation for a productive partnership is to focus in the initial meeting on building a relationship. As we discussed in chapter 4, this initial focus on who faculty and student partners are as people helps build the foundation of trust necessary for realizing the potential of pedagogical partnership. It is helpful for both faculty and student partners to:

- **Introduce yourselves and say something about why you are interested in this work**. What interests, skills, hopes do both student and faculty partners bring? What are the faculty partner's perceptions, questions, and hopes for teaching in this context? What are the student partner's perceptions, questions, and hopes for learning in this context? How can pedagogical partnership address these?

- **Share educational histories and experiences**. This is a great time for student partners to begin to understand the trajectory of their faculty partner's career that led to this moment—their experiences in other institutions and the current one. It is also a great opportunity for student partners to talk about their experiences as students in the institution and offer faculty partners a sense of the culture of the institution.
- **Keep the initial discussion focused on you two as people.** While it is tempting to jump straight to the work at hand, and some partners do that, it is helpful to provide insight into past experiences and current contextual information that can situate the pedagogical work.
- **Take time to ask how other things are going**—research, courses, how you are feeling about the class you are focused on. Slowing down to make space for some of these more personal exchanges, before partners get into talking about specific things they want to focus in on, can make a big difference.
- **Establish ways of checking in as people.** The dynamic that student and faculty partners establish at the outset will shape how the relationship unfolds over time. Throughout the partnership, remember to focus on relationship. Keep in mind that partnership is not just transactional. By taking time to engage as whole people, not just as teachers and students, partners will be better able to build a strong and trusting connection that will enable the part of the work that is focused on exploring teaching and learning. A former student partner articulates the importance of that kind of human focus:

> In one of my partnerships our entire first meeting was talking about ourselves as people, and then we moved into talking more about the class, goals, etc. This made for a really strong foundation in the partnership and

our conversations about the class ended up being more honest.

—Sasha Mathrani,
former student partner in SaLT
(personal communication)

How can student and faculty partners establish a focus for their work?

Once student and faculty partners have established rapport and begun to build some trust, they can move to focusing on the pedagogical work. As part of the initial meeting, before the student partner begins visiting the faculty partner's class, clarify what the faculty member's teaching and learning goals are for the particular course upon which the partnership will focus. In the SaLT program, student partners ask questions such as:

- What are the course goals?
- What does the syllabus include and look like? (for more information about the course, how goals are portrayed in the syllabus, etc.)
- What are some specific pedagogical goals you have within the course?
- What kind of learning experiences do you want students to have and why?
- What do you see as my role in helping you to explore these pedagogical issues?
- What do you want me to focus on initially in my classroom observations?

Based on the faculty partner's responses to the questions above, the student and faculty partner can formulate a clear statement of what the initial focus of the partnership will be. For example, a student partner might say, "Based on what you've shared, it sounds like XX is important to the success of this course and your students. Perhaps that should be our initial focus as we begin this partnership?" Whatever initial focus partners identify will likely evolve and change over the course of the semester, but it is helpful to name a starting place.

Depending on the kind of relationship the student and faculty partners build, it might be possible for student partners to propose areas of focus. This is a delicate negotiation, since even within the overall construct of pedagogical partnership, some faculty can experience such student-proposed foci as presumptuous and impositional, while others welcome any proposed area of exploration students generate. It can be quite difficult to predict which foci will be perceived as inappropriate and which will be welcomed, so, as always, the key is careful listening and respectful communication.

What are some common areas of focus for pedagogical partnerships?

Many student and faculty partners select a focus for their partnership that is specific to the context of the discipline, student population, or institution in which they work, so there are as many areas of focus as there are partnerships. A few broad categories into which many foci might fit include building more inclusive classrooms, encouraging engagement and contribution to classroom discussion, and teaching in the context of social and political complexity. Here is a sample of foci that student and faculty partners have explored:

- Classroom environment/culture
    - » Practices to use in the beginning of the year to establish classroom culture and build student-professor relationships
    - » What constitutes good stress/pressure vs. bad stress/pressure?
    - » How to create a positive classroom culture where it is okay to not know all the answers (and the way a professor's use of language impacts this)
    - » How to bring in a professor's personality into the classroom (what's the best balance between sharing one's personality and staying more distant?)
- Pedagogical transparency
    - » How to make pedagogy explicit and invite students into this discussion if they want to join it
    - » How to recognize and explain intentions (e.g., a faculty partner tended to make hand gestures—rolling his hands, tapping on the table) that struck his student consultant as stress inducing,

but he meant them as encouraging, so he explained his intent to the students enrolled in his course)
- Classroom conversations
  » How often students are called on, how often students volunteer to talk
  » Who students look at when talking
  » Interrupting students
  » How to make participation more accessible and inclusive (think-pair-share, time to write, etc.)
- Assessment and evaluation
  » Alternative ways to think about feedback and revision
  » How to structure tests, assignments, and activities to maximize learning and participation

We offer some selected readings related to these common areas of focus in the "Selected Reading Lists" resource.

What should the student partner role and responsibilities be in any given partnership?

A student partner in the SaLT program offers the following reminder to other student partners:

> Remember that as a student partner you have valuable insight as an external student who is an advocate and liaison for not only the students enrolled in the course and your faculty partner but also for transformative pedagogical tools that may be overlooked. No matter what may seem "small" or "large" to you, as long as you are consistently engaging in material and engaging in dialogue as well as questioning your assumptions, your work is impactful. (Excerpt from informal feedback)

Typically in the SaLT program, student consultants visit their faculty partners' classrooms once per week and take observation notes, but not everyone has employed this model. We discuss two possible models for classroom-focused partnership below:

- Classroom observations plus weekly meetings
- Weekly meetings plus other forms of exploration and dialogue

Should student partners visit their faculty partner's classrooms?
Most classroom-focused pedagogical partnerships through SaLT and other programs include classroom observations, but sometimes this is not the best or even a possible approach, such as when faculty teach courses with confidential content (as in schools of social work). Although it might seem counterintuitive, sometimes partnerships in which the student partner does not visit their faculty partner's classrooms can prompt deeper reflection. When the faculty partner needs to convey to the student partner what is happening in the class, the partnership can feel more collaborative, as the student partner strives to imagine what the faculty partner describes, having to listen deeply for what is explained and what might be overlooked. Instead of the student partner doing the work of analysis based on observation, the work of analysis has to happen between the partners.

Here are two possible approaches for student and faculty partners to consider:

- **Classroom observations plus weekly meetings**
  If the student partner will visit the faculty partner's class once a week, will they
  » silently take observations notes only?
  » participate sometimes as well (and if so, when and how)?
  » send the observation notes prior to the weekly meeting or bring the notes to the weekly meeting?
- **Weekly meetings plus other forms of exploration and dialogue**
  If for whatever reason the faculty partner prefers not to have weekly visits to their classroom, or if they want to add some of the following to classroom observations, the student partner can employ one or more of these alternative ways to collaborate and be in dialogue:

» Focus in the weekly meetings on the faculty partner describing to the student partner their pedagogical practices and rationales.
» The student partner can research pedagogical practices in the faculty partner's field or discipline and discuss findings and recommendations with them. This can be research into pedagogical approaches with which faculty are not familiar but want to be, or it can be research into practices in which faculty already engage to gather evidence for such approaches.

If you decide that classroom observations will be a component of your partnership program, the "Visiting Faculty Partners' Classrooms and Taking Observation Notes" resource provides detailed guidelines regarding how student partners can be introduced to the faculty member's class and what the student partner's classroom observations notes can look like.

Should student partners interact directly with students enrolled in the course?

Whether student partners interact directly with students enrolled in the course is up to the faculty partner. Some faculty members ask their student partners to share their email addresses, meet regularly with students enrolled in the course, conduct regular or only midterm feedback, and more. Other faculty members prefer that student partners have no direct contact with students in their classes because they want students to come directly to them as instructors rather than have an intermediary.

Student and faculty partners can discuss the pros and cons of various approaches and make a decision together, but student partners should not initiate contact with students enrolled in the class if the faculty member has not agreed to this. As we discussed in chapter 4 under the heading, "How do you practice professional and confidential communication?", students enrolled in faculty members' courses may approach student partners uninvited. In the SaLT program, we emphasize the importance of student partners listening to whatever input is given and offering to share it anonymously with faculty partners but not sharing what faculty partners discuss or trying to explain what faculty partners are trying to achieve, which would constitute a violation of the confidentiality of the partnership.

How often should student and faculty partners meet?

Ideally, student and faculty partners should meet once a week for 30-60 minutes. Meeting right before the faculty partner's class is not generally a good time, although some people have made it work. Here are some guidelines to keep in mind about meetings:

- Student and faculty partners should identify a time to meet each week and, as we discussed in chapter 4 in terms of professional communication, if either one is unable to make the meeting, they should let the other know as far ahead of time as possible.
- If the student partner takes observation notes, student and faculty partners should agree about whether the student partner will send the notes ahead of the meeting or bring them to the meeting.
- If the student partner does not take observation notes, student and faculty partners should agree on how they will focus their discussions, as suggested above.

Some student and faculty partners find that they want to meet more often at some times during the term and less often at other times. It makes sense to work around the flow of the term and the other demands on both partners' time, but it is also important, if at all possible, to establish a regular meeting time so that energy isn't spent on, or frustration generated over, that logistical dimension of the work.

How might student and faculty partners structure their weekly meetings?

In the SaLT program, we recommend that student partners open the weekly meetings by asking their faculty partners to identify what they think went well in their most recent class and what areas they might want to focus on for further refinement or improvement. For some student and faculty partners, that general opening is enough to get the conversation going. For others, a more focused prompt is helpful. Sasha Mathrani, a former student partner in SaLT, reflects: "In my experience, it is important to be specific when inviting faculty perspective. Simply asking, 'How do you feel about how last class went?' does not always bring out much. It is helpful to return to some of the key 'focuses' from the beginning, or if the faculty member mentioned a particular concern, ask them about that" (personal communication).

If the student partner is visiting the faculty partner's classroom, this opening discussion can be followed by discussion of the observation notes taken by the student partner. Student and faculty partners can either work through all the notes, if that is the faculty partner's preference, or the student partner or the faculty partner can identify some particular points to focus on. Some faculty partners appreciate it if their student partners write short summaries of key issues at the end of the observation notes or separately so that discussion can focus on those.

Some opening questions student partners can ask:
- Given your pedagogical goals for the course, how do you think this last class went?
- Thinking about your request that we focus on [topic or issue identified by faculty partner], what's your sense of how the class went in relation to that issue?
- Which moments or segments in the most recent class felt particularly effective to you?
- What experiences do you want students to have in your classroom and what should they do to prepare for those?

Some approaches student partners can use to conclude weekly meetings:
- Ask about focus: Given what we have discussed today [noting examples], would you like me to keep the same focus for my next observation or shift my attention to something else?
- Offer appreciation/affirmation: I really appreciated your explanation of why you designed the main class activity the way you did. If I had been a student in the class, that would have helped me so much because . . .

If the student partner is not visiting the faculty partner's classroom, these weekly meetings will be informed by the faculty partner's descriptions of what is happening in their classroom. In this case, the student partner's role is to ask questions, invite reflection and analysis, and offer suggestions based on what emerges from the faculty partner's description.

Some opening questions student partners can ask:
- Given your pedagogical goals for the course, can you describe parts of the class that seemed to you to move toward meeting those goals?
- Were there moments or segments in the most recent class that felt particularly engaging and effective to you? Can you describe them to me and explain why they felt engaging and effective?
- What experiences do you want students to have in your classroom and what should they do to prepare for those?

Some approaches student partners can use to conclude weekly meetings:
- Ask about focus: Given what we have discussed today [noting examples], what would you like me to think about between now and our next meeting?
- Offer appreciation/affirmation: I really appreciated your explanation of why you designed the main class activity the way you did. If I had been a student in the class, that would have helped me so much because . . .

Should student and faculty partners revise the approach or focus of their partnership as the term progresses?

Some student and faculty partners in the SaLT program move through the entire term using the same observation note format, shifting focus as the term progresses. Others find that by week 8 or 10, or even sooner sometimes, they are ready for a change of focus and format. Here are some options for shifting focus:
- The student partner can experiment with different note-taking approaches to make new aspects of the course visible for them and their faculty partner (see "Mapping classroom interactions" below and the "Mapping Classroom Interactions" resource.
- The student partner can visit a different class the faculty partner is teaching, if the student partner is available to do so.
- The student partner can research particular pedagogical approaches or threshold concepts within the faculty partner's discipline and discuss how they might inform teaching in this or another course.

SELECTING APPROACHES TO CLASSROOM-FOCUSED PARTNERSHIPS | 169

- The student partner and faculty partner can begin to plan courses for future. They can use the template for backward design (Wiggins and McTighe 2005, *Understanding by Design*) or the guidelines offered by L. Dee Fink (2013) in *Creating Significant Learning Experiences* to think in concrete ways about how to apply what they have explored during the semester's work to another semester's courses.
- The student partner can respond to the faculty partner's syllabus for the next course they will teach or a course they will be revisiting and note what seems especially inviting and "promising" (see Lang's [2006] discussion of Bain's concept of "The Promising Syllabus") or confusing or puzzling and would benefit from revision or expansion.

How can student and faculty partners conclude their partnerships?

There are several aspects of concluding the partnership that student and faculty partners will want to consider. These include the following:

- Student partners may conduct the final feedback for the class, using the college or university's form or a form the faculty partner develops with the student partner. This approach affords the same benefits as the student partner conducting midterm feedback and also gives the student partner a chance to say thank you and good-bye to the class.
- The student partner can compose an annotated list for the faculty partner of things they learned, accomplished, and might take forward—basically, a validating list of what the faculty partner did during the term as well as a few (maybe one to three) ideas about what to continue to work on. We explain this in the section called "Creating end-of-term annotated lists" below and in the "Representing What Student and Faculty Partners Have Explored" resource.
- Student and faculty partners will want to have a final conversation in which each one:
  » shares what they got out of the partnership; and
  » asks for some feedback about the work (i.e., What did I do that was particularly useful? What could I have done more of

or better?). This latter conversation is particularly important to make the exchange feel reciprocal—so both partners are getting feedback on their teaching and learning within the partnership.
- In the SaLT program, student partners write letters to their faculty partner articulating what they got out of the partnership—lessons they learned, insights they gained, aspects of the relationship they appreciated, or ways the partnership experience enriched them as learners, teachers, or people. See the section below called "Writing thank-you letters" and the "Representing What Student and Faculty Partners Have Explored" resource for details. Sometimes faculty partners also write letters of appreciation, and we recommend this form of reciprocity.
- Have a final meeting in which both partners share appreciations, takeaways, and letters of appreciation.

What can student and faculty partners do to make the most of their partnership?

The following points are, from Anita's perspective, particularly helpful in thinking about how to make the most of partnerships.
- **Create personal connections.** Once student and faculty partners have gotten to know one another, they can create personal connections throughout the partnership. Reference moments like "I remember when you mentioned . . . I can see that applying in this situation where . . ." It is okay and even deepens the personal connection to spend some of the weekly meeting time talking about non-class-related topics. It is part of building the connection that makes the partnership stronger.
- **Develop the capacity to "read" your partner and share your insights in a way that is accessible.** The observation notes student partners take give them the perfect opportunity to reflect on and pick out main themes that stood out and main points to draw their own and their faculty partners' attention to. Both partners can practice "reading" one another and framing the points they want to make in a way that the other can hear. There is a time and place

for everything, so gauging what makes sense to relay to a partner when, given the time frame and the feeling of the partnership, is important.

- **Draw on and generate resources.** Student partners can review the resources provided by the director of the program, and the reflections peers offer in weekly meetings can also serve as a resource. In turn, faculty partners can respond to as well as ask for input from all the student partners who participate in the weekly meetings, not only their own student partner.
- **Don't be afraid to ask questions!** If either a student or a faculty partner is nervous, confused, or puzzled about anything, they should speak up. The weekly meetings of student partners are support sessions as well as the primary resource for gathering a wealth of student perspectives on pedagogical and curricular questions. Faculty partners find, in the same way, that the weekly meetings with their student partners can become an important source of support.
- **Be intentional about building skills.** When student partners are in weekly student partner meetings, they can think about the strengths they identified during the student partner orientation and go through how they have been applying or could apply them in their partnership. Similarly for weaknesses, they can consider how they can strengthen their approaches through the interactions they have with their faculty partner and the program director, as well as during student partner meetings. Once again, the weekly meetings between student and faculty partners can provide the same kind of forum for faculty partners, affording them an all-too-rare opportunity to think about and affirm their strengths and the further capacity they are building.
- **Affirm yourself.** Partnership can be emotionally demanding, so it is essential that student and faculty partners not be hard on themselves when things may not seem to be going well. Remember, each individual student and faculty partner has unique insights and contributions to make to the partnership. Find ways to step back, name, and appreciate what each brings to partnership, and

try to identify and celebrate what the partnership and the individuals within it are achieving, even if that sometimes only feels like surfacing struggles or frustrations.
- **Translate what you learn in partnership beyond partnership—in courses, after graduation, and in professional life.** Student and faculty partners can think about the cumulative skills they are developing as their partnership continues and think about ways they can name those experiences when explaining what partnership means. Partners can ask themselves questions like: How have you grown? Can you name these skills? What are the outcomes of your partnership? This reflection is useful to students as they apply for jobs and for faculty as they approach moments of review.

What techniques might student and faculty partners use?

The techniques described here provide student consultants the opportunity to bring their unique perspectives as students and their heuristics as knowers to bear on what unfolds in classrooms. Because they are students themselves but are positioned as observers of teaching and learning, rather than learners of subject matter, they have a unique vantage point and time to focus on patterns of interaction. Students in the class should know that all observations are for the purpose of analyzing classroom environment and dynamics with the goal of making them as inclusive as they can be.

Below is a set of approaches that student and faculty partners have developed in the SaLT program. These include taking observation notes, mapping classroom interactions, gathering feedback, creating end-of-term annotated lists, and writing thank-you letters.

Taking observation notes

Reading observation notes is, in one faculty partner's words, like "looking in a mirror, only better" (quoted in Cook-Sather 2008, 473; see also Abbott and Bean 2017). Observation notes provide a play-by-play of the class session as described from a student perspective and offers a student's reflections on and questions about what unfolded during the class session. If you decide that classroom observations will be a component of your partnership program, see the "Visiting Faculty Partners' Classrooms and Taking Observation Notes" resource for detailed guidelines. This resource provides a description of the SaLT approach to note-taking, as well as sample observation notes. It addresses these questions:

- How should student partners be introduced to the faculty member's class?
- What should the student partner's classroom observation notes look like?
- What helps student partners gain confidence in note-taking?
- How might observation notes be written up?

Mapping classroom interactions

Classroom mapping captures the physical space of a classroom and how faculty and students occupy it in a way that descriptive, written notes cannot. As Abbot, Cook-Sather, and Hein (2014) explain: "This approach moves the patterns of participation from abstract notions to concrete representations, and it provides detailed records to which faculty and their consultants can return and use to inform consideration of what changes in pedagogical approach might be beneficial." As another faculty member who used classroom maps explains:

> Having the maps as a point of reference made it easier for me to facilitate the class and assess student performance because I was not forced to do both concurrently. Over time, I could trace patterns in students' engagement, note who commonly responded to whom, and even anticipate the types of in-class work that would best engage this group. (Corbin 2014, 2)

See the "Mapping Classroom Interactions" resource for detailed instructions for how to map and sample maps.

Gathering feedback

Student partners are especially well positioned to gather feedback from students enrolled in their faculty partners' courses. They can collaborate with faculty in formulating questions that are likely to evoke constructive responses, they can put students enrolled in the course at greater ease, they can deepen students' metacognitive awareness and deepen their learning, and they can provide feedback that is more candid and reliable than impersonal, end-of-term feedback (Cook-Sather 2009; Marquis et al. 2018a).

In the "Gathering Feedback" resource we address these questions:
- How can faculty partners decide if they want to gather feedback?
- What goals do faculty partners have for gathering midterm feedback and do their questions match their goals?
- How can faculty and student partners prepare for the emotional demand of receiving feedback?
- How can faculty and student partners plan to communicate to students ahead of time that student partners will gather feedback and share it with faculty partners?
- What approaches might faculty and student partners take to gathering feedback early in the term?
- What approaches might student and faculty partners take to gathering midterm feedback from students enrolled in a course?
- How do faculty and student partners process and share back the midterm feedback?

Creating end-of-term annotated lists

Typically, student partners spend a full semester—or longer—with their faculty partners. Over that time they gain a deep sense of their faculty partner's pedagogical commitments, classroom approaches, ideas about curriculum, and much else. They gather many hours' worth of observation and conversation notes, and they are in a unique position to make sense of all of these.

One of the final responsibilities of student partners in classroom-focused partnerships through the SaLT program is to draw on all their notes to create annotated lists or other representations of what they hope their faculty partner will be able to celebrate and also to keep working on in the future. To create such an annotated list, student partners read back through all of their observation notes, notes from weekly meetings, and any other resources. They can also ask their faculty partners to revisit

SELECTING APPROACHES TO CLASSROOM-FOCUSED PARTNERSHIPS | 175

and reiterate their original goals from the beginning of semester and to identify goals they have going forward. These questions can help student partners shape their annotated lists.

Some student partners present their annotated lists as shown in this example from one of Melanie's partnerships:

> **Pedagogical Strategy:** Small Group Discussions
>
> **Description:** You often have the class break into smaller groups to discuss. Sometimes, you have the groups already assigned while other times you have students count off to form these small groups. You travel between the groups to hear from and participate in their discussions.
>
> **Benefits:** Some students feel more comfortable in smaller settings. Small group discussions give a larger variety of students the chance to participate. Small group discussions also allow for students to get to know each other better and see how other students investigate texts.
>
> **Potential Drawbacks:** Sometimes, students wouldn't really talk to one another or try to answer the question, but would instead wait until you had arrived at their group and expect you to answer the question for them.
>
> **For Next Time:** It might be helpful to have students always work in the same groups and to have these groups be connected to student writing as well. It also might work if you only sat with one group (as a full group member) rather than floating between the groups and therefore giving some students the chance to simply "wait" until you arrived at their group and gave them the "answers."

Student partners might also use a kind of annotated outline format. For instance, Melanie's annotated list mapped out practices that she and her faculty partner discussed and that the faculty member used in her class, and she then included with each practice a short annotation describing each item and affirming how her faculty partner used it effectively to accomplish her goal of creating a dynamic and inclusive learning environment. One annotation read:

> **Pedagogical Transparency**
>
> *Assignments as skill-building*
> You've talked explicitly to students this semester about how the assignments for the course build on one another and provide opportunities for students to develop their skills. I think this is a really wonderful and helpful way for you to structure the assignments, and I think talking about it with the class allows them to be more critically aware of how they are applying different skills to each assignment. They can also take away a greater sense of what they have learned in the course.
>
> *Your role during small group work*
> I appreciated that you articulated to students what you would be doing while they discussed in pairs or small groups. I think it was meaningful that you let them know that you would be standing by taking notes to bring back to the large group so that they weren't worrying about what you were doing. By being transparent in this way, small group discussions are able to continue as you move around the classroom.

Melanie's full annotated list can be found in the "Representing What Student and Faculty Partners Have Explored" resource.

Another student partner in the SaLT program, Crystal Des-Ogugua, developed a different approach. As she wrote to her faculty partner: "This is a compilation of observed efforts you took to set up a positively functioning classroom environment. I have condensed my notes/observations into a chart that shows how you impacted classroom discussions, student comprehension of materials/content, and students' responsiveness in class" (personal communication). Crystal developed a key that included:

- **Teacher-Student:** Efforts made by the teacher that directly impact the student

- **Student-Student:** Efforts made by the teacher that encourage and promote student-to-student interaction and learning
- **Student-Classroom:** Efforts made by the teacher to promote student participation and interaction with the entire classroom environment
- **Teacher-Classroom:** Efforts made by the teacher to engage and improve the entire classroom environment
- **(Potential Section) Student-Self:** Efforts made by the teacher to facilitate and engage student self-development

An example of her chart can be found in the "Representing What Student and Faculty Partners Have Explored" resource.

Other student partners have taken alternative approaches, such as creating websites through which their faculty partners can easily navigate. Faculty and student partners can decide which format is preferable given the aspects of pedagogy they have focused on and what kind of representation would be most useful to faculty partners in future.

Writing thank-you letters

For the majority of the semester, dialogue between student and faculty partners is focused on faculty members' practice, affirmation, and growth. Of course, many partners regularly discuss what student partners are learning as well, but the main focus is on the faculty members' pedagogy. At the end of the semester, all student partners in the SaLT program write their faculty partners personal letters that include thanks for what student partners gained through the partnerships—as learners, as future teachers (some of them), and as people.

The gratitude student partners articulate reinforces the positive aspects of the relationship they have built with their faculty partners as well as clearly names the benefits to the student partners. An excerpt from one consultant's letter is reproduced in the box below:

> "Thank you for being in this relationship with me and for helping to create this opportunity in which I have been able to so grow my self-confidence and sense of self-worth. Thank you also for making this a truly reciprocal relationship: You have quickly become one of

> my most valued mentors, and I am so grateful that this relationship will continue after we both (I, more immediately) leave the physical space of [Bryn Mawr and Haverford Colleges]. Your interest in and support of all that I do means a lot more than I can say."
>
> —Student partner in the SaLT program
> (personal communication)

Although student partners may have thanked their partners for the opportunity to work with them throughout the semester, the final letter formalizes that gratitude, separates it out from the flow of the work together, and marks it as particularly meaningful while also explaining that meaning. Writing the thank-you letter is an opportunity for student partners to pause and articulate for themselves what they have learned from this partnership. As the culminating communication from student partners to their faculty partners, these letters constitute a positive ending to the partnership, sounding a note of appreciation and gratitude that reverberates into the future for the faculty partners. It also opens the door to the possibility of informal collaboration in the future, which can be reassuring for faculty moving forward. While the benefits of the approach may also accrue to the student partner, we propose that the receipt and reflection on gratitude has mutual benefits for the faculty partner as well. In the "Representing What Student and Faculty Partners Have Explored" resource, Melanie and Anita offer additional guidelines for writing thank-you letters.

YOUR TURN

Preparing for partnership:

How can student and faculty partners in your context best lay the foundation for a productive pedagogical partnership?

Establishing a focus for partnership:

How can student and faculty partners establish a focus for their work?

Do the common areas of focus for pedagogical partnerships listed in this chapter resonate in your context, or do you anticipate other areas you might want to name?

Selecting approaches:

What should the student partner role and responsibilities be in any given partnership? Weekly observations and meetings or only meeting? If observations, mapping? Gathering feedback? End-of-term annotated lists? Thank-you letters? Other possibilities?

What are the pros and cons of asking student partners to interact directly with students enrolled in the course?

What can student and faculty partners do to make the most of their partnership? Which of the points listed in this chapter would support productive partnership in your context?

7 WHAT APPROACHES MIGHT STUDENT AND FACULTY PARTNERS TAKE TO CURRICULUM-FOCUSED PARTNERSHIPS?

This chapter provides the complement to chapter 6, in which we discussed classroom-focused pedagogical partnerships. Drawing once again on the SaLT program model, as well as examples from other contexts, we discuss in this chapter curriculum-focused partnerships. We describe the four forms curriculum-focused partnership typically take in SaLT and programs like it: co-planning a course before it is taught; co-creating or revising while a course is unfolding; redesigning a course after it is taught; and making explicit and challenging the hidden curriculum. We also discuss who might participate in curriculum-focused pedagogical partnerships, what the focus of such partnership work might be, and the process of embarking on curriculum-focused partnerships. Whereas chapter 6 offered guidelines, this chapter offers description and examples.

What forms can curriculum-focused pedagogical partnerships take?

The terms used to name curriculum-focused work differ across country and context. A course in the United States, for instance, is called a module in the United Kingdom. A syllabus is generally understood to be an outline or overview of a course or module. We chose to use the term "curriculum" as the overarching concept in this chapter to signal the substance—the what—of any given course or module, and the term "course" because we are situated in the United States. This is both a regional choice as well as an effort to distinguish this discussion from our discussion of pedagogical process—the how—in chapter 6. These are, certainly, not so clearly distinguishable, but for the purposes of differentiating the two kinds of pedagogical partnership we discuss, we embrace here the more encompassing concept of curriculum and the US term "course."

The kind of curricular co-creation student and faculty partners might undertake will be informed by their understanding of what curriculum is. That may seem obvious, but there are many conceptualizations of curriculum ranging from the most common—the content delivered—to a "blueprint for achieving restricted objectives" (Kegan 1978, 65) to a perspective on content (Schubert 1986) to a course designed through the running of it (Pinar 2004). Fraser and Bosanquet (2006) define curriculum as a co-construction of knowledge between learner and teacher (see also Bovill, Bulley, and Morss 2011). There are also different sets of principles that might inform curriculum development, such as the eight core feminist principles Chin and Russo (1997) identified—diversity, egalitarianism and empowerment, self-determination, connection, social action, self-reflection, and integrative perspectives—or the Aotearoa New Zealand government's tertiary education strategy that has as one of its priorities to enable Māori to achieve education success as Māori (see Berryman and Eley 2017 for a discussion of this).

Regardless of how it is conceptualized and of the approach student and faculty partners take to developing it, curriculum "always represent[s] an introduction to, preparation for, and legitimation of a particular form of life" (McLaren 1989, 160), and the way a course is designed provides structures and supports for particular ways of thinking, learning, and being. When students and faculty co-create curriculum, the ways of thinking, learning, and being the courses support are informed by more than the inherited, disciplinary, or individual faculty member's ways of thinking about curriculum.

As Bron, Bovill, and Veugelers (2016, 1) argue, "When students are involved in curriculum design they offer unique perspectives that improve the quality and relevance of the curriculum. . . . Enabling students to have a role in curriculum design requires that the curriculum is regarded as a process instead of a predetermined, externally established product." There is a growing number of examples of curricular co-creation at the class, course, and degree program levels (Bovill 2017a, 2017b;

Bovill, Cook-Sather, and Felten 2011; Lubicz-Nawrocka 2018). These are instances of faculty and students sharing power and responsibility in the design and redesign of curriculum (Mihans, Long, and Felten 2008; Smith and Waller 1997) in what Bergmark and Westman (2016, 29) describe as "students' opportunities to partake in educational decision-making and students' active participation in educational activities." Such an "ecology of participation" (Taylor and Bovill 2018, 112) supports co-creation *of* the curriculum (co-design of a program or course, usually *before* it is taking place) and co-creation *in* the curriculum (co-design of learning and teaching within a course or program usually *during* its taking place) (see Bovill et al. 2016). As Bovill and Woolmer (2018, 409) point out, "the ways we think about curriculum impact upon our perceptions of the possibilities and scope for involving students, the focus of any co-creation, and ultimately upon the learning experience of students."

Research and reflections on efforts to co-create curriculum suggest that the process is demanding, can be destabilizing, and can be deeply rewarding, including outcomes such as shared responsibility, respect, and trust; learning from each other within a collaborative learning community; and individual satisfaction and development (Lubicz-Nawrocka 2018). The challenges such work poses to faculty partners include shifting thinking about who is responsible for curriculum in what ways—a shift that requires thinking about and distributing power in a different way. But faculty are not the only ones who might find that challenging. Delpish et al. (2010, 111) suggest that "students are accustomed to, and often comfortable with, assuming a relatively powerless role in the classroom, just as faculty are trained to believe that their disciplinary expertise gives them complete authority over the learning process. When faculty or students challenge these habits, students and faculty must confront fundamental questions about the nature of teaching and learning" (see also Felten 2011; Glasser and Powers 2011). One of the consistent findings of research on student-faculty partnership is that co-construction requires the development of vocabulary and the confidence to collaborate with faculty (Cook-Sather 2011b; Cook-Sather, Bovill, and Felten 2014; Delpish et al. 2010; Mihans, Long, and Felten 2008). The two students quoted below capture their experiences of curricular co-creation:

> "I guess you feel more important.... Throughout the course we worked in those groups of four to create our learning portfolios, to create our reading lists, all these things. I've ended up being best friends with those people in my group, when I hadn't really formed many good friendships with people on my course until now, so it's been a great opportunity in that respect as well. It comes back to the classroom not just being a cold environment; it's a place where you're friends. It does make a difference. You're more comfortable and feel safer."
>
> —Student (quoted in Lubicz-Nawrocka 2018, 54)

> "I also learned a bit more about responsibility. I think having that close interaction, that close engagement with professors, you're held accountable for more.... I think there was less room for me to casually do it or just pass by, which in other classes that's easier to do if there's less accountability and trust that's made, that bond."
>
> —Student (quoted in Lubicz-Nawrocka 2018, 57)

Drawing on SaLT projects and other curriculum-focused pedagogical partnerships, we describe four kinds of curricular co-creation student and faculty partners might consider either separately or in some combination: co-planning a course before it is taught; co-creating or revising while a course is unfolding; engaging in course redesign after a course is taught; and making explicit and challenging the hidden curriculum of a course.

Whereas the previous chapter addressed pedagogical partnerships focused on classroom practice and offered extensive detail regarding how student and faculty partners might work together, this chapter offers more general frames for conceptualizing curriculum-focused pedagogical partnership. Because the focus in this chapter is on co-creating content and less on processes that unfold within the classroom, how student and faculty partners develop these partnerships will depend more on the subject matter and disciplinary norms.

Co-planning a course before it is taught

When student and faculty partners, sometimes on their own and sometimes in collaboration with others, work together to conceptualize and plan a new course, they bring to bear different sources of expertise. Lori Goff and Kris Knorr (2018) describe how they developed an applied curriculum design in science course at McMaster University in Canada that had as it goal to engage students as co-creators of curriculum. As they explain: "From the outset, there was a strong desire to involve students in developing a course that would benefit students transitioning into first-year Science" (Goff and Knorr 2018, 114). Their process included gathering feedback from students to inform the conceptualization of the course and then working in collaboration to develop the various components of the course. In this case, the course design team included faculty, students, and educational developers from McMaster's Teaching and Learning Center. In their words: "Faculty members bring a perspective on what disciplinary content and skills students need to know, while students have a perspective on what they find to be meaningful and engaging learning opportunities. Educational developers can help bring these two perspectives together through good practice in course and curriculum design" (115).

To create a context in which the co-creation of this course could take place, the educational developers designed a third-year course in applied curriculum design in science and invited third- and fourth-year students to apply. The early weeks of the course focused on science education, instructional design, and course design principles. The students enrolled generated lists of topics that they found most interesting and collectively identified skills that they felt they would have benefited from learning during their first year at the university. Groups of ten students each worked with two faculty disciplinary experts and two educational developers to develop stand-alone, week-long units "that aimed to engage first-year students in a miniature research investigation on a topic they selected" (Goff and Knorr 2018, 115). These teams also co-created learning outcomes, outlines and resources, and a form of assessment for each unit.

Through a different process in the SaLT program, undergraduate student Yi Wang and faculty member Yonglin Jiang (2012) co-created Cultural History of Chinese Astronomy, a course that they chose to design drawing on Jiang's expertise as a professor of East Asian studies and Wang's knowledge from her hobby, astronomy. They co-created the syllabus for the course, which, as they explain, "covered major parts of our personal interests such as astrology and the astronomical political system" (Wang and Jiang 2012, 1). Jiang acknowledged that "emphasizing 'equal partnership'... did not mean I would give up the leading role in the relationship" (2). He took the lead on "identifying issues, locating and selecting materials, structuring the course, organizing course activities, designing assignments, and more" (3). He emphasized, though, that alongside him, his student partner "was playing a leading role in identifying the issues of the field and enriching my understanding of astronomy" (3). Furthermore, he explained, "because of her student status and perspective, she could facilitate a smoother working relationship between me and the whole student body in class" (3).

This kind of "equal partnership" in course design has been embraced by other participants in the SaLT program. Some faculty, having worked with student partners on one course, invite that student partner and other students to help imagine and design other courses. Students bring expertise of all kinds, as Wang and Jiang (2012) describe above, and their engagement in co-creating new courses ensures that their experiences, energy, and insights help shape educational experiences for other students. In some cases, these student partners have subject matter knowledge and in others they do not. Student partners can bring a wide range of knowledge to course design, such as what might engage students from different cultural and educational backgrounds. A faculty member describes how he partnered with students in course design:

> That first class on the history of women's higher education with a strong emphasis on the history of Bryn Mawr College ... was a collaborative effort put together with the help of students who had taken others of my courses and the student consultant who was then working with

me on my class on the History of Philadelphia, Erica Seaborne. Erica and I agreed to . . . bring the group of students together and craft a course together from scratch. We thought about the readings, the assignments, the ways in which the class would operate, the speakers we would invite, the places we would visit and the students who would be invited to take the class. We agreed to invite the teaching assistant for the course and several other students who had taken multiple courses with me to a meeting. I put on the table the idea that I wanted them to imagine a course that would be conducted along lines that would maximize their learning. I told them that everything was open for revision. (Shore 2012, 1)

In another co-creation effort, Alison spent a semester co-planning a course called Advocating Diversity in Higher Education with Crystal Des-Ogugua, who was, at the time, an undergraduate and student consultant through SaLT. This was an education course, but Crystal was seeking neither teacher certification nor the minor in educational studies offered through the Education Program at Bryn Mawr and Haverford Colleges. Rather, she and Alison met when Crystal became a student consultant through SaLT. Her experience as an underrepresented student in the context of the college and a seasoned student consultant ensured that she brought essential perspectives to a course with a focus on advocating diversity in higher education.

Alison and Crystal met weekly, talked through the goals and aspirations of the course, created the overall structure, selected readings, and designed assignments (Cook-Sather and Des-Ogugua 2017). Melanie took the class that Alison and Crystal created. In the box below is an excerpt from an article that Alison, Crystal, and Melanie wrote about how co-creation can unfold not only between faculty and student consultants but also between faculty and students enrolled in their courses as part of a larger institutional process of change:

> "As a smaller more 'manageable' version and representation of society, the institution has the potential to be the site of innovative change. If we think of higher education, individual courses, and pedagogical partnerships as 'as-if' places (Walker 2009, 221), places 'where long term goals of social change are lived inside the institution as if they were already norms for society' (Bivens 2009, 3), we can use those spaces to behave the way we want to live in the wider world (Cook-Sather and Felten 2017a). Each of these 'as-if,' liminal spaces can become what hooks (1990, 342) calls 'the site of radical possibility, a space of resistance' (quoted in Green and Little 2013, 525). Within such spaces we can cultivate 'expanded moral sympathies, deepened democratic dispositions, and a serious sense of responsibility for the world' (Hansen 2014, 4). If students, faculty, administrators, and the institution as a whole work in partnership to actualize changes in a bounded space, it provides these actors with the tools to create change in the 'outside world.'"
>
> — Cook-Sather, Des-Ogugua, and Bahti 2017, 384

If student and faculty partners co-plan courses in these ways, bringing multiple experiences, perspectives, and sources of expertise to the planning process, the likelihood increases that the course will reach a greater diversity of students. Furthermore, if students who enroll in the course know that it was co-planned with students, they perceive the course as modeling and enacting a way of thinking, learning, and being that values students as collaborators. This co-creation *of* the curriculum models one kind of sharing of power and responsibility (Bergmark and Westman 2016; Bovill et al. 2016; Bovill and Woolmer 2018; Mihans, Long, and Felten 2008; Smith and Waller 1997).

Faculty and student partners who choose to engage in this form of co-creation may want to use the template for backward design (Wiggins and McTighe 2005, *Understanding by Design*) or the guidelines offered by L. Dee Fink (2013) in *Creating Significant Learning Experiences* to break the co-planning process down into intentional and manageable steps. When students and faculty respond to some of the questions included in such approaches—such as, "What are important learning goals for the course?"—they can ensure that both student and faculty perspectives inform the development of the course, as opposed to student partners operating only in more of a supportive or responsive mode.

Co-creating or revising while a course is unfolding

Co-creation can also take place as a course is unfolding (Cecchinato and Foschi 2017; Monsen, Cook, and Hannant 2017; Sunderland 2013). Reasons for engaging in such co-creation include maximizing learning, building on the power of multiple perspectives, realizing a more democratic approach, or some combination. We describe two ways such co-creation can unfold: with the students enrolled in the course, and with a student partner not enrolled in the course.

Co-creating with students enrolled in a course

While faculty can plan courses for maximum learning based on previous experiences of teaching in general and teaching a specific course in particular, any conceptualization of curriculum beyond delivery of content acknowledges that who is in the course matters in how the content is engaged with. Every individual student and the group as a whole will have particular interests, needs, hopes, and more regarding the course curriculum. It is therefore worth considering the extent to which the course should be planned in advance and the extent to which it might be co-created as it unfolds. For instance, Vicki Reitenauer describes how she strives "to become accountable to my students for the power I hold to frame and initiate an experience in which I am asking them to choose to participate" (Cates, Madigan, and Reitenauer 2018, 38). One of the ways in which she does this is to collaboratively develop course content. She and a student, Mariah Madigan, who partnered with her in this project, reflect on that experience:

> "Mariah and her colleagues in the class teach us content through sharing their projects and linking their chosen topics to the overarching themes of the course, among other content-contributing assignments. My intention in this pedagogical intervention is to disrupt students' expectations that course content is a fixed and

> impenetrable force that acts upon them and to catalyze students' active participation in designing course content as curators of knowledge."
>
> —Cates, Madigan, and Reitenauer 2018, 38
>
> "The outcome of this experience for myself, as a student, grew beyond the project. I began the term floundering, unsure if college was the right place for me, unsure if I was capable, and disconnected from campus. After this course, I found confidence that I did not have before. I became more involved on campus and more engaged in my classes and with professors. I began learning how to get what I needed out of college, rather than producing work that felt meaningless just for a grade."
>
> —Cates, Madigan, and Reitenauer, 2018, 41

When working with students enrolled in a course, some faculty plan the entire course but make adjustments in response to student input as that curriculum unfolds. Other faculty plan only the first half or three-quarters of a course, leaving the remaining portion to be co-created—or entirely created—by the students enrolled. Still others prepare an outline with basic goals and structures for assignments and then co-create the entire course with the students enrolled. These approaches are certainly the most compatible with institutional structures and expectations. Many faculty must submit a complete syllabus prior to the semester in which any given course is taught, including all assignments and assessments spelled out in detail. Even within such prescribed and restrictive conditions, though, co-creation can unfold regarding some of the details of assignments and assessments. Faculty can gather student feedback and adjust the work of the course without straying from the original syllabus. In institutions that allow more latitude and for faculty who are committed to co-creating more of the curriculum, an approach through which the first portion of the course is planned and the latter portion left open to co-creation might be preferable. A faculty member and graduate student at the University of Kansas explain their approach to co-creation:

> Initially, Dan [Bernstein] designed and taught this course solo, first at the University of Nebraska-Lincoln and then at the University of Kansas. In his role as the Director of the Center for Teaching Excellence at the University of Kansas he met and began collaborating with Sarah [Bunnell], who was a doctoral student in Psychology and graduate assistant at the teaching center at the time. Within the first year of Sarah's work at the Center and second year of graduate study, they began co-teaching and co-designing the course. This collaboration was further enhanced through ongoing partnerships with undergraduate students who had previously completed the Conceptual Issues course. Students often approach Dan at the end of the term with an interest in becoming involved in his research program, and since our shared research was pedagogical and the course was our "laboratory," we invited several students to contribute their insights to the design of the course. We met weekly with our undergraduate collaborators, in both the semester leading up to the offering of the course and while the course was being taught. We discussed in detail the goals that we had for student learning for each section of the course, what was working well (and not as well as we would like), and ways in which we could maximize student learning and engagement with the material. (Bunnell and Bernstein 2014, 1)

Some course co-creation efforts have as their explicit purpose to democratize the curriculum creation process. For instance, Bell, Carson, and Piggott (2013, 503-504) describe an approach through which a professor "drew on her background in deliberative democracy to create an opportunity for the students to give feedback" on a unit and "collectively decide" in a large group on a "final list of suggested changes" to the unit. This approach is reflected in Bergmark and Westman's (2016, 29) conceptualization of curriculum as "students' opportunities to partake in educational decision-making and students' active participation in educational activities." The teacher of the course in a university in Sweden upon which Bergmark and Westman report emailed students enrolled in the course to invite them to co-create it and then worked through the ongoing negotiation necessary to enact co-creation. As they write: "This openness to the students' earlier experiences and views on how to plan, enhance, and construct the course teaching can be considered a democratic value." Such an approach, they continue, demonstrates "an appreciation of otherness and diverse perspectives which involves the recognition of others' skills and competence" (Bergmark and Westman 2016, 33). The faculty member who undertook the co-creation offers her perspective:

> [For me, co-creating curriculum] means meeting and really listening to the students, to use your tact, be open. . . . Today, I take smaller steps than I did the first time. I've also learned to anticipate their anxiety, and I explain things beforehand and am clear on what choices there are, what my openness and their influence means in a democratic perspective, what my responsibility is and so on. (Faculty member quoted in Bergmark and Westman 2016, 37)

Like all pedagogical partnership, such co-creation efforts require faculty and students to rethink and revise their traditional institutional positions. This is challenging enough in Western contexts but even more so in Eastern contexts, where, as Kaur, Awang-Hashim, and Kaur (2018) explain, cultural values are rooted in respect for hierarchy, humility, polite attitude, and tolerance (Nguyen 2005) and can inhibit students from questioning, contradicting, or challenging teachers' knowledge or perspective (Cheng 2000; Pagram and Pagram 2006). Reporting on a study of four different courses for a master's degree program in education at Universiti Utara Malaysia, Kaur, Awang-Hashim, and Kaur (2018) describe how students enrolled in the courses had the option to co-plan and co-teach with their instructors particular units in the courses. Like other students who have participated in pedagogical partnership, these students reported experiencing deeper learning, a more engaging classroom environment, a sense of empowerment, increased competence, and enhanced relationships with instructors. Similarly, while students felt many of the doubts and uncertainties we discussed in chapter 1, the experience of partnership alleviated them and supported the students in recognizing their capacity to contribute to curricular co-creation and to feel more connected to the faculty with whom they work (see also Kaur and Yong Bing, forthcoming).

The course Alison co-designed with one of her student partners, Crystal Des-Ogugua, was also co-created with students enrolled in the course, including during the semester in which Melanie enrolled in the course. Students selected which readings they would complete and annotate for the rest of the class each week, chose how they would fulfill the assignments, and assessed their progress and achievements. In the box below we describe one assignment from that course as an example of how co-creation can unfold in partnership with students enrolled in a course.

> One assignment for Advocating Diversity in Higher Education was developed in an effort to access the experiences that students have at the intersections of their academic experience (fostered in and outside the classroom), their social experience, and their personal backgrounds, experiences, and identities that shape them beyond the campus. In particular, the goal was to create a forum for marginal voices to be heard and respected by putting them in a place where they can inform classroom pedagogy and student learning. Alison's student partner and co-creator of Advocating Diversity, Crystal, invited sixteen members of the campus community who claim a diversity of identities to participate in one-on-one, structured interviews through which they named the dimensions of their identities and how those shape how they navigate the social and political landscapes of their campuses. Drawing on students' own words from the interviews, Crystal composed anonymous but detailed articulations of the individual student experiences—verbal portraits—which became required reading for the course. Crystal

also created a template for use as one option for the fieldwork component of the course.

Completing these interviews was the option Melanie took up as one of twenty students who enrolled in the course in the Spring 2016 semester. Melanie (and other students enrolled in the course) completed additional interviews, using and modifying Crystal's template, all of which also became required reading for the course. Often, we would post around the classroom walls actual sheets of paper with key statements from interviewees—again, anonymous, verbal portraits—that completed these sentences:

I am . . .

To me, diversity on campus . . .

Times when my campus or its culture is unsupportive, or negatively affirms my identity:

Times when my campus or its culture is supportive, or affirms my identity:

What I'd like to see in the future . . .

Students enrolled in the course walked around the classroom, read the interviews, sat and reflected silently on and/or wrote to themselves about what they had read, and then talked as a whole group.

In preparation for conducting her interviews, Melanie created new questions that focused on individual students' experiences of inclusion and exclusion in their learning environments (which mostly meant in the classroom). She had been exploring strategies for promoting inclusive classroom environments during a student-faculty partnership through the SaLT program, and shifting the direction of the assignment for Advocating Diversity in Higher Education allowed her to continue pursuing her interest in inclusive pedagogy. At the same time, the focus of the interview assignment on individual experience allowed the students she interviewed to speak from their own perspectives, which gave them a space to tell their story similar to the space created by the original set of interview questions.

Melanie's approach to this assignment was informed in several ways by the co-creation process that shaped Advocating Diversity. Because students enrolled in the course had many options for completing a fieldwork component of the course, they were able to shape their choices to align with personal interests and goals for engagement with campus communities. As Melanie shaped her interview questions, she participated in a co-creative relationship with both Alison and Crystal. Alison offered students flexibility and space to design their own fieldwork projects, which informed and were informed by other course content. And although Crystal was not physically present in Melanie's class, the structure and intention of her original assignment and interview portraits provided the framework for Melanie's fieldwork.

The process of conducting the interviews offered its own form of co-creation. While Melanie developed a set of questions prior to conducting her first interview, these questions shifted over time in response to the ideas and perspectives of participants. Each conversation shifted her own viewpoint and gave her new ideas to consider. The interview as both fieldwork for the course and intervention in the wider campus community raised awareness, affirmed a diversity of experiences and voices, and extended the co-creation through which the intervention was created.

—Excerpted and adapted from
Cook-Sather, Des-Ogugua, and Bahti 2018

Co-creating with students not enrolled in a course

When faculty co-create courses with student partners who are not enrolled in the courses, they may experience some similar and some different sharing of power and responsibility. For instance, Anita spent a semester in such a partnership with Kathy Rho, a visiting instructor at Bryn Mawr College, who taught Making Space for Learning in Higher Education, a course that Alison had created and taught for many years and in which Anita had enrolled the previous semester. Not only was this partnership Kathy's first time working with a student consultant, but it was also her first time teaching at Bryn Mawr College. Anita, at the time, had not experienced a partnership where her role evolved beyond the usual structure of weekly check-ins, note-taking and synthesis, and student consultant meetings. Also, like Crystal, who had worked with Alison to co-create Advocating Diversity in Higher Education, Anita was not pursuing teacher certification or a minor in educational studies. However, her extensive experience as a student consultant and someone who had taken the course uniquely prepared her to be a student partner in this expanded way.

Through this partnership, Anita's role expanded to include active re-framing of students' general perceptions of an idea through providing reflective questions as well as encouraging each student's individual reflection by connecting the class's theories to current educational expectations. Because this was such a new and eye-opening experience for both of them, Kathy and Anita decided that Anita's role in framing reflective questions could transition into her teaching a topic from the syllabus to the students. This initiative inspired Kathy to invite students enrolled in the course to choose a topic from the syllabus and teach it to the class in a way that linked the content to each student's unique teaching style. This shift was also in service of the goals of the course; it provided some practical application of pedagogical considerations embedded in the course readings with opportunity to reflect on that meaning in practice of the topics after. Students also began to actively ask for their peers' feedback through reflective questions and group work.

Through this co-creation effort, Kathy and Anita learned to be understanding of each other's roles and also flexible in how the curriculum was delivered and taken up throughout the semester. Not only did the partnership provide insight into how the rest of the semester would unfold, it encouraged students to become co-creators as well and consistently to reflect on and understand their distinctive teaching styles by assessing their values and goals. Reflecting on a co-curricular experience at the University of California at Berkeley, Sutherland (2013) sounded some of the same notes, arguing that a student engagement approach to pedagogy includes students as active participants in curriculum design.

Redesigning after a course has been taught

Starting in 2005, faculty, students, and academic development staff at Elon University developed a variety of approaches to partnering in "course design teams" (CDT) that co-create, or re-create, a course syllabus. While each team's process varies, typically a CDT includes one or two faculty members, between two and six undergraduate students, and one academic developer (Delpish et al. 2010; Mihans, Long, and Felten 2008; Moore et al. 2010). Faculty members initiate the redesign process, inviting the students and developer to co-construct a team. Students usually apply to participate in a CDT, motivated by a desire to contribute to a course they have taken or that is important to the curriculum in their disciplinary home. Once the CDT is assembled, they use a backward design approach (Wiggins and McTighe 2005), first developing course goals and then building pedagogical strategies and learning assessments on the foundation of those goals.

This co-creation approach includes multiple students in part to balance out the power that is unevenly distributed among students and faculty. It also includes an academic developer to add another perspective as well as ensure that the process is organized and, if necessary, mediated. One group, which included faculty, students, and an academic developer, described their experience this way:

> At times in our discussions, the professors became the learners and the students became the teachers—a complete flip from what was the norm. Throughout this process, students' comments and suggestions about the student experience were honored; however, the team also deferred to the professors' content expertise periodically. By working together to take full advantage of all of the team's expertise, we began to understand the true meaning and importance of shared power through collaboration. (Mihans, Long, and Felten 2008, 5)

Looking back on their course redesign process, this same team reflected:

> Students on the course design team gained significant new disciplinary knowledge, developed what Hutchings (2005) calls their "pedagogical intelligence" ("an understanding about how learning happens, and a disposition and capacity to shape one's own learning"), and became more capable of and confident in expressing their own expertise in academic settings. . . . We, as faculty, also have changed. We have learned the value of really listening to our students. We now teach all our courses somewhat differently because we are more attuned to student needs and expertise, and we have wholeheartedly embraced the concept of student collaboration in course design. (Mihans, Long, and Felten 2008, 8)

Other approaches to course redesign have emerged in other contexts. For instance, Charkoudian et al. (2015), a faculty member and three undergraduate students at Haverford College, engaged in a semester-long redesign process through which they revised course content, assignments, and methods of assessment for Charkoudian's first-semester organic chemistry course. During their first meeting, they identified seven different themes, decided to dedicate two weeks to each theme, and scheduled weekly meetings to discuss the needs they identified within each theme and actions to meet those needs. Working with her student partners allowed Charkoudian, in turn, to work with the students enrolled in her course as "a part of a team . . . to achieve the course objectives" (9).

Another faculty member at Haverford College, in the French Department, worked with a student who had taken the course to reflect on and revise particular aspects of it. Both the faculty partner and the student partner write about that process:

> "This spring semester I have been working with a student from a course I taught in the fall (Grammaire avancée, conversation et composition: Tous journalistes!) to reflect upon certain aspects of that course. This course is a freshly renovated course with material, topics, and approaches that I took on for the first time this past

semester. For this and other reasons, I wanted to work with a student from the course to find out how she (and possibly others) felt about the material covered: How did her writing improve? In what ways did she feel that certain assignments developed critical thinking skills? How was the pace, sequence, timing, volume of work? How did my pedagogical goals align with the assignments? Before getting to these questions, I first asked my student partner, Joanne Mikula, to look back over the syllabus and reflect upon the course. In turn, Jo annotated the syllabus with her reactions to assignments—what was helpful and what was not, and why. We then met together and openly discussed her notes; I explained my goals for certain assignments and what I had hoped to accomplish, she considered that, and together we imagined other possibilities for the pace of the course, the order of certain assignments, the way certain assignments were presented, etc.

After this first 'task,' I asked Jo to look more in depth at specific assignments and answer some of the questions I mentioned above. While our goals for the course lined up for the most part, there were certain areas where Jo (and other students) felt we could have moved more quickly through the material (e.g., writing a code of ethics) or where the material presented was confusing or less easy to follow (e.g., some grammar exercises and archival news articles). Consequently, I asked Jo to help me reformat some of this material; she has translated several ethical passages from English to French and is fixing some formatting issues with archival material to make it more accessible to the students.

Working with a student partner in this way gives me tremendous insight as to how students regard the material, and where I need to push or expand. In all, I believe our collaboration has provided me with the specific and in-depth feedback I need to make certain changes to my course material and its structure, which (I hope) will ultimately help the course to flow more smoothly and with the best possible outcomes to my objectives."

—Kathryn Corbin, Haverford College, United States (personal communication)

> "I really enjoyed getting the chance to work with Professor Corbin. Our partnership gave me a window into the teaching process and all the work that goes into preparing a course for students. Working with Professor Corbin also helped me develop skills that extend beyond our partnership. For example, my work translating pieces for her has honed the way I approach writing in French and helped me recognize more of the fundamental structural differences between English and French. Finally, I have enjoyed our partnership simply because I now feel that Professor Corbin is someone I can consult about my courses and my future with French."
>
> —Joanne Mikula, Haverford College, United States (personal communication)

In these cases of course redesign, the student partners had subject matter knowledge. In all cases, student and faculty partners worked together to structure courses to be inclusive of a diversity of students who come from a variety of backgrounds, bring a wide range of interests, and benefit from courses re-conceived at the intersection of student and faculty partners' perspectives.

Making explicit and challenging the hidden curriculum

A final example of how co-creation of curriculum can unfold is through navigating challenging or controversial content (Brunson 2018; Daviduke 2018) and always bringing to any curriculum an equity lens. This kind of co-creation makes visible and begins to deconstruct the hidden curriculum—a term coined by Philip Jackson (1968) to capture the idea of the unintentional lesson taught that nonetheless reinforces inequities. The hidden curriculum resides in the "gaps or disconnects between what faculty intend to deliver (the formal curriculum) and what learners take away from those formal lessons" (Hafferty, Gaufberg, and DiCroce 2015, 35); most commonly, what learners take away is a sense that people like them are not reflected in the subject matter, that they may not have the capacity to master the course content, and that they do not belong in the course or discipline.

Within the sciences in particular, there is danger of reinforcing patterns of content selection that excludes and does not value underrepresented students. As a student majoring in the social sciences and a woman, Natasha Daviduke (2018) knew nothing about the cultural norms and classrooms practices of the natural sciences, yet all three of her pedagogical partnerships through the SaLT program were with faculty who taught in STEM disciplines. This lack of familiarity gave her a unique perspective. As she explains, "I had sat in the very same seats as the students in my partner's course and wondered how basic STEM concepts were relevant to my learning and my goals" (Daviduke 2018, 153). Because she had "been one of these students," she had experience and perspective that informed her feedback to her faculty partners on how they developed components of their curriculum. She describes the work of her first partnership this way: "With the students in mind, we worked to build space for deeper discussion into the course, attempted to place concepts and examples into a relevant context, and strived to provide a clear structure for academic success." Working to reach and include a diversity of students, Daviduke and one of her faculty partners created a feedback system to, in essence, invite the students to co-create the course, as she explains:

> We devised a system for gathering consistent, pointed feedback from students in order to address issues with the course in real time. Our goal was to reimagine how to teach an introductory STEM class with a sensitivity to students' learning needs and a consideration of the type of thinking they would be asked to do in higher-level courses. We received rich, informative feedback and were able to develop a number of innovative solutions to students' challenges. (Daviduke 2018, 155)

This attention to the structure of the course—to the way the course was designed, and the kinds of opportunities students had to engage with the curriculum—is one way to surface and begin to address the mostly unintentional ways that STEM curricula are unwelcoming to underrepresented students. Attention to "STEM's culture and its structural manifestations" (Ong, Smith, and Ko 2017, 2), of which curriculum is one example, can support faculty partners in countering those norms (see also Perez 2016).

While the hidden curriculum can be embedded in disciplinary histories and biases, it can also reside in faculty conceptualizations of their curriculum regardless of discipline. Another student partner in the SaLT program describes the challenge her faculty partner faced when, based on student feedback, he realized that, "For the first time in his thirty plus year career, he was unsure about whether he was fit to teach his subject matter" (Brunson 2018, 2). Teaching a course that included underrepresented perspectives in a discipline that is typically among the most inclusive, this faculty member nevertheless "worried that his class was not inclusive enough and that he lacked an understanding of what his students were experiencing that was necessary to create a successful learning environment." Specifically, Mary Brunson (2018) explains, her partner "wanted to know if there was a way that he could create a curriculum that would make him more 'in touch' with his students."

Brunson and her faculty partner worked to name, explore together, and conceptualize how to create curricular structures through which the faculty member and the students enrolled in his course could engage with the course content, which positioned him and his students very differently. Brunson had not taken this course, and she was not completing a major in this faculty member's discipline. Nevertheless, she was able to work with him to analyze and revise the course in ways that reassured him and improved the experience of the students enrolled in the course. Power relations are inscribed in formal mechanisms such as curriculum (Bernstein 2000), and faculty and students perceive this from different angles. By working to examine the curriculum as well as creating more partnership opportunities within the class, this partnership demonstrated how "inviting students to participate in curriculum design changes power relations, providing opportunities for voices that are often marginalized to speak and those who customarily hold positions of power to listen and hear" (Bron and Veugelers 2014, 135). Throughout their yearlong partnership, this student-faculty pair worked, like Daviduke (2018) and her faculty partner, to create curricular structures that endeavored to counter the "hidden curriculum," whether disciplinary or relational, that threatened to undermine student learning and their more general experiences as people. Catherine Bovill and Cherie Woolmer (2018) reflect on this challenge:

> We need to consider the wider societal context within which universities operate and how they influence curriculum. As Shay and Peseta (2016, p. 362) argue, we need to question "in what ways do our curricula give access to the powerful forms of knowledge that students require not only to successfully complete their degrees, but also to participate fully in society?" ... On the one hand, whichever theories and whoever's interests are dominating curricular discourse will have a significant impact on the opportunities that are available for students to co-create curricula. On the other hand, co-creation *of* and *in* the curriculum have the potential to bring new voices and perspectives into discussion of curricula and to challenge existing ways of thinking about knowledge and curriculum. (Bovill and Woolmer 2018, 10)

This work in the curricular arena necessarily intersects with work in the pedagogical arena. One of the recommendations generated by student and faculty partners in the pilot project that launched the SaLT program was framed in this way: "The development of intellectual and critical spaces into which underrepresented—and well-represented—students can enter is facilitated by the use of inclusive examples." Student and faculty partners who participated in the pilot pointed out that "it helps students tremendously when faculty members include examples that connect to students' own lives and when faculty don't make assumptions about shared experiences among their students." Student and faculty partners offered illustrations of this, cautioning against "assum[ing] a uniform or narrow cultural context" and emphasizing the importance of both "draw[ing] on analogies from common social themes, especially when explaining complex concepts" and "encompass[ing] everyone's experience" (Cook-Sather and Des-Ogugua 2018, 10).

One student partner describes the effect of such approaches through a description of the practices of her faculty partner in the natural sciences:

> [My faculty partner] never assumed sameness. She never said it in a way that would make you feel bad if you weren't a part of the group she was talking about because she would try to include you in another way. I had never seen that before—someone who was always so conscious of how you are framing things. . . . It was so refreshing to be able to come in and never feel like you are an outsider because you don't match up with the mainstream. (Student partner quoted in Cook-Sather and Des-Ogugua 2018, 10)

Each of these examples of making explicit and challenging the hidden curriculum reflects ways in which student partners paid close and careful attention both to their faculty partners' pedagogical commitments and to the ways in which the curriculum might be undermining or working against those and, in particular, disenfranchising or disadvantaging some students. Each example also illustrates how faculty partners trusted and valued their student partners' insights, revisiting their curricular approaches within the new frames student partners offered and also co-created with their faculty partners.

Who might participate in curriculum-focused pedagogical partnerships?

Who participates in curriculum-focused partnerships depends on which type of curricular co-creation you want to engage in. Typically, faculty initiate the course design or redesign process, since it is usually faculty who have primary responsibility for the curriculum.

In the case of co-planning a course before it is taught, faculty may invite a group of students who have taken similar courses, a group of students who might be the intended population to enroll in the course, and librarians, instructional technologists, or others who could bring expertise and insight regarding how to create resources and structures. This is a proactive approach: seeking partnership before the curriculum of the course is run (Pinar 2004).

Co-creation of courses while they are unfolding can take place in planned and anticipated ways or in response to recognition of the need for revision of what had been planned. In the first case, the faculty member teaching the course needs to think through how to invite students to participate in such a co-creation effort, as Ulrika Bergmark and Susanne Westman (2016) described. When a faculty member decides to revise or reconceptualize while the course is unfolding, it is also necessarily in partnership with students enrolled in the course. This is a responsive approach embraced in recognition that the course needs to change direction. Other collaborators might still be brought in, but it is primarily the faculty member and students working together who conceptualize and enact the change in direction.

Engaging in course redesign after a course is taught typically involves the faculty member who taught the course and some subset of the students who completed it. Faculty who have redesigned courses in partnership with students have been deliberate about inviting a range of students into such partnership: those who succeeded easily, those who struggled, those who had a particular critical perspective, etc. Those choices send strong messages both to the students involved in the redesign and to other students who are aware of the redesign process.

Finally, in the case of making explicit and challenging the hidden curriculum, faculty might invite any of the partners noted above but also students who have no knowledge or experience in the course content but might have a particular perspective, based on their own identities, experiences, and studies, who could bring a missing angle or set of insights to the exploration.

What might be the focus of the partnership work?

The focus of curriculum co-design might be informed by any number of factors: institution- or department-wide curricular revision mandates; faculty and student partners' own interest in developing a new course or re-imagining an existing one; or a particular assignment or set of assignments within a course but not the whole thing. The focus of the design or redesign will depend on the course goals and also on who leads the design or redesign. Below are some examples of different ways to focus curriculum design and redesign.

Should student and faculty partners identify a particular issue (e.g., alignment between pedagogy and assessment) or can it be a more open redesign process?

There are many ways to approach co-design, and we offer just three examples below: when students and faculty draw on their lived experiences and identities to co-create from the ground up; when faculty invite students to re-imagine how best to structure engagement with course content; and when students are the source of content for the course.

When Alison and Crystal co-designed Advocating Diversity in Higher Education, the goal was not only to bring to bear their different perspectives as faculty member and student but also to draw on their lived experiences based on their different identities to create a set of curricular components that would speak to and invite the voices of a diversity of students. So, from the outset, the goals themselves as well as the curriculum were co-created.

Focusing on reconceptualizing curriculum, when Charkoudian (2015, 1) decided to redesign her first-year chemistry course, she was guided by the questions: "Did the overall structure of the course make sense? Did my forms of assessment align with my course objectives? What could I do to improve this class for future students?" These questions came from her own teaching experience and perspectives, and she sought the learning experiences and perspectives of students who had taken the course. In the box below we include snapshots from their semester-long process. We highlight Weeks 1, 4, and 6 of their collaboration to offer glimpses of the range of topics they addressed, and we include framing comments and transitions in italics to convey the overall arc of the co-redesign process:

Lou Charkoudian, Assistant Professor of Chemistry at Haverford College, explains the approach she took in collaboration with three undergraduate students who had taken her organic chemistry course, Anna Bitners, Noah Bloch, and Saadia Nawal:

During our first meeting, we identified seven different themes and decided to dedicate two weeks to each theme. We scheduled weekly meetings on Thursday mornings to discuss our progress and any challenges encountered by the student consultants. We identified "needs" within each theme and brainstormed "actions" to meet these needs. The themes, needs, and action items that we covered over the course of the semester are outlined below along with some reflections on each. Taken together, these illustrate the ways in which the student consultants' insights shaped my rethinking of multiple aspects of the course.

We identified key needs as a group by examining the course objectives and assessment strategies outlined in the syllabus. The course objectives included students being able to do the following by the end of the semester:

1. Recognize, name, and draw the structure of all general classes of organic compounds found in biological systems.
2. Predict the reactivity of a molecule in a biological system based on its chemical structure.
3. Understand the fundamental organic reactions that underpin life.
4. Determine reactions that can be carried out to accomplish a specific biological transformation.
5. Predict the mechanism of organic biological reactions.
6. Draw parallels between how synthetic chemists make molecules versus how nature makes molecules.
7. Locate, read, and understand primary journal articles and scientific review articles.
8. Present the biosynthetic pathway of a natural product.

Assessment strategies included three midterm exams throughout the semester, one final exam, a final presentation on a topic related to the organic chemistry of biomolecules, pre-lecture quizzes, and weekly problem sets.

We asked ourselves: Did these different tasks fulfill the objectives of the course and help students learn the material? What could be improved upon? What would be helpful for future students?

Week 1: General organization
Need: Incorporate feedback from last semester.
Action: Reviewed end-of-semester evaluations and pull out constructive feedback. Discussed general design of course and brainstormed ways for improvement. Areas identified for improvement included: General timing of major assignments (exams and poster presentations), balance between assigning practice problems versus exercises designed to think about key concepts, and the role of the "Chemistry Question Center" in enabling student learning.

Weeks 2 and 3 focused on poster presentations and pre-lecture quizzes.

Week 4: Problem sets
Need: Engage students in answering questions at the interface of chemistry and biology that do not simply have a "right" and "wrong" answer.
Action: Created a set of qualitative open-ended "key concept" questions that can be included in the weekly problem set assignments. The "key concept" question writing was a collaborative effort that took place during one of our weekly meetings.

Week 5 focused on exams.

Week 6: Lecture Notes
Need: Students commented that it would be useful to highlight key concepts and topics covered in each lecture.
Discussion: After reflecting on the semester as a whole, we reviewed the syllabus and discussed the flow of the course. Looking back, we were clearly able to see the progression and flow of material; however, we thought it would help students if they could see the progression more clearly as they moved through the semester. We therefore brainstormed methods to make this flow more

apparent and decided to make the lecture design more transparent to the students.

Action: Clearly articulated key concepts/topics from each lecture and created a list of objectives ("by the end of the class you will be able to . . .") to be shared the students at the beginning and end of each class.

Week 7 focused on reflection on the process of the co-redesign experience and yielded the insights that all four participants share in the essay they published, cited below.

Charkoudian, Lou, Anna C. Bitners, Noah B. Bloch, and Saadia Nawal. 2015. "Dynamic Discussions and Informed Improvements: Student-Led Revision of First-Semester Organic Chemistry." *Teaching and Learning Together in Higher Education* 15. https://repository.brynmawr.edu/tlthe/vol1/iss15/5/.

A third option for a focus is what students bring. A faculty member might have a general idea about a course they want to teach, but they might invite a group of students to help identify what the curriculum might include, following the students' lead in conceptualizing and designing the curriculum.

What techniques from classroom-focused pedagogical partnerships might you use to inform curriculum redesign?
If student and faculty partners are focusing on revising while a course is unfolding or making explicit and challenging the hidden curriculum as a course is unfolding, or even if they are redesigning a course after it is taught, they may want to use some of the techniques that student and faculty partners use in classroom-focused partnerships (discussed in detail in chapter 6 and in the "Visiting Faculty Partners' Classrooms and Taking Observation Notes" resource, "Mapping Classroom Interactions" resource, "Gathering Feedback" resource, and "Representing What Student and Faculty Partners Have Explored" resource). These include:
- taking observation notes;

- mapping classroom interactions (in whole-group and small-group constellations);
- gathering feedback (after a class session, at the midpoint of the term, or at other times); and
- creating annotated lists of practices explored and to explore.

What will the process look like?

As student and faculty partners begin to imagine a curriculum-focused pedagogical partnership, they will want to consider which and how many people should participate; how much time they can spend; what forums they need to create; how often they will meet; who will be responsible for what; and how they will move from identifying issues to enacting revision. We discuss each of these below.

Which and how many people should participate?

If student and faculty partners engage in the first or third form of co-creation—co-designing a course before it is taught or redesigning a course after it is taught—they will want to consider which faculty members and which students, as well as, perhaps, which staff members, might be involved. Will it be a single faculty member who plans to develop or revise a course? An entire department? A cross-disciplinary group? Will it be a group of students who have taken courses in the area of study? Students without knowledge of the subject matter? Students who have generally been successful? Students who have struggled? Students who are underrepresented at the college or university? Will it be members of the library, information services, a dean's office, a diversity officer, a member of access services, or another staff member? Student and faculty partners can ask themselves not only which and how many people should be involved but also why. What individual or institutional perspective might particularly enhance the process and outcomes and not have been included in previous conceptualizations and reconceptualizations of the course?

If student and faculty partners engage in the second form of co-creation—redesigning as the course unfolds—they will want to think carefully about whether all or just some students in the course will be involved. It is important that no inequitable structures or opportunities are created around the course revision, so we recommend that, for this kind of partnership, all students have the option to be involved. Perhaps the students, faculty, and staff involved can think together about a range of options for involvement. To give all students the same opportunity for contribution, student and faculty partners can consider holding regular focus-group discussions within and outside of class, creating an anonymous suggestion box, and inviting informal and formal midterm feedback. Some institutions have created student ambassador positions: a role for students in the course that include checking in with other students enrolled to gather feedback to be shared with the instructor.

How much time should student and faculty partners spend on the curriculum development or revision process?

All four versions of curriculum development and revision we discuss here typically unfold within the span of a single term or over the summer. There are two main reasons to spread the work over a full term or to concentrate it when most classes are not in session. First, given the professional work everyone has—teaching and taking classes, undertaking research and holding jobs—few would have time to devote concentrated periods to the development or revision process during terms when classes are in full session, so it is important to think about how to spread the work out over the term or concentrate it in the summer months when there are, in many contexts, typically fewer classes. Second, it is helpful to create a structured, attenuated process so that thinking can proceed as well as circle back as each component of the course is considered and reconsidered.

What forums do you need to create for curricular development or revision?

The examples we describe above offer a range of forms that curriculum-focused pedagogical partnership can take, but regardless of the form, student and faculty partners will want to think about the face-to-face and virtual forums they create for engagement and collaboration, and they will want to consider the purpose of each forum they create. Alison,

Melanie, and their co-author Crystal Des-Ogugua state their purposes in co-creation:

> During both the co-planning and the classroom-based co-creation phases of Advocating Diversity in Higher Education, as we experienced and watched the toll that ongoing protest takes on students (Ruff 2016), we had as our priority to affirm a diversity of students in the Bryn Mawr and Haverford College communities and to inform all members of the course regarding those students' identities and experiences of belonging or alienation. This approach complements recent discussions of utilizing students' funds of knowledge as assets for disciplinary learning (Daddow 2016) by using those sources for co-creation and for education regarding identities as well. (Cook-Sather, Des-Ogugua, and Bahti 2018, 378)

How often should student and faculty partners meet?
If student and faculty partners engage in the first or third form of co-creation—co-designing a course before it is taught or redesigning a course after it is taught—they may want to follow the approach student-faculty teams in the SaLT program have typically used: meeting either once a week or once every two weeks during the term or once every few days, either in person or virtually, during the summer. Regularly planned meetings give all parties involved an opportunity both to analyze and to reflect as well as to confer with others involved to keep the focus clear, monitor progress, and make any changes to the approach that might be necessary. Richard Mihans, Deborah Long, and Peter Felten explain their approach:

> The Center for the Advancement of Teaching and Learning paid students $450 stipends and, since we met over the noon hour, box lunches were provided at each meeting. Our team was formed, [and] the meeting schedule

was set (twelve meetings over three months). (Mihans, Long, and Felten 2008, 4)

If student and faculty partners engage in the second form of co-creation—redesigning as the course unfolds—they will be meeting regularly anyway for class sessions. The amount of in-class or outside-of-class time spent on revising the curriculum will depend on the kind and extent of revisions they want to make.

If they engage in the fourth kind of development and revision—making explicit and challenging the hidden curriculum of a course—the partnership work will depend on whether the revision is linked with any of the other three or independent. If the partnership is with students enrolled in a course, the project might become a curricular focus in and of itself. If the partnership is with a student not enrolled, then it might take the form of the weekly observations and meetings described in chapter 6.

Who should be responsible for what?

While the emphasis in this work is on collaboration, that can include dividing up components of the work and distributing tasks. Alternatively, it may be that everyone wants to engage with every aspect of the work, and then the collaborative time is spent comparing perspectives, negotiating decisions, and implementing. Who takes on what responsibility should be an ongoing conversation in co-creation because, as Delpish et al. (2010, 111) explain, taking on new roles challenges old habits:

> Students are accustomed to, and often comfortable with, assuming a relatively powerless role in the classroom, just as faculty are trained to believe that their disciplinary expertise gives them complete authority over the learning process. When faculty or students challenge these habits, students and faculty must confront fundamental questions about the nature of teaching and learning.

Confronting those fundamental questions can cause conflict but can also lead to new insights and approaches. In their discussion of the course redesign process in which they engaged, Mihans, Long, and Felten (2008) describe how at first the student and faculty perspectives were in conflict, but then by using Wiggins and McTighe's backward design course development template, they came to a place of being able to respect and draw on both perspectives:

> As we co-created the framework for the course, we found that students were simultaneously gaining expertise as learners and increasing their disciplinary knowledge and skills. For example, one student wrote, "The whole backwards design plan, I'm really now a huge advocate for that. . . . At first I was skeptical, but I've definitely come around to . . . believing that this is the best way to go about [curriculum design]." (Mihans, Long, and Felten 2008, 5)

How will student and faculty partners move from identifying issues to enacting revision?

As part of a plan for curricular development or revision, student and faculty partners can include a schedule of steps, building on the structure they create and also identifying a set of outcomes, which might change as their work unfolds but that can serve as a set of loose goals to begin with. Charkoudian and her students provide one example of such a schedule in the box on pages 207-209.

If student and faculty partners are revising a course as it is unfolding, they will enact the changes in real time, but we recommend that faculty members, interested students, and any staff members involved keep notes as the course unfolds and confer once the course is over regarding what was revised and how those changes might be carried forward.

A list of readings about curriculum-focused partnerships can be found in the "Selected Reading Lists" resource.

YOUR TURN

What is your definition of curriculum?

Given your definition, which forms of curriculum-focused pedagogical partnership can you imagine pursuing in your context?
- Co-planning a course before it is taught?
- Co-creating or revising while a course is unfolding (either with students enrolled in the course or students not enrolled)?
- Redesigning after a course has been taught?
- Making explicit and challenging the hidden curriculum?
- Other forms?

Who might participate in curriculum-focused pedagogical partnerships on your campus—faculty, students, librarians, IT staff, others?

How will participants in your context decide on the focus of curricular co-creation?
- Responding to institution- or department-wide curricular revision mandates?
- Drawing on the lived experiences and identities of students and faculty to co-create from the ground up?
- Faculty inviting students to re-imagine how best to structure engagement with course content?
- Other drivers or inspirations?

What techniques from classroom-focused pedagogical partnerships might you use to inform curriculum redesign? Revisit:
- Chapter 6
- "Visiting Faculty Partners' Classrooms and Taking Observation Notes" resource
- "Mapping Classroom Interactions" resource
- "Gathering Feedback" resource, and
- "Representing What Student and Faculty Partners Have Explored" resource

What might the process of curricular co-creation look like?

- Which and how many people should participate?
- How much time should student and faculty partners spend on the curriculum development or revision process?
- What forums do you need to create for curricular development or revision?
- How often should student and faculty partners meet?
- Who should be responsible for what?
- How will student and faculty partners move from identifying issues to enacting revision?

8 HOW MIGHT YOU MANAGE THE CHALLENGES OF PARTNERSHIP?

We have focused in the majority of this text on the promises and possibilities of pedagogical partnership, but it is also important to name and address the challenges we and others have encountered. In this chapter, we identify the most common challenges to developing pedagogical partnership. These include managing everyone's complex schedules and lives, differentiating teaching assistants and student partners, considering diversity of identities and roles, acknowledging and managing the emotional labor involved in partnership, and what to do if something challenging happens.

What are the most common challenges to developing pedagogical partnership?

Bovill et al. (2016) identified three complex and overlapping challenges to engaging in pedagogical partnership: resistance to co-creation of learning and teaching; navigating institutional structures, practices, and norms; and establishing an inclusive approach. We summarize each of these challenges here.

There are many forces that can prompt resistance to change and innovation, the first challenge to developing pedagogical partnership, and the forms of change and innovation that pedagogical partnership require can be particularly challenging. Among the forces that work against embracing pedagogical partnership are faculty members' own experiences as students, the expectations of current students, and inherited practices from colleagues (Hughes and Barrie 2010). Two factors in particular that "determine innovation resistance are habit toward an existing practice and perceived risks associated with the innovation"

(Sheth and Stellner 1979, 1). Custom and common practices alongside "the perceived personal and institutional risks of redefining traditional [faculty]–student roles and relationships inform the challenges [faculty] and students experience in co-creating learning and teaching" (Bovill et al. 2016, 199).

Faculty are often concerned about finding time for pedagogical partnership work on top of already heavy workloads. They may wonder how students can contribute meaningfully to designing learning and teaching when those students do not have subject or pedagogical expertise (a concern shared by many students). And they might wonder whether or not students should have a voice in elements of learning such as assessment. Students also have worries about what they bring to partnership, how much emotional and intellectual labor, and time, are required, and how to navigate the complexities of the role that can lead to resistance, including why they should step out of their (often comfortable) traditional role in order to engage in co-creation and how they as students will benefit from this different approach.

Paul Trowler and Ali Cooper (2002, 229, 230) note that faculty assumptions regarding the "nature of students in higher education (including their abilities and preferences)" and "what is, and is not, appropriate practice in teaching and learning situations" can influence their receptivity to innovation. Lynley Deaker, Sarah J. Stein, and Dorothy Spiller (2016) point to the tendency of faculty to resist forms of professionalization that they may experience as oppressive (see also Quinn 2012). Endeavoring to understand the potential sources of both faculty resistance (Ntem and Cook-Sather 2018) and student resistance (Keeney-Kennicutt, Gunersel, and Simpson 2008) can help address those resistances. As Kelly Matthews (2019, 4) suggests, we can welcome questions about partnership that might seem like resistance as an opportunity to engage in a "shared thinking process that brings new people into the partnership conversation as we think together about supporting, growing, and sustaining genuine partnership praxis."

A second common challenge to developing pedagogical partnership is how to work within and in some cases against institutional structures. While some institutions seek innovative change, others may adhere to institutional structures, practices, and norms that are in tension with co-creating learning and teaching. Partnership challenges "existing assumptions and norms about working and learning in higher education, and offers possibilities for thinking and acting differently by embracing the challenges as problems to grapple with and learn from" (Healey, Flint, and Harrington 2014, 56). As Bovill et al. (2016, 200) argue, "Even at institutions where teaching is a high priority, an orientation towards co-creation may be novel since it falls outside traditional views of student and [faculty] roles."

Similarly, many of the expectations and practices structured into institutions do not accommodate partnership, either conceptually or literally. As Beth Marquis, Associate Director (Research) at the Paul R. MacPherson Institute for Leadership, Innovation and Excellence in Teaching at McMaster University in Canada, notes:

> I've heard people raise questions about how partnership fits with established institutional practices—everything from the need to have pre-established learning outcomes on a syllabus through to documentation for career progress (e.g., we have a spot for "supervision" on our forms, but co-curricular partnership doesn't really fit anywhere and thus has to be squeezed in/left off). The notion of students as co-inquirers also isn't really clearly reflected in things like ethics forms or grant processes. (Personal communication)

Rigid role boundaries are an additional institutional structure that can pose a challenge that can make it difficult not only to embrace partnership approaches but also to develop "more nuanced and complex conceptions of identity that go beyond the dichotomous 'student/staff' binary" (Mercer-Mapstone, Marquis, and McConnell 2018, 18). The questions we pose in chapter 2 are intended to help with navigating that challenge.

A final challenge Bovill et al. (2016, 203) identified is "how to strike a balance between inclusion and selection (Felten et al. 2013)." In most cases, although there are exceptions, faculty are typically the ones who invite students into pedagogical partnership. As Bovill et al. (2016, 203) argue, "This raises difficult questions of how they determine whom they will invite and which students have the capacity to contribute." We discuss this in some detail in chapter 7, focused on curriculum-based pedagogical partnerships, but it is a theme throughout the book, especially as the literature on equity-focused pedagogical partnerships expands (Cook-Sather 2019b; Cook-Sather and Agu 2013; de Bie et al. 2019; Marquis et al., under review; Gibson and Cook-Sather, forthcoming; Marquis et al. 2018b).

How might you manage everyone's complex schedules and lives?

This is by far the most difficult logistical challenge of pedagogical partnership. Finding literal meeting times and making the emotional as well as intellectual space for pedagogical partnership work requires planning and flexibility and a capacity to sit with complexity and uncertainty.

What is the best way to approach scheduling?

Scheduling is always complicated, and when you are working with complex faculty, student, and program director schedules in which you are trying to integrate a new set of activities, it is even more complicated. A practical way of managing this logistical challenge is to plan as far in advance as you can, knowing that some shifts may be necessary once terms get underway.

In the SaLT program, Alison endeavors to match student and faculty partners who plan to engage in classroom-focused partnerships in the semester prior to the onset of their partnership work. In chapter 5 and in the "Inviting Faculty and Students to Participate in Pedagogical Partnership" resource, we include examples of messages to send to prospective faculty partners to try to get a sense of who might participate. Once program directors have a sense of faculty partners, typically fifteen to twenty per semester in the SaLT program but smaller at some places and potentially much larger at other institutions, they can reach out to invite student partners so they have the right number of participants and can have all partners matched, at least provisionally, before any given semester begins. For the most part, faculty working with students in curriculum-focused pedagogical partnerships do their own selection and scheduling with only two, three, or, at most, four or five people involved, if they are outside of class, and everyone involved if they are within classes.

It is often the case, though, that a last-minute course change undoes all that planning, or a faculty member might decide at the last minute that they want to participate, and that's where the flexibility has to come in. Alison also endeavors to plan the weekly meetings with student partners during the summer or over winter break, but last-minute schedule changes often necessitate rescheduling these meetings once the term is underway. Also, because of the number of student partners per term and the complexity of everyone's schedules, as well as Alison's desire to ensure that all student partners have sufficient time and space to speak during meetings, she typically schedules three or four separate meetings per week. She attends all the meetings, but student partners attend only one meeting per week.

How might you think about time?

Time is at the root of the scheduling challenge. But time is not a simple quantity. As Cook-Sather, Bovill, and Felten (2014) noted, one of the questions faculty most frequently pose about pedagogical partnership goes something like this: "I have enough to do already without having to set up all these meetings with students; wouldn't it be quicker to do this on my own?" We reproduce in the box below the response we generally offer to this question:

> "It depends on how you think about time. People typically find time for the things they consider most important. Working with students as partners in the design or revision of a course probably takes more time than doing these alone. However, time investments up front can pay off later as students take a more active role in the learning process (Wolf-Wendel et al., 2009), and working in partnership with students rather than working against them actually saves time as students assume more responsibility for

> the learning, as well as sometimes the teaching, that happens in a class. The time you spend creating and building partnership that enhances student engagement and accountability is time you save later on: repeating or clarifying when students don't understand; reviewing with students during office hours; responding to drafts of student work; and coping with the frustrations of teaching disengaged students."
>
> —Cook-Sather, Bovill, and Felten 2014, 17

Time spent in pedagogical partnership working through curricular and pedagogical questions can not only save time later in the ways described above, it can also be a source of energy and inspiration that makes time *feel* different. If all participants conceptualize and contribute to facilitation of pedagogical partnership in the ways we discussed in chapter 4, the "Ways of Thinking about Listening" resource, and the "Ways of Conceptualizing Feedback" resource, focusing in particular on listening, affirmation, and constructive feedback, all the time spent not only on pedagogical partnership but on all aspects of work can feel more fulfilling.

Should you insist on differentiating teaching assistants and student partners?
This will depend on your context. Berea College has considered this question deeply, because of their unique structure, and their discernment process is useful to everyone. Leslie Ortquist-Ahrens, director of Berea's pedagogical partnership program, explains how they thought through this question:

> Each year between 150-200 students serve as teaching assistants, learning assistants, or tutors for their labor positions at Berea College. As my colleague, Anne Bruder, and I puzzled about how to pilot a pedagogical partnership program, we decided to start with those faculty members who were already assigned teaching assistants, most of them in a first-year writing sequence taught by faculty from across the disciplines with a TA unlikely to be in their

field. To do so would ensure that each faculty member and each student had a partner, and it would guarantee that their schedules would line up (one of the biggest challenges otherwise) so that students could observe at least one class a week. In the pilot for the program, all pairs consisted of faculty members and their assigned or chosen TAs.

While this arrangement satisfied most participants—in fact, many found it gave them new and exciting ways to work well with one another—we, as program co-facilitators, did have some qualms. A first set of concerns involved what were inherently complex role definitions and power relationships. Navigating the dual roles TAs/student partners inhabited proved challenging at moments for a few, and it became important for partners to name their current mode or role very intentionally as they engaged in one aspect of the work (e.g., serving as a teaching assistant) vs. another (serving as a partner). Students wondered aloud with their faculty partners, if they should be serving as the TA or as the partner at various moments in class or in dialogue with one another, and, for a few, this was distracting. Other partners found the movement between roles unproblematic and fluid. For most faculty participants, the relationship established with a student partner who was also a teaching assistant provided insight into how to build a better and more productive relationship with any teaching assistant in the future. In fact, we have heard this insight echoed again and again, whether or not a faculty member has worked with a partner who was a TA or not.

A second area of concern for us involved the power dynamics in play for students who had complex and ongoing relationships with faculty partners as their TAs (who would be evaluated in that role, though not in the student partner role) or as those few students in the faculty member's field who might take a course from the faculty member in the future. Students wondered together in the group meetings whether sharing something with a faculty partner that was hard to hear might negatively affect an evaluation in the future. To date, participants have not reported problems around

> these power dynamics in practice, but we are remaining vigilant, and we call faculty-TA partners' attention to the potential challenge they could face and encourage ongoing open dialogue.
>
> But another major area of concern that emerged as we sought to use a pre-existing teaching assistant program to structure student-faculty partnerships was even greater than these. Because many, many faculty members don't have a TA or tutor assigned to work with them, they would never be able to participate in a promising and rich experience, unless we were able to develop a way for students to participate without being TAs. This challenge led us to reassess how we might establish partnerships for faculty and students who weren't already in a working relationship. A course promised to allow for broader access to the program for both those with and without faculty/TA relationships.
>
> —Leslie Ortquist-Ahrens, director of the Center for Teaching and Learning and director of faculty development at Berea College, United States (personal communication)

Berea College's structure is rare, and it is unlikely that many institutions will have exactly the same challenges, but the questions Leslie raises are ones everyone should consider. For instance, navigating the dual roles of TA and student partner might be smooth and fluid for some students, as has been the case at Berea thus far, or it might put students in very difficult and even detrimental positions, if they and their faculty partners are unable to develop a productive partnership dynamic. A student in the latter situation who plans to major in that discipline could feel vulnerable and even decide not to pursue a degree in that major, which would be a very unfortunate and even damaging outcome of pedagogical partnership.

A related problem is that, since many TAs do grading, having the same person in the role of TA and student partner might unintentionally reproduce the power dynamic and hesitation to share candid feedback that students enrolled in the class can experience with professors. In contrast, a student partner with no "stake" or evaluative role in the course can work in a liminal space with faculty to share their learning process and feedback.

An additional concern is that, very often, students who are selected as TAs in a course are those who have succeeded in that coursework in the past (understandably so—a student who never quite understood a major threshold concept in the field would probably not make the best support for their peers struggling with this same threshold). But it can be extremely valuable to work in pedagogical partnership with those students who do not feel confident in the discipline, or who have struggled through their academics, because they may more clearly be able to identify challenging moments in the class and notice peers who face those same struggles.

A further consideration is whether the insights of a student familiar with the content, and in fact playing a role in helping students learn it, will be able to offer the perspective of someone distant from or unfamiliar with the content. As we have mentioned, the vast majority of faculty partners in the SaLT program have found it useful to have student partners not in their disciplines. Those who have not found this arrangement useful have tended to be looking for content-focused rather than pedagogy-focused conversations. The exception, of course, is in advanced courses and in curriculum-focused partnerships. At McMaster University, enough faculty members have found working with students in their disciplines to be beneficial that the Student Partners Program offers faculty the choice of whether they would prefer a student partner in their discipline or one from outside the discipline.

In addition to scheduling and time, what about energy?

Planning for the emotional and intellectual demands of partnership is a less obvious dimension of this work, but no less real. A number of years ago, a new faculty member who participated in the SaLT program said that she found participating in pedagogical partnership some of the most stimulating intellectual work she had undertaken. Having the opportunity to analyze her pedagogical practice was deeply invigorating for her and has been so for many faculty.

While many faculty are energized by the work, some find the anticipation of it, and sometimes the work itself, stressful and exhausting. The same is true for student partners, who regularly report that this is some of the most demanding intellectual and emotional—and the most meaningful—work that they undertake as undergraduates, but that it can also be intellectually and emotionally draining. Marquis, Black, and Healey (2017, 727) found that exhaustion was a theme in their research as well. As one student put it: "on an interpersonal level the partnerships can be a little taxing when you are confronted with like direct conflict... or you're working with someone who doesn't really want to change."

It is helpful for everyone involved in pedagogical partnership work to remind themselves and one another that the intensity of the work is temporary, and the goal is to generate a set of insights and approaches that can be developed over time, not all at once. Being reminded that an experience is bounded often helps people generate energy and focus. Taking regular opportunities to reflect, too, as we discuss in chapters 4 and 5, can help participants gain perspective and feel re-energized.

What considerations might you take into account regarding diversity of identities and roles?

Pedagogical partnership intentionally and radically complicates traditional roles and relationships (Cook-Sather 2001), and in so doing, it both throws institutional and wider social identities into relief and calls for the forging of new identities (Mercer-Mapstone, Marquis, and McConnell 2018). Part of the complexity in all of this is that people who might seem the most likely to take on partnership roles might actually reinforce some of the traditional identities and relationships structured by institutions of higher education. Likewise, those who take on partnership roles are likely to have multiple identities, roles, and relationships that might overlap and even be in conflict with one another. Finally, once partners forge particular pedagogical relationships, they may be loath to expand those to include others. We discuss these considerations below.

How do you get a diversity of student partners, not just the "best" students/frequent flyer students whose voices are already represented or attended to?

Often when Alison listens to colleagues talk about developing a pedagogical partnership program, she hears a familiar refrain: Let's start with those students already in leadership positions. This is an understandable impulse. Students in those roles already have some experience working within the institutional structures in roles other than "only student," they may have developed some capacity and language for talking with faculty and administrators, and they have demonstrated investment. The problem is that they may also be the people whose voices are always heard, who have access already, whom institutions of higher education were designed to serve, and who have figured out how to navigate and succeed in higher education.

In chapter 5 and in the "Inviting Faculty and Students to Participate in Pedagogical Partnership" resource we discuss how program directors might invite prospective student partners or respond to their requests to participate. The first point we make is about how the SaLT program got started: through focus groups and other discussions that included traditionally underrepresented and underserved students and focused on how to support the development of more inclusive and responsive classrooms. This kind of framing from the outset, similar to what Smith College did (in identifying a commitment to designing a support structure through which their faculty members and student consultants could engage in pedagogical partnerships around bias interrupters and inclusive curricular development) or what Florida Gulf Coast University did (in focusing on the potential of pedagogical to foster belonging for students and faculty) sends a strong message that the pedagogical partnership program will invite and value a diversity of voices.

In addition, when asking faculty for recommendations for student partners, it is important to be clear about the explicit and implicit goals of the program—e.g., to facilitate dialogue across differences of identity, position, and perspective (Cook-Sather 2015); to develop a more inclusive learning environment (Smith College); to foster a sense of belonging (Florida Gulf Coast University); to create multiple initiatives through which students and faculty co-create teaching and learning—so that those recommending student partners think about a diversity of students to recommend. The sample messages inviting faculty to recommend student partners for participation in pedagogical partnership included in chapter 5 and in the "Inviting Faculty and Students to Participate in Pedagogical Partnership" resource offer examples of language that can signal clearly to faculty what particular partnership programs emphasize.

It is also useful to be aware of students' perceptions of facilitators and barriers to seeking out partnership opportunities. Students in a study conducted by Beth Marquis, Ajitha Jayaratnam, Anamika Mishra, and Ksenia Rybkina (2018) identified the following facilitators of becoming involved in pedagogical partnership work: flexible program structure, perceived approachability of faculty partners, previous experience, and established networks. Barriers to participating that students identified included: lack of time available to dedicate to partnerships, perceived ineligibility for and competitiveness of positions, and lack of awareness of student-faculty partnerships. Marquis et al. (2018b, 76) recommend that those who facilitate pedagogical partnership programs find ways "to take into account the variable levels of confidence that students might have had a chance to develop as a result of their experiences and social locations." Program directors, faculty partners, and student partners can all give these factors consideration and develop approaches for encouraging students who might not otherwise feel inclined or qualified to participate.

Finally, we recommend that you ask student partners for recommendations, particularly for students whose voices are not generally heard. Students will not only have perspectives on who those people might be in their particular institutions but will also benefit from the opportunity to give that question careful consideration or reconsideration in the context of pedagogical partnership.

What might you do about peer relationships between student partners and students enrolled in classes?
Complex, multiple relationships are likely if not inevitable at small institutions but can happen anywhere. As we mentioned in chapter 5, we

emphasize in the SaLT program the importance of students keeping their faculty partners' confidence while also offering to share student feedback anonymously with faculty partners. Here we expand on the challenge of maintaining professionalism, friendship, and transparency.

When student and faculty partners meet to establish the goals and parameters of their work, as discussed in chapter 4, as well as in chapter 6 for classroom-focused pedagogical partnerships, they need to be clear on what role the student partner will play in the class—how actively involved they will be, in what ways, if any, they will interact directly with students enrolled in the class, etc. These initial agreements will frame any interactions student partners have with students enrolled in the course. If the faculty partner feels strongly that the student partner should be in dialogue only with them and not with students enrolled in the course, it might be helpful for the student partner to proactively explain that to any peers or friends who are in the class, indicating that their pedagogical partnership is with the faculty member, and while they can listen to and share anonymous feedback from their friends, they cannot be in conversation with their friends about what faculty partners say. If faculty partners are comfortable with more communication between the student partner and students enrolled in the course, then the proactive approach is to make that clear and explicit.

In any case, faculty partners need to be aware that this is a challenging aspect of pedagogical partnership for student partners, especially in residential educational institutions, where students spend their lives sharing space, food, time, sleep—where they are always together. Likewise, student partners need to develop a heightened awareness to ensure that they are not unduly influenced by what their friends might have to say. This complexity can be an ongoing topic of conversation between faculty and student partners, and it is an issue that program directors will want to address in the regular meetings of student partners. Sophia Abbot, former student partner in SaLT and former fellow for collaborative programs, the Collaborative for Learning and Teaching at Trinity University, Texas, describes how she navigated this complexity:

> I navigated this somewhat myself, and then navigated it even more when I was in classes with faculty with whom I'd partnered and found myself still translating the goals of my professor to my peers and working as an advocate between the professor and students. It's a role that's hard to escape and especially complicated by the small school setting, which means one may interact with one's faculty partner (past or present) in many different roles and relationships. (Personal communication)

What are the benefits and drawbacks of staying in the same partnership over time (i.e., for more than one semester)?

Many faculty who work with a student partner for one semester want to continue with that same student partner in the next or in a subsequent semester. There are both benefits and drawbacks to this approach.

The benefits are that faculty have developed a rapport with the student partner, the student partner has learned about their faculty partner's pedagogical commitments and goals, and the partners therefore have a foundation on which to build. There is a sense of trust, empathy, and safety, and there is not the need to start over, build a new foundation, and invest the emotional labor that a new partnership demands. For student partners, staying in the same partnership builds a sense of empowerment and expansion. They can contextualize any new pedagogical issues that arise and see growth and change over time that they can feel excited to support and affirm, and they can build on the foundation they have established to work on different aspects of teaching.

The drawback of this approach is that neither faculty nor student partners have the opportunity to gain a different perspective, and variety is part of professional development for both partners. The faculty partner does not have the opportunity to learn from a different student's perspective, and the student partner does not have the opportunity to see different disciplines, teaching styles, and classroom dynamics. Particularly if student partners are hoping to continue in education, they do not have the opportunity to think about all of this diversity in relation to their own pedagogical commitments and aspirations.

Therefore, we recommend that faculty and student partners consider what the greatest benefit will be of continuing a partnership or starting afresh. They can discuss this question with other faculty and student partners, with the program director, and, of course, between themselves.

What kinds of emotional labor are involved in partnership?

Most students and faculty embarking on pedagogical partnership are focused on the intellectual and professional labor that will be required. However, pedagogical partnerships involve both anticipated and unexpected emotional labor on the part of faculty partners, student partners, and program directors. Acknowledging this from the start makes experiencing and carrying the weight of that engagement less surprising and more manageable.

What kind of emotional labor might faculty partners experience?

The emotional labor faculty partners experience depends on many variables and can evolve and shift over the course of partnerships. Prior to and when first embarking on partnership, faculty partners might experience a kind of anticipatory anxiety and disorientation. For instance, as we mentioned before, some faculty in the SaLT program talk about having a sense of "anxious expectancy of classroom observation as a (real or perceived) form of benevolent surveillance" (Reckson 2014, 1) and experiencing "the disconcerting presence in the classroom of a student consultant" as an "unnerving conjunction of counselor, coach, and court stenographer" (Rudy 2014, 2). Faculty partners might feel uncertain, vulnerable, and self-conscious at the thought of a student sitting in their classes to observe the teaching and learning and talking with them about their pedagogical or curricular practices. Reflecting back on the start of her partnership, a faculty partner in SaLT wrote: "Before I began meeting with my consultant, I have to admit that the prospect of opening my classroom to the critique of another was intimidating. I felt vulnerable and more self-conscious about my teaching than I ever have before" (Conner 2012, 8).

These are understandable feelings. Faculty rarely emerge from "pedagogical solitude" (Shulman 2004) and even more rarely (unless they are in the field of education) talk in deep and extended ways with students about teaching and learning. Furthermore, most visits to a faculty member's classroom are for some form of evaluation, so it is difficult not to carry that expectation over to pedagogical partnership and student partner observations. Until faculty and student partners establish frames, modes, and rhythms for classroom visits and weekly meetings, as we discuss in chapters 6 and 7, faculty partners may feel all of what participants in the SaLT program describe above and more.

Once faculty partners do get to know their student partners, though, and learn how to work together, they will likely find, like the majority of faculty members in SaLT and other programs, that they experience a shift from investing emotional labor to benefitting from emotional support. The faculty partner quoted above, who felt disconcerted by his student partner's presence, came to experience his student partner as "an inside/outside character in the class, a liminal and unexpected figure foreign to traditional teaching and central to raising pedagogical awareness" (Rudy 2014, 5). Instead of continuing to feel anxious about being under surveillance, the faculty partner quoted above who worried about being monitored found that her student partner "offered observation without judgment—a rare gift—and along with it, a sense of camaraderie and shared purpose" (Reckson 2014, 1). And finally, the faculty member who had felt vulnerable and self-conscious found that she moved to a place where "the sole feeling that washes over me is gratitude" (Conner 2012, 8). While most faculty experience this shift, not all do, and program directors, student partners, and faculty themselves should be prepared for a range of responses to the emotional challenge of this work.

In addition, the emotional labor faculty partners might experience will vary depending on the nature of the course or the pedagogical issues upon which they focus. Is it a course they have taught many times and about which they feel relatively confident? Is it an entirely new course about which they already feel overwhelmed and uncertain? Is it an elective within which they have a fair amount of freedom, or is it a required course in a sequence upon which other faculty depend? Are they concentrating on aligning assessment with pedagogical approaches, or are they focusing on what pedagogical approaches make their classroom more inclusive and responsive to traditionally underrepresented and underserved students? All of these will contribute to the sense of emotional labor that faculty need to invest in and through the partnership.

As we discuss in chapter 6 and in the "Gathering Feedback" resource, it can be particularly challenging to hear student perspectives through midterm feedback. It is important that the faculty partner prepare for this and that student partners consider how best to support their faculty partners and help interpret student feedback. One of the reasons this process is so emotionally charged is that students are rarely asked to offer feedback and so they can have a lot of pent-up feelings. An important lesson to take from this, and a way to help mitigate the intensity of the focused feedback offered at the midterm moment, is to have more opportunities for feedback scattered throughout the term, as we discuss in chapter 6 and the "Gathering Feedback" resource.

The emotional labor of pedagogical partnership will also vary for faculty partners, as everything does, not only based on the nature of their work with their student partners but also on the ways that various aspects of their identities intersect with the values and norms of their field, their institution, their department, and individuals on their campus, including their student partners. Faculty partners of color in particular have talked about the emotional labor in which they must engage in so many arenas, most intensively, typically, in supporting students of color. Working in partnership can be a relief. One faculty partner in the SaLT program, a woman of color, who taught courses in the humanities that enrolled a majority of students of color, explained that for her students "to see my consultants, who were both students of color, come in and to know that students of color can be authorities in the classroom, was incredibly transforming and powerful for the students who were actually participating in the class." Working with these student partners of color, this faculty member felt able to share the emotional weight she felt, and she voiced her relief at recognizing that she "can share the responsibility for what happens in the classroom with students . . . [and she need not] be the only voice speaking" (quoted in Cook-Sather and Agu 2013, 279). A faculty member in the natural sciences described her work with her student partner, also a person of color, in similar terms:

> [My relationship with my student partner] supported the "bravery" needed to question the traditional boundaries of what is discussed in an undergraduate physics class. Whereas many humanities classes can encourage critique of which authors are included or excluded from a syllabus and why, or how societal factors influence the construction of a canon, the self-view of physics as a linear accumulation of objectively-necessary skills, and of success in physics as based solely on aptitude in these skills, can restrict discussion of social issues in the classroom. (Perez 2016, 2)

However, not all faculty of color experience partnership this way. A student partner, also a person of color, reflected:

> New POC faculty have trouble letting go of their perceived all-encompassing control. My partner had very specific ideas about how she wanted everything to go, which led to inflexibility. I think sometimes new faculty insecurities get the best of them and lead them to a very defensive/resistant attitude. (Quoted in Ntem and Cook-Sather 2018, 89)

The emotional trajectory from anxiety and vulnerability to greater comfort, confidence, and gratitude, and the variation in kind and intensity of emotional energy invested that depends on interactions of identities, can be further complicated by pedagogical disagreements, destabilizing feedback from students enrolled in the course, or other challenges that arise. For instance, one faculty partner described the frustration she felt and the emotional effort it required "to disentangle my consultant's interpretations of the classroom from her observations." Although this was initially exhausting and frustrating, the emotional effort this faculty member invested yielded "many useful and unexpected lessons" (Anonymous 2014, 1). This is certainly the potential payoff of emotional investment.

Indeed, once faculty learn to work with their student partners, the vast majority describe feeling that they can share the emotional weight of teaching with their student partners. In the words of one faculty partner in the SaLT program: "Just talking to someone every week really energized me to fully commit to my own teaching goals and made me think about how I can do better at what I am doing and what kind of identity as a teacher I want to develop" (Oh 2014, 1). Nevertheless, the emotional labor will feel different for each faculty member, and we urge student partners and program directors to keep this in mind.

What kind of emotional labor might student partners experience?

Faculty partners' sense of being able to share the emotional weight of teaching with their student partners is mirrored in student partners' descriptions of carrying that weight. If we had to identify one experience that is most unexpected among student partners, it is this experience of the emotional labor required for the role. Many students seek out the role because they are interested in teaching and learning or because they want a meaningful, well-compensated job on campus. Virtually none of them realizes ahead of time how much emotional labor will be involved.

For many student partners, the emotional labor will begin, like faculty partners', with a sense of uncertainty and anticipation regarding this new role and how to do it "right." Reflecting on her work, one student partner in the SaLT program wrote: "When I participated in the student consultant orientation before embarking on my journey of partnerships, I listed one of my apprehensions regarding participating in partnerships as *using the wrong words or tone to communicate with my faculty partner*" (Mathrani 2018, 2). The deep respect for faculty and high levels of awareness the vast majority of student partners bring to this work contribute to their capacity as student partners and contribute, as well, to the emotional labor involved in doing the partnership work.

Another aspect of the emotional labor for student partners is related to self-confidence and sense of capacity. The role of student partner itself, with its insistence on student knowledge, capacity, and agency, is so anomalous and unfamiliar for most people that it takes some time to adjust emotionally as well as intellectually. Another student partner in the SaLT program wrote: "My faculty partner was incredibly knowledgeable in her field and I felt a little intimidated. What did I have to offer?" (Alter 2012, 1). Students in every institution for which Alison has consulted, whether small liberal arts institutions or large state schools, have expressed this uncertainty and have felt a huge emotional weight lifted when they are reminded that they are in the role *because* they are students as well as people with a wide range of lived experiences and insights to share.

Student partners will have these and other worries—about approaching their partners in the best way, about what they have to offer, and more. We recommend that student partners try to keep in mind that the emotional labor they invest in attending to these important questions, while potentially draining at first, can become energizing as they experience themselves growing into the role. We also recommend that they remember to affirm their efforts and achievements early and often, and that their program director offer such affirmation, too. Their faculty partners may not be as consistent in doing so, although many are, not because they do not value their student partner's efforts but rather because they are managing their own emotionally demanding process.

The emotional labor continues as student partners grow into the shift in role and responsibilities that being a student partner requires. At their first meeting with their faculty partners, they will need to tune their attention to the faculty partner's level of comfort, receptivity, flexibility, and more and to develop or refine ways of engaging that are at once respectful of the faculty partner as a person and a professional and productively challenging. Student partners cannot decide those things for themselves; they have to figure them out in relationship with their faculty partner. One student partner, Amaka Eze, describes this process in an excerpt from an essay she wrote about her four different partnership experiences:

> "In my first partnership, the professor with whom I was paired focused in her research and teaching on areas that are of interest and importance to me, too. However, this professor did not find

the approach to classroom observation typically employed by SaLT student consultants to be a good fit for her needs. At first I found this unexpected challenge disorienting, as I had been prepared to follow the guidelines offered to student consultants to help me navigate my first partnership. But after my first week of in-class observation, the professor asked me to change my note-taking style to better fit her classroom comfort.

While I don't purport to understand the complexities of professorship, I can empathize with the kinds of anxieties that might surface as one enters into a new teaching environment, intensified by being observed by a student consultant. To avoid undermining the development of trust and the miscommunications that can arise when people feel vulnerable, I came back with a new system for observational notes that focused entirely on the kinds of thematic pillars that emerged from class time, as opposed to any direct commentary on her teaching strategies. I re-focused my attention, drawing on the same attentiveness but representing what I saw differently, so that it was more directly linked to my faculty partner's pedagogical commitments.

The approach I developed emerged only after a series of difficult conversations between Alison, director of the SaLT program, and the professor with whom I was working, and me. I had to revisit my expectations regarding the best way to reflect the classroom environment and dynamics back to my faculty partner, and it was important that I find a way to do that through which I could continue to try to build trust with her. Through listening carefully to how she spoke about her pedagogical goals and looking for examples in class that appeared to be supporting students' pursuit of those goals, I was able to focus my observations in a way that felt more manageable to my faculty partner and thereby allowed us to focus on analyzing how she could continue to create structures for the kind of student engagement she hoped for."

—Amaka Eze, student consultant in SaLT
(Eze 2019, 1-2)

Student partners will need to think, throughout their partnership, about what they feel very strongly about and want to persist in finding ways to address with their faculty partners and what, for their own health and well-being, they might need to let go. As one student partner in SaLT explained: "I have learned to let things go (for my own sanity) and also the beauty of re-adjustment. [My faculty partner and I] spent weeks reframing our relationship/what she wanted me to do for her, which has resulted in a much more fruitful partnership" (quoted in Ntem and Cook-Sather 2018, 88).

Another catalyst for emotional labor is the insight student partners will gain into what happens "behind the scenes"—how hard faculty work, the kinds of pressures they are under, the way institutions can function to dehumanize. This glimpse behind the scenes may, as it has done for student partners in the SaLT program and other programs like it, cause student partners to feel greater empathy for faculty—another kind of emotional investment they might not anticipate. Student partners can feel overwhelmed, frustrated, indignant, and a desire to be helpful on their faculty partner's behalf. They might find themselves becoming "faculty advocates," as one student partner in the SaLT program put it, who feel compelled to stand up for as well as support faculty. This impulse and the capacity to act on it can carry over into relationships beyond the pedagogical partnerships, as Yeidaly Mejia (2019) describes in an essay she wrote about how the skills she developed as a student partner equipped her to address a complex set of issues in a course in which she was enrolled.

There is also emotional labor in handling the way in which partnership contrasts other experiences. As student partner Alise de Bie (de Bie and Raaper 2019) writes:

> My most positive experiences of partnership have also been the most devastating because they created a stark and significant discrepancy: There was now a wider and more visible and felt gap between my typical experiences of harm on campus (and within the medical system) and the possibility—arrived at through partnership—that

things didn't have to be that way and could, very feasibly and concretely, be different.

This contrast has been noted by other student partners in a variety of ways (see Cook-Sather and Alter 2011, for instance), and it also requires attention and processing. In her blog post (de Bie and Raaper 2019), de Bie raises an important set of questions from which the above excerpt is drawn and which can inform such processing.

Like faculty partners of color, student partners of color have described the particular emotional labor they experience. If a student partner is a person of color working with a faculty member who is white, they may experience one kind of emotional labor. One student partner in the SaLT program, a person of color, explained: "Many people, faculty included, are unused to checking their privileged identities regularly. When student partners ask this of them it can be overwhelming and again lead to defensiveness" (quoted in Ntem and Cook-Sather 2018, 89). That defensiveness requires, in turn, more emotional labor from students. Another student partner in SaLT, also a person of color, reflected:

> We've seen in the consultant meetings how emotionally vulnerable some of my peers are willing to be in our partnerships in order to think about justice [and] racial or gender equality. It's very moving to see my peers give themselves so much, give so much of themselves in their partnerships to make professors understand, to give professors perspective on their experience. (Student partner quoted in Ntem and Cook-Sather 2018, 92)

Students of color working with faculty members of color might find that the emotional labor takes a different form. Student partners might not have realized the extent and intensity of the demands on faculty of color, whose reaction to them might be like that of the faculty member quoted above who found solace and support in her student partners of color and realized she need not be the only voice speaking to issues of equity and inclusion. On the other hand, student partners might encounter unexpected forms of resistance from their faculty partners that result from discrepancies between their sense of the responsibilities of faculty of color and the sense those faculty members have themselves of the appropriate amount of time and energy to invest.

It is essential that student partners never feel that they need to do this emotional work alone. Consider creating a buddy system whereby experienced student partners are paired with newer student partners or two new student partners are paired to provide regular support and a confidential space within which to confer. One of the most important functions of the regular student partner meetings is to get support from other student partners and the director of the program. Student partners should never hesitate to share what they experience, wonder about, worry about, and want to celebrate. No struggle and equally no accomplishment is too big or too small for this forum. In many partnership programs, faculty, staff, or student facilitators of these weekly meetings ask student partners to respond to prompts that make space for student partners to capture, reflect on, and process their emotions and thoughts. If student partners find themselves needing such space, they can suggest a prompt to whoever is facilitating the meetings. Likely as not other student partners will need, and certainly they will benefit from, the creation of such space for reflection and processing. One SaLT student partner reflects on her experience of emotional labor and the importance of naming, affirming, and compensating it:

> [Working in partnership makes] invisible things visible. I know I have been doing a lot of emotional labor here since the beginning, I know that, I will name that, but it's usually been unrecognized institutionally. . . . [Partnership] makes that work visible. It's paid. And then discussing it in the weekly meetings and feeling like we are all doing this work. So we're being affirmed in doing this work for the institution and also for each other. (Student partner quoted in Cook-Sather 2018b, 927)

It is easy to feel overwhelmed by the emotional demands of partnership, but one of the key functions of the weekly student partner meetings is to help reframe everything that happens as a learning experience that prepares student partners not only for professional life but for life, period. It is these reframings and reminders, current and former student partners reiterate, that make the emotional labor required for this work manageable (Eze 2019; Mejia 2019).

What kind of emotional labor might program directors experience?

The vast majority of the emotional labor for program directors takes the form of supporting student partners and faculty partners. As the faculty and student partners with whom program directors work will experience the emotional labor described above and other forms, program directors will need to be present to and supportive of them. Program directors are the people who see more than one side of the partnership work: the student side through the weekly meetings with student partners, the faculty and staff side through whatever interaction program directors might have with them, their own experiences as a faculty or staff member, and the institutional perspective regarding what implications individual partnerships and this work collectively can have.

The most regular demand on program directors' emotional energy—and equally the most energizing aspect of this work—will be the weekly meetings with student partners. It requires deep, genuine attention to support their partnership work, and while it can sometimes feel like being present in that way requires more energy than program directors themselves have, if they think of those meetings as times for sharing responsibility—one of the premises of partnership—even the most demanding, difficult meetings can become energizing and strengthening.

Occasionally, a misunderstanding or some kind of tension may arise between student and faculty partners. As we discussed in chapter 5, it is important that faculty and students know that program directors are there to support them and help mediate any difficult situations that arise. In her role as director, Alison has occasionally met with faculty and student pairs together, or with faculty and student partners separately, to talk through these misunderstandings and tensions. In the majority of cases, revisiting the premises of pedagogical partnership, affirming each person's perspective, and helping them better understand the other's perspective will help partners get back on track.

The most energy-depleting experience program directors may have is when a faculty or student partner does not experience the program director's efforts as genuine or successful, and does not trust or believe them for whatever reason, no matter how hard they might work to create such trust; the program director may feel that they cannot find a way to reach that person. In these situations it is essential that program directors have trusted colleagues to talk to about the emotional drain of these dynamics. If they try to carry the emotional weight alone, it is likely to enervate them and eclipse the rest of their work. It has certainly been the case for Alison that when a single person or partnership is struggling, it is difficult to keep in mind that the others are doing wonderfully well.

Finally, program directors may experience the emotional labor of working to create, sustain, or grow a program that may be countercultural in their institutional contexts and that may have to compete for resources. Because pedagogical partnership work is human, relational work, there is virtually no aspect of it that does not require negotiation. Furthermore, because by design, as well as by default, pedagogical partnership often exists in liminal spaces, the lack of stability, a source of freedom and flexibility on the one hand, can also create a sense of unmooredness (Ahmad and Cook-Sather 2018). In regard to this form of emotional labor it is helpful to be in dialogue with other directors or people who can serve in the role of consultant, as Alison does for numerous institutions. Alison and her colleague, Arshad Ahmad, reflect on their choice to take on this emotional labor:

> The sense of responsibility that prompted us to risk embracing leadership of teaching and learning institutes committed to pedagogical partnerships among students, faculty, and staff . . . [informs] our stories. . . . [We hope these] reveal a deeper understanding of risk and uncertainty as they intersect with responsibility in relation to the professional choices we have made to help us better navigate in forging new and more widespread

pedagogical partnerships. (Ahmad and Cook-Sather 2018, 2)

What should you do if something challenging happens?

Because pedagogical partnerships require intense and demanding emotional as well as intellectual work, there are likely to be moments of tension, challenge, miscommunication, or other stress. This is not only because the partnership work itself is intensive but also because when the perspectives of students and teachers are brought into dialogue around issues of teaching and learning, rather than kept largely separate from one another and focused on content from their respective angles, and when people endeavor to work across differences of identity, position, and perspective (Cook-Sather 2015), issues arise that otherwise might have remained invisible or unnamed. As Floyd Cheung, director of the Sherrerd Center for Teaching and Learning and the pedagogical partnership program at Smith College suggests, "Properly handled and with a little luck, confronting concerns via the partnership model might address some problems that may never have come to light in any other way" (personal communication).

The first thing to do when challenges arise is to remind those involved to return to the basic principles that underpin partnership and to remind them that pedagogical partnership is first and foremost a relationship, that all relationships need intentional work to make them functional, and that tensions or challenges usually have their origin in some assumption or misinterpretation or some gap in communication. Virtually any challenge, if left unaddressed, can fester and undermine confidence, trust, productivity, and the potential of pedagogical partnership. When addressed as a learning opportunity, however, virtually any challenge can contribute to realizing the goal of pedagogical partnership: to facilitate dialogue across positions and perspectives that deepens understanding in all directions and helps make teaching and learning as engaging, effective, and inclusive as they can be.

If faculty or student partners experience a challenge or some form of discomfort in relation to pedagogical partnership work that feels sensitive and especially vulnerable-making for that person or for the other person or people in the partnership, we recommend that they address it first in confidence with the program director. If there are personal, ethical, or legal implications beyond the scope of the partnership program, the program director needs to be made aware of those and manage them through the proper institutional and legal channels. For less dire but nonetheless tricky situations, the program director may have a sense of larger context or particular complexities with any given faculty member, student, class, or department.

While the general recommendations above apply to both faculty and student partners, we offer some more specific scenarios below to help you think about what such processes might look like.

What might faculty partners do if something challenging happens?

The majority of challenges that faculty partners have experienced have had to do with clashes of expectations between them and the students enrolled in their courses or between them and their student partners. Clashes of expectations between faculty and the students enrolled in their courses are often surfaced or made explicit because the pedagogical partnership encourages forms of analysis, feedback, and dialogue that might not unfold otherwise.

One such challenge is brought into relief by the presence of the student partner. Sometimes students in a course approach a student partner with concerns rather than going directly to the faculty member. Even if a faculty member has indicated a desire for such mediation, they can sometimes change their minds or grow concerned about this. If faculty partners encounter such a challenge, we recommend that they have a candid conversation with both their student partner and with their class to clarify hopes and expectations. Such a challenge, while it might first appear to be a problem, might actually turn out to be a useful occasion to make hopes and expectations, and reasons behind them, more explicit to students.

A second example of a challenge some faculty partners experience concerns the observation process and the accompanying notes. We mention in chapter 1 that a common assumption faculty partners make is that they will be under surveillance by their student partners, and the observation notes can either dispel or exacerbate that fear. Upon receiving their first set of notes, some faculty partners can feel relief and excitement at the focus and the useful detail offered. Others can feel overwhelmed by the detail and even more vulnerable. It is up to faculty partners to decide and convey what form, kind, and extent of notes are most helpful to them. We encourage faculty partners to give the detailed, time-stamped descriptions and analyses a try, but if such notes are too overwhelming or otherwise not useful, faculty partners can agree with their student partners on another approach, such as short reflections on the key pedagogical issues the faculty partner identifies.

A final example of a challenge that some faculty partners experience is a disagreement between themselves and their student partners regarding pedagogical practice. These can arise around personal or disciplinary commitments and can cause tension. One faculty partner describes her experience of such a conflict:

> "From the beginning of our partnership, I realized that my consultant's view of the ideal classroom differed from my own. I was indeed getting a new perspective, but I wasn't sure how well the consultant's perspective mirrored the experience and expectations of other students in my classroom. As a student of education, my consultant was bursting with ideas for how to run a classroom. The ideal classroom that she described involved a spirited and free-flowing discussion, punctuated by activities that further fueled student engagement. My classroom, in contrast, was punctuated by periods of silence as my students struggled to digest difficult material before offering a contribution to the discussion. How to interpret these silences and their implication for the classroom experience became a point of contention between me and my consultant. What my consultant interpreted as confusion and disengagement, a problem in need of a solution, I interpreted as a necessary part of learning philosophy. Where my consultant saw confusion, I saw students slowly beginning to master the

> material, improving in both reading comprehension and in their ability to raise effective criticisms. At first I found it frustrating attempting to disentangle my consultant's interpretations of the classroom from her observations. In spite of this initial frustration, my consultant and I worked together to find ways to make our partnership productive, and I gained many useful and unexpected lessons through the process. Perhaps the most useful insight concerned the role of silence."
>
> —Anonymous 2014, 1

A challenge such as this, born of a pedagogical disagreement, can also become a source for learning and growth, as this faculty member makes clear, but only if faculty engage with the challenge or disagreement in a productive way (Abbot and Cook-Sather, under review).

All of these examples illustrate the importance of clarifying assumptions and commitments. Any one of them could have devolved into a greater challenge because of lack of communication and clarification. But when faculty partners remain engaged and work to clarify, the outcomes are productive.

What might student partners do if something challenging happens?

It is common for student partners to have a concern about a faculty partner's pedagogical practice. We recommend that student partners bring these concerns to the weekly, confidential meetings with the program director and other student partners, where they can get a sense of whether the reaction is a personal, individual one or whether others share the concern. Either way, student partners can work with the group on how to address the concern in a respectful and productive way with their faculty partner or, if it seems better for the partnership and the students enrolled in the course, they may choose not to address it and think about how to turn the struggle they are having with the practice into a learning experience for themselves. Many student partners have found this process to affirm their concerns and equip them with language and confidence to address them, and just as many have realized that their concerns stemmed from assumptions they were making or lack of understanding of the professor's or others' perspectives, and get just as much from that experience. For instance, one student partner felt strongly that her faculty partner should be looking for more opportunities for students to participate in discussion until she realized that she was imposing her own preferred way of learning on others. We include her explanation of this realization:

> I had always known that there were different kinds of learners and that different students had different learning styles. But there was always some part of me that believed my way of learning—through discussions—was superior. As I stepped back and analyzed this belief, I realized I had assumed that people who didn't speak frequently in class were perhaps the slightest bit lazy or the slightest bit dull.... After analyzing... mid-semester feedback from [my faculty partner's] class and realizing the assumptions I had been making, I no longer thought my quieter classmates were lazy or less motivated and no longer did I worry they weren't getting enough out of their college education. Instead, I began to realize that their classroom experiences and desires were just as valid as mine, and it was that "aha" moment that forced me to stop thinking about my role as "identifying opportunities for discussion" and see it instead as an opportunity for "seeing moments of learning." (Gulley 2014, 2)

Another form student partners' concerns can take is when a faculty member appears to be engaging in a pedagogical practice that the student partner worries is detrimental to students for other reasons, such as causing discomfort or intellectual and emotional harm to students already underserved by higher education. Another student partner explains such a scenario:

> During one of the weekly meetings . . . [my faculty partner] shared an idea he had for a class he was planning to teach next semester: that he wanted to start the class with a very difficult assignment to show the students they had a lot to learn. However, he said he did not want to tell the students the assignment was intentionally difficult. I thought this lack of transparency was not ideal in the classroom, and I believed professors should always be transparent with their students. I did not talk about why I believed this—partly because I wasn't sure, I just felt it—I just told him I believed so. After talking about this uncomfortable conversation in my weekly student consultant meeting, I figured out why I felt this idea was not ideal for the classroom. The next time I met my faculty partner I told him I had thought about our previous conversation and the reason I did not agree with his idea was that making an intentionally difficult assignment would disproportionately hurt students from marginalized backgrounds. Students who are questioning their place in a natural science classroom will immediately be discouraged if they are not given any reason for such a difficult assignment. When I framed my belief this way, with a clear reason behind it, my faculty partner immediately changed his focus and began to think about his practice differently. (Mathrani 2018, 5)

In both these cases, student partners had a strong feeling or belief and experienced a challenge because that feeling came into conflict with a faculty partner's practice. Both worked through those concerns, with their faculty partners and with support in the weekly meeting of the program director and student partners, and both were able to find ways of managing the challenge that respected everyone involved.

A third challenge that student partners might face is when their faculty partner asks them to take on responsibilities outside the parameters of the partnership. This can be completing the readings for a course, for instance, or making copies or some other administrative but not pedagogical or curricular task. It can also include doing extra research or writing with and for the faculty partner that were not part of the agreed upon set of responsibilities the faculty and student partners discussed at the outset of the partnership or as it unfolded. If a student partner feels that a faculty partner is asking such things, they can begin by trying to address the concern directly with the faculty partner. If that does not resolve the issue, the student partner should consult with the program director, who can either offer advice for how to address the issue with the faculty partner or talk with the faculty partner directly.

Other challenges may emerge in other contexts and with different groups of participants. The ways to address them generally have qualities in common, however: reflect and communicate, rather than make assumptions and try to manage the challenges alone.

What might program directors do if something challenging happens?

Program directors will find themselves mediating the kinds of challenges described above. Most important is that they try to get a sense of each partner's perspective and experience and support both. Because most of these challenges emerge as a result of some assumption or misinterpretation or some gap in communication, the program director's primary role is to clarify different perspectives and to support communication. This can include meeting or talking with student or faculty partners separately or mediating a conversation between them. In either case we recommend framing the challenge as an opportunity for deeper understanding of differences—of perspective, of experience, of goal—and deriving greater insight from the differences to take forward into future learning and teaching encounters.

While the majority of challenges program directors manage will be of the kind described above, less often, but occasionally, they may experience faculty partners questioning or rejecting the premises and practices of the pedagogical partnership program. In these cases, the first step is to try to negotiate directly with the faculty members involved. If this does not work, it is important that program directors also seek support from trusted colleagues and, if there are programmatic or institutional implications, from senior administrators. Alison and her colleagues, Cathy Bovill and Peter Felten, addressed this issue, and we reproduce their advice:

> *How should participants and facilitators manage the intersection of different perspectives and the disagreements that can arise at those intersections?*
>
> Welcome them. Listen carefully to them. Learn from them. We are used to having differences and disagreements divide us, but a key goal of student-faculty partnerships is to elicit contrasting perspectives and then to use those to foster deeper understanding and clarify or expand practice. (Cook-Sather, Bovill, and Felten 2014, 181)

Can partnerships fail?

When supporting colleagues and institutions in developing pedagogical partnerships, Alison often gets asked what happens when partnerships fail. From our perspective, a partnership can only fail if you don't show up and don't engage. Otherwise, virtually anything that happens can offer insight that can inform teaching and learning.

In order to turn whatever happens into a learning experience, it might be necessary to seek the support of the program director or others. Sometimes moments of miscommunication or vulnerability can feel like failure, but if they are addressed, they can be turned into insights. As Anita and Alison discuss in relation to resistances and resiliencies that student partners have experienced, what begins as self-doubt and a sense of having failed can turn into a clearer sense of what needs to be addressed and revised to allow learning to happen (Ntem and Cook-Sather 2018).

References related to managing the challenges of partnership are included in the "Selected Reading Lists" resource.

YOUR TURN

What are the most common challenges to developing pedagogical partnership?

How might you manage everyone's complex schedules and lives?

Should you insist on differentiating teaching assistants and student partners?

What considerations might you take into account regarding diversity of identities and roles?

We note the various kinds of emotional labor involved in partnership. Which of these do you anticipate in your context, and are there other kinds you can imagine?

What should you do if something challenging happens?

9 HOW MIGHT YOU ASSESS PEDAGOGICAL PARTNERSHIP WORK?

In their chapter on assessment in *Engaging Students as Partners in Learning and Teaching: A Guide for Faculty*, Cook-Sather, Bovill, and Felten (2014) focus on assessing processes and outcomes of student-faculty partnerships. As in that discussion, we use the term "assessment" as the root of the word suggests—to sit beside, to step back from, and to analyze the progress of. We are aware that in the UK and Australia, assessment generally refers to grades, and evaluation generally refers to this more iterative process of reflection and improvement. However, writing in the US context, we use assessment in the sense we define above.

In this chapter, we reproduce some of the assessment approaches and questions included in *Engaging Students as Partners in Learning and Teaching* because they are those used in the SaLT program. In addition, we focus on other less formal, day-to-day ways to assess the work of pedagogical partnership.

What approaches can all participants take to assessing the partnership work as it unfolds?

As we have endeavored to make clear throughout this book, the work of engaging in pedagogical partnership is logistically, intellectually, and emotionally demanding. Because all partners put so much into partnership, it is beneficial and enlightening to consider how they might regularly assess how they personally are engaging in the work, what they are getting from it, and where they might revise their approaches. Assessing is critical both for affirming what is going well and why and also for gaining perspective on what revisions might be necessary to improve, deepen, or extend the partnership work.

In addition to the approaches we describe below, we suggest that both faculty and program directors consider gathering feedback from students informally, such as at lunches or in office hours. Students might share thoughts in a more extemporaneous way in these informal venues.

How can student and faculty partners regularly assess their partnership work?

Both student and faculty partners will be steeped in the daily work of thinking about pedagogical practice or curriculum design and redesign. Because doing such work in collaboration may feel so unfamiliar for most partners, a lot of their energy will be focused on preparing for and processing the observations and feedback. If partners focus only on the content and not the process of these collaborations, it can be easy to get overwhelmed by the work and to lose perspective on it. Therefore, we recommend that both student and faculty partners find ways to regularly step back from and reflect on their partnership work.

Student and faculty partners might want to set aside a few minutes each week to do some reflection on their own time. They can perhaps create a section in a notebook or a folder on their computers for "Partnership Reflections" and just enter ideas, thoughts, questions, worries, celebrations—anything that relates to their partnership work and that they want to capture, think through, or remember. Setting aside a time each day for such reflection can be illuminating and energizing, especially if partners are sure to include affirmations of their own and one another's efforts.

One semester in SaLT, all student partners committed to writing, every evening before they went to sleep, three things that they felt positive about in relation to their partnership work (this is a variation on a positive psychology intervention). After a few weeks, they reported feeling more generally positive (consistent with research in positive psychology) as well as better able to notice and affirm what was going well in their partnerships. Faculty partners might consider engaging in this practice as well.

In the following sections of this chapter we offer specific recommendations for making the most of partners' weekly meetings, generating questions that foster reflection and the role of the program facilitator in supporting such reflection, creating particular forums and practices to support student partners, and representing the reflective work of both student and faculty partners to external audiences.

How can student and faculty partners make the most of their weekly meetings?
Regular (ideally weekly) meetings are the most consistent forum student and faculty partners have for assessing how their work is going. We recommend that during initial meetings, student partners ask faculty partners about their pedagogical goals, what learning experiences they hope students in their class will have, and other questions intended to afford faculty partners the opportunity to assess, articulate, and analyze their pedagogy. Similarly, if faculty partners' focus is curriculum development or revision, they will want to articulate clearly—and invite student partners to articulate—what it is they hope to develop or revise. These are rare opportunities for reflection, dialogue, and (re)articulation of pedagogical and curricular visions and goals, and we encourage faculty partners to take full advantage of them in spoken conversation and to keep records of them as well.

As the partnership unfolds, the observation notes (for classroom-focused partnership) and course development or revision (for curriculum-focused partnership) will provide the main focus for the weekly meetings. Seeking and attending to one another's perspectives can both clarify and complicate in productive ways the perspectives both partners have. As one faculty partner in the SaLT program explains:

> Receiving and reading [my student partner's] comments has provided me the opportunity to reflect on what has happened that week in the class. Our conversations have likely been helpful, both as a venue in which to discuss possible courses of action in the classroom and also in justifying certain decisions—or recognizing that another course of action would have been better. (Cook-Sather, Bovill, and Felten 2014, 234)

The practical benefits of these weekly meetings are complemented by more affective benefits. A faculty partner working with her student partner, Natasha Daviduke (2018, 154), addressed the question of energy and enthusiasm for teaching: "Weekly meetings with my student partner kept my spirit up about designing the best lesson plans I could."

For detailed advice from student partners about making the most of weekly meetings (as well as partnerships overall), see the section called "Making the most of your partnership from start to finish" in the "Guidelines for Student and Faculty Partners in Classroom-focused Pedagogical Partnerships" resource.

What questions might facilitate reflection on the shared work of pedagogical partnership?

In addition to taking advantage of reflective times they themselves can create and those offered by partnership programs, student and faculty partners may want to have semi-regular check-ins that are intentionally reflective and offer a chance to step back from the regular work of pedagogical and curricular analysis. During one of their weekly meetings, student partners can pose questions tailored to the particular relationship they have developed with their faculty partners. Such questions might take the following forms:

- What has surprised you most about our work on your class/course?
- What are you most excited about in relation to this work, and what are you most frustrated by?
- To what extent is the observation format we are using allowing us to best capture and reflect on the pedagogical issues we have identified?
- Does the way we structure our weekly meetings feel productive, or shall we experiment with a different structure?
- What has each of us done to engage and facilitate in constructive dialogue, and what might we do more or differently?

Student and faculty partners should be sure to craft whatever questions they pose in ways that are constructive, rather than asking about what their faculty or student partner likes or dislikes. The focus should be on what will best further the pedagogical partnership work.

What role can program directors play in student and faculty partner reflections on their work?
Student and faculty partners should not hesitate to reach out to their program directors and ask for a meeting or a virtual conversation if there is anything that they want to delve into more deeply or to troubleshoot. In the SaLT program, Alison often meets or talks with student partners who have particular issues they want to celebrate, plan for, reflect on, or otherwise process. This can be especially helpful to student partners if they: are new to the role and feel uncertainty or confusion; are experiencing particular challenges with their faculty partners that feel too sensitive or complex to address in the weekly meetings with student partners; or are thinking about how to carry into a different context the principles and practices of the partnership work they have done as undergraduates.

Likewise, the program director is a resource for faculty partners to consult. While faculty partners' primary relationship is with their student partners, there may be times when faculty partners want a faculty colleague's perspective or need to check in about how the partnership is going. If there are issues to discuss with the program director about student partners or how the partnership work is unfolding, it is always better to raise them early rather than wait until simple misunderstandings or miscommunication intensify into conflict or tension. In the SaLT program, Alison often confers over email or in meetings with faculty who have particular issues they want to celebrate, plan for, reflect on, or otherwise process.

What particular forums and practices might student partners use?
Because this work is so countercultural and challenging in asking students to assume consulting responsibilities, student partners need consistent, ongoing support in this partnership work, such as regular—weekly in the SaLT program—meetings of the program director and other student partners. One student partner in the SaLT program captures what virtually every student partner asserts: "Our weekly meetings have been the most important aspect of this experience. Being able to bounce ideas and problems off my peers is such an incredible help because I gain insight from multiple perspectives" (Cook-Sather, Bovill, and Felten 2014, 229).

This guide recommends that program directors provide regular prompts in the weekly meetings with student partners to encourage and support just such reflection. The "Sample Student Partners Course Syllabus" resource, "General Guiding Principles for Weekly Reflective Meetings of Student Partners" resource, and "Sample Outline of Topics for Weekly Meetings of Student Partners" resource provide examples of prompts for reflection. When the program director provides such a prompt—such as "What strengths and capacities do you bring to partnership?" early on in the term and "How can you re-energize yourself or your partnership?" as the term starts to wind down—student partners should take the time to engage these prompts with all their attention. We recommend that student partners really push themselves to capture as many of their thoughts and feelings as they can.

Although program directors may ask student partners to draw on their responses to such prompts in group discussion, these reflections will be primarily for student partners themselves, so student partners should write to themselves honestly. Doing so will ensure that they name and process what they are experiencing and consequentially learn much more from their reflections than if they just plow ahead. The kind of metacognitive awareness student partners will develop through such articulation and analysis will not only help them process the experiences they are having but also help them develop awareness, language, and confidence within and beyond their partnerships (as we discuss in the "Outcomes of Pedagogical Partnership Work" resource). Experienced student partners recommend keeping these responses to the prompts and reflections in one place and looking back on them to trace their own growth. Such tracing is an important part of assessment.

In addition to these forms of self-assessment, student partners might want to consider the kind of assessment they can offer to and receive from other student partners. Every time they pose a question such as, "What do you think about how I am approaching this issue?" or offer a response to a similar question that other student partners pose, they are engaging in assessment and also affirmation, both of which are essential to sustaining energy for this work. It can be helpful for program directors and other student partners to point this out, since when a student partner poses or responds to such a question, the focus can be on the content and not so much on the benefits of the process. Student partners can also take the initiative to request or propose prompts—or simply bring up issues—that they feel would be especially beneficial to themselves and to other student partners to address in their weekly meetings or in confidential conversations with other student partners outside the weekly meetings.

At the midpoint or earlier, the program director may ask student partners to step back and assess what they have accomplished. Questions such as "What do you feel good about accomplishing so far in your role as a student partner? What has your faculty partner accomplished that you can particularly affirm?" give student partners an opportunity to self-assess as well as assess the work with faculty partners. Again, getting distance on and articulating these things helps make them more real and allows student partners to deepen their awareness of what they are getting out of the experience.

Why might student and faculty partners want to keep a record of their reflections?
Both student and faculty partners in SaLT have indicated that they find it very useful to keep track of the kinds of regular reflections we advocate above, revisit them over the course of the partnership, and then look back over all of them at the end of the partnership. Doing so affords student and faculty partners perspective along the way and also the long view from the end of the partnership, which is almost always quite rich and full of growth.

As Sophia Abbot explains regarding the work she did in leading the Tigers as Partners program at Trinity University, "Some students have kept journals about their work throughout the partnership. These can be used as tools to track progress (of both faculty and student partners), themes that recur throughout the partnership, process challenges, celebrate successes, and as reminders that things can and will change when the partnership feels 'stuck' or challenging" (personal communication).

Faculty partners have similar and different reasons for keeping records of reflections. Teaching is such a demanding job, and it is impossible for faculty partners to keep track of and remember what they think through if they don't keep some sort of record of their thoughts, clarifications, and revisions. The various resources student partners can generate for faculty partners—observation notes, end-of-term annotated lists, and thank-you letters from pedagogy-focused partnerships (all discussed in the "Representing What Student and Faculty Partners Have Explored" resource), and new sets of curricular approaches, activities, and assessments from curriculum-focused partnerships—serve as resources as faculty partners move ahead with affirming and revising their practice.

It is helpful if faculty partners organize the resources in some way. Many faculty partners have created portfolios of work that include plans, reflections on them, student partners' notes, and overall takeaways from the partnership work. Below is one example of a table of contents of such a portfolio:

Table of Contents
1. Changes and Takeaways for Future Courses
   a. Changes made to syllabi
   b. Changes made to course structure
   c. Confidence boost: Things I kept the same (because I need to remember I'm doing many things well!)

2. Weekly Reflections
   a. My overall observations of weekly reflections

3. Collaborations with Student Consultant
   a. Things that can help balance students from different levels
   b. Research on social stereotypes in the classroom
   c. Videos for course

4. Student Consultant Observations

When faculty gather and reflect on the work they have done with their student partners, they clarify their practice, as this faculty partner in the SaLT program asserted: "I am much more aware of the atmosphere in my classroom and better able to point out and articulate (to myself or others) what is and is not working the way I want—in particular because

I'm more aware of my goals in the first place" (quoted in Cook-Sather 2011a, 3).

Keeping track of and analyzing reflections also provides language for and examples of the work the partners have done, which can be included on resumes and in job applications, in conference or class presentations or discussions with other students, faculty, and administrators, and in other professional forums. Finally, these reflections can also inform the thank-you letters student partners write their faculty partners (see chapter 6 and the "Representing What Student and Faculty Partners Have Explored" resource for detailed discussions of those letters) and letters faculty partners might write their student partners. A former SaLT student partner, Alexandra Wolkoff, captures the usefulness of looking back at her reflections: "In looking back upon my semester-long partnership with a new faculty member, I see myriad ways that she came to trust herself and move toward becoming the teacher she wants to be . . . and I see the theme of trust characterizing my own trajectory of growth: as a teacher, learner, interlocutor, and person" (Wolkoff 2014, 1).

How can student and faculty partners represent their work to external audiences?

Student and faculty partners regularly talk about how challenging it can be to explain what they do in the SaLT program to others—students who have not participated in partnership, faculty unfamiliar with the program, and prospective employers. Khadijah Seay, former post-bac fellow in Berea College's student-faculty partnership program, developed an activity to address this challenge. Leslie Ortquist-Ahrens, director of Berea's partnership program, explains:

> During Khadijah Seay's second semester as a post-bac fellow, she developed a valuable activity for students in the final part of the course. Reflecting on how challenging it had been for her to describe and explain on her resume and in a cover letter her experience as a student consultant, she urged us to invite students in the course to practice doing so for their final portfolio. Each student

was asked to imagine a post-graduation path—either graduate or professional school or a career direction—and then think about how they might describe the work they had engaged in through the program in a resume, application, graduate school statement, or cover letter. Students brought their drafts to class, and together we workshopped all of them. In this way, they not only had a chance to practice and develop their own, but they also saw models from other students.

—Leslie Ortquist-Ahrens,
director of the Center for Teaching and Learning
and director of faculty development at
Berea College, United States
(personal communication)

Alison regularly invites both student and faculty partners to write about their work for publication in the journal she created for this purpose, *Teaching and Learning Together in Higher Education*. Many faculty and student partners in the SaLT program have published essays in this venue, as have participants in partnership programs at institutions in Aotearoa New Zealand (Bourke 2018), Australia (Matthews 2017b), Hong Kong (Chng 2019; Seow 2019; Sim 2019), Italy (Frison and Melacarne 2017), and the United States (Goldsmith and Gervacio 2011; Oleson 2016; Torda and Richardson 2015). How can program directors both support assessment and assess their own facilitation of partnership work?

Many program directors, including Alison, find that the weekly meetings with student partners regularly prompt reflection and assessment. The questions student partners bring, the insights they have, the challenges they wrestle with, and the ingenuity and empathy they bring to this work will regularly inspire program directors to step back and analyze what supports such deep engagement and what might better support it. In other words, the reflective spaces program directors create for student partners in turn create a reflective space for the program directors themselves. Sophia Abbot echoes this assertion:

> I encourage program directors to answer for themselves the same reflective prompts they share with students. Especially if directors ask students to share part of that reflection with the group, I've found it valuable to also share my reflection/growth/learning/challenges with the student partners because it means the sharing is more reciprocal, I am more humanized, and student partners don't feel I'm asking them to share challenges or anxieties (in other words, be emotionally vulnerable) without doing any of that emotional labor myself.
>
> —Sophia Abbot, former SaLT
> student consultant and
> former post-bac fellow,
> Trinity University, United States
> (personal communication)

Likewise, any time program directors have a conversation with a faculty partner or someone else in the institution who raises questions, offers thoughts, or proposes new directions for the partnership work, those program directors can take such input as an occasion to step back and assess, in an informal way, what the implications might be for any such question, thought, or proposal. It is generative to have such conversations with faculty, student, and program director colleagues beyond one's home institution. Talking with people doing similar work in other contexts can offer a new perspective, affirm an approach, or simply deepen understanding and awareness (see Marquis, Black, and Healey 2017 and Marquis et al. 2018a for discussions of how the International Summer Institute on Students as Partners at McMaster University provides such opportunities).

Occasionally, Alison has invited past participants in SaLT, both faculty and student partners, to gather for informal reflection sessions or sent around reflective prompts. For instance, one year she sent the following questions to former faculty partners:

- Please complete the following statements and speculate about or explain any connections you see to your work through the partnership experience:
  » I am more aware of . . .
  » I am more comfortable with . . .
  » I work and/or interact with students/faculty . . .
- I am less comfortable and/or I am concerned by . . .
- Please describe 1–3 pedagogical or curricular approaches or practices you have developed or revised since participating in the partnership and any ways in which your work through the partnership informed those.
- What do you need over time to sustain partnerships? Ideally, what kind of follow-up support would you like to have?
- If you could make one statement to share with others (students, faculty, administrators, funders) about this work, what would it be?

Faculty and student partners who have participated in such informal assessment conversations or surveys consistently say that such reflection and recollection inspires them to return to the insights they gained through their partnership work and to renew their efforts to try to be more reflective in general. They also indicate that, until they joined the conversation or addressed the questions, they had not remembered what an impact the partnership work had on their practice. This is a further illustration of the power of simply opening space and offering an invitation to reflect.

Another way that program directors can assess the way the partnership work is unfolding and the lessons that can be learned from the work is to develop research projects that provide an opportunity to delve in to aspects of the partnership work. Alison regularly does such research in collaboration with student partners. Here is a partial list of the kinds of things they have explored together and the forms of publication that their explorations have taken:

- An opinion piece co-authored with Olivia Porte called "Reviving Humanity: Grasping Within and Beyond Our Reach" and published in the *Journal of Educational Innovation, Partnership and Change* that pushes back on the idea of the "hard-to-reach" student by arguing for the potential of pedagogical partnerships to support a reciprocal "reaching across" the spaces between students and faculty (Cook-Sather and Porte 2017).
- A creative dialogue co-authored with Sasha Mathrani called "Discerning Growth: Mapping Rhizomatic Development through Pedagogical Partnerships" that uses the concept of rhizomatic development—the spreading of an interconnected, subterranean array of influences—to describe growth that can occur through engaging in pedagogical partnership; to be published in an edited collection called *The Power of Partnership: Students, Faculty, and Staff Revolutionizing Higher Education* (Mathrani and Cook-Sather 2020).
- A research article co-authored with Anita called "Resistances and Resiliencies in Pedagogical Partnership: Student Partners' Perspectives" published in the *International Journal for Students as Partners* that explores Anita's idea that forms of resistance can be turned into forms of resilience within the structures and processes of pedagogical partnership (Ntem and Cook-Sather 2018).

Each of these publications took an idea that emerged in the context of pedagogical partnership work and offered an opportunity to assess that work by analyzing it within a new frame or metaphor that threw new issues into relief and contributed to the development of theories of partnership praxis (Matthews, Cook-Sather, and Healey 2018).

What approaches might you take to assessing the process and outcomes of partnership work at the individual, programmatic, and institutional levels?

In previous sections of this chapter, we have focused on what differently positioned participants in partnership can do to assess partnership work from their respective positions and mutually informing experiences. Here we focus on processes of gathering feedback and on creating structures for assessing outcomes.

What might you ask regarding the way pedagogical partnership is unfolding?

These questions are primarily for faculty and student participants in the program. The goal is to offer opportunities to step back and ask questions about the process in which they are engaged—reflection that would likely not happen if there were no specific prompts that made space for such reflection. Below, we provide some sample formative assessment questions student and faculty partners might want to address as partnerships are unfolding.

> **Sample Formative Assessment Questions for Participants During Partnerships**
> - Faculty engaged in designing or redesigning a course with students might ask: Do you feel that our collaboration has given you meaningful opportunities to share your perspectives, and to understand my perspectives, on assignments and activities for this course? How could we structure our work differently to ensure even more interchange?
>
> - Students in the role of consultant to a faculty member teaching a course might ask their faculty partners simple questions such as: Do you want to continue to focus on this particular aspect of your teaching? Is the kind of feedback I am offering useful? Should we shift the focus of our work?
>
> - Faculty developers might ask both faculty and students: Are our meetings structured and facilitated in a way that elicits both faculty and student perspectives on the issues we are exploring? If so, what is most effective in making that dialogue happen? If not, how could these sessions be structured or facilitated differently?
>
> Cook-Sather, Bovill, and Felten 2014, 197

Student and faculty partners may also want to ask assessment questions at the end of their partnerships. These, too, are primarily for participants and for those facilitating the partnership forums—internal analyses of what is working well and what might be revised to better support participants. In the following box are sample end-of-term questions used in the SaLT program to assess processes of partnerships.

> **Sample End-of-Semester Questions to Assess Process of Partnerships**
> - Looking back over the way the partnerships were structured and supported, which aspects contributed most positively to your experience and which would you recommend revising and how?
> - What were the most significant benefits and challenges you experienced in working with a student partner/faculty partner? In what way, if any, has what you learned shaped your practice as a teacher and a learner? In what ways might it inform your future thinking and practice?
> - Insights:
>   » For faculty partners: What are the most important **pedagogical insights** you gained or deepened? How have they (further) informed your practice, and how do they position or prepare you to continue to develop as a teacher?
>   » For student partners: How has this partnership informed your experience as a student?
> - Beyond specific pedagogical insights, what **overall benefits** did you derive from this opportunity? Why are these important?
> - What advice do you have for me and the college about how to best support faculty partners/student partners in the future?
> - What advice do you have for student partners that I could pass along to next year's and subsequent participants?

- What advice do you have for faculty partners that I could pass along to next year's and subsequent participants in partnerships?

- Any other comments?

Many programs do informal check-ins with student and faculty partners at midterm and request formal feedback on the program at the end of the term, for assessment purposes. These data can be vital when it comes time to ask for budget increases for the program.

What more formal structures might you create for assessing outcomes?

Cook-Sather, Bovill, and Felten (2014) suggest that is useful to facilitate formal moments of reflection and feedback that are intended to involve an audience beyond the partners themselves, such as interested colleagues and funders. As they explain: "This situates the partnership work within a larger frame and allows for comparison of experiences with other student-faculty partnerships and documentation of the process of partnerships unfolding." They suggest that "this kind of assessment addresses basic questions about what is working and needs to be affirmed and what should be revised. Responses are useful to participants, but they also engage other stakeholders in conversations about the process of partnership" (Cook-Sather, Bovill, and Felten 2014, 198). The box below offers examples of such formative assessment questions:

Sample Formative Assessment Questions for Participants and To Inform Conversations with Others

- What were your expectations as you approached this partnership, and how have they been met or not met thus far?

- What do see as the most, and the least, effective practices within this partnership?

- What do you see as the emerging outcomes of this work?

- What appear to be some of the meaningful questions or issues that this partnership seems not to be addressing, and how might we engage those?
- What insights about teaching and learning have you derived from your reflection on this partnership?

Cook-Sather, Bovill, and Felten 2014, 198

If responses to these questions are going to be included in presentations or publications beyond the campus, it is important to secure approval from the institution's ethics board and to secure participants' consent before gathering the data. Alison has consistently sought such approval for studies of student partners' experiences within the SaLT program and has both conducted research and published findings in collaboration with students (e.g., Cook-Sather and Abbot 2016; Cook-Sather and Agu 2013; Cook-Sather and Alter 2011; Cook-Sather and Des-Ogugua 2018; Cook-Sather and Luz 2015). In most contexts, gathering of data for internal purposes does not require ethics board approval, but it is always good to check with local ethics boards before proceeding.

While a great deal of the assessment work program directors do is qualitative, some colleagues are beginning to create approaches that might help "measure" some of the findings of qualitative assessments. Bill Reynolds, director of the Lucas Center for Faculty Development at Florida Gulf Coast University, explains his approach:

> The partnership literature suggests that student consultants benefit from partnership programs by becoming more self-confident, having increased sense of agency, and experiencing a greater sense of belonging. To evaluate these variables in a new partnership program at Florida Gulf Coast University we are asking students to complete pre- and post-tests of the College Self-Efficacy Inventory (Solberg et al., 1993), General Self-Efficacy Scale (Schwarzer & Jerusalem, 1995), School Belonging

Scale (Vaquera, 2009), Sense of Belonging to Campus Scale (Hurtado & Carter, 1997), and the Academic Locus of Control Scale (Curtis & Trice, 2013). We're interested in measuring change in faculty attitudes as well, but we haven't yet identified the appropriate constructs to measure.

—Bill Reynolds, director,
Lucas Center for Faculty Development,
Florida Gulf Coast University, United States
(personal communication)

When might informal assessment inform more formal review processes?

We have emphasized that it is essential that the work student and faculty partners do be confidential—that they create together a brave space for exploration and experimentation (Cook-Sather 2016b). Therefore, the majority of the work they do will not be made public. There are, however, ways in which that private work can inform public processes.

Anecdotal reports

Administrators have shared anecdotally that faculty who participate in partnership do better at moments of review. Since the advent of the SaLT program, for instance, far fewer faculty at Bryn Mawr and Haverford Colleges experience concerns about their teaching at initial review than prior to the advent of the program, and those who do have concerns tend not to have taken up fully the opportunities the program offers (see chapter 8 for a discussion of this challenge). There is no way to correlate participation in SaLT with better outcomes at moments of review, and Alison has insisted that it would be counterproductive and even detrimental to try to measure outcomes in this way while also creating brave spaces for faculty, but the anecdotal evidence is there.

Faculty requesting student partners to write letters for reappointment

Another way in which informal assessment might inform formal processes of review is when faculty partners ask student partners to write letters for them. This is, of course, voluntary and entirely up to individual faculty members, but numerous faculty partners in the SaLT program, the Tigers as Partners program, and other partnership programs have asked their student partners for such letters, since, as they explain, no one else has had such extended exposure to their classroom or curricular approaches or such extended dialogue with them about their pedagogical and curricular practices.

Students requesting faculty partners and director to write letters
A final way in which informal assessment might inform formal processes is when student partners ask their faculty partners or program directors to write them letters of recommendation for jobs and graduate school. Alison receives many such requests because, as student partners explain, working so closely with them in this context affords her insight into their capacity and commitments as little else on campus can do.

YOUR TURN

As you think about developing or extending pedagogical partnership work in your context, what approaches can you imagine all participants taking to assessing the partnership work as it unfolds, and why would you use those particular approaches?

How will student and faculty partners regularly assess their partnership work?
- How will student partners make the most of weekly meetings with other student partners and the program director, and how will faculty partners make the most of weekly meetings with their student partners?
- Why will student partners want to keep a record of their reflections?
- What questions might facilitate reflection from student and faculty partners on the shared work of pedagogical partnership?

What role can program directors play in student and faculty partner reflections on their work, and how might these encourage their own reflections?

What approaches might you take to assessing the process and outcomes of partnership work at the individual, programmatic, and institutional levels?

What might you ask regarding the way pedagogical partnership is unfolding?

What more formal structures might you create for assessing outcomes?

When might informal assessment inform more formal review processes?

CONCLUSION

In this final chapter, we offer some recommendations for how to use this book's supplemental resources and address why the challenging work of pedagogical partnership is worthwhile. Our discussion of the resources includes recommendations for which resources might be of particular use if you want to: structure conversations with campus stakeholders about the possibility of developing a pedagogical partnership program; consider options and institutional structures for supporting pedagogical partnership, both when programs launch and in terms of sustainability; compare how different kinds of institutions have launched pedagogical partnership programs; begin to craft detailed structures for participant engagement; and dig into the various approaches student and faculty partners might take if they are focused on classroom practice. There are, of course, many other questions you might want to address and ways you can draw on the resources, but this set of recommendations gives you a place to start.

Our discussion of why such challenging work is worthwhile offers a reminder of the benefits to faculty, students, program directors, and institutions that we discussed in the opening chapters. It also reaffirms the potential of pedagogical partnership to afford perspective, value differences, promote both/and rather than either/or thinking, and support life-affirming practices—if we are willing to embrace "hope in the dark" and to make our roads by walking.

How might you use this book's supplemental resources?

Throughout this text we have pointed you to the thirty-five additional resources posted online. If we think of this core text as the central living space of this work, where you can engage in dialogue with yourself and others about pedagogical partnership, you might think of the resources as adjoining rooms. Each one opens a door to a space within which you can contemplate, work with, build on, extend, and otherwise explore and apply what we mention in the core text but cannot address in detail for reasons of space.

You will, of course, make your own way through those additional resources, exploring what is of interest to you and leaving closed the doors that open onto details that are less compelling. Here we make a few suggestions for how to draw on those additional resources.

- **To structure conversations with campus stakeholders about the possibility of developing a pedagogical partnership program**, pair the "Checklist for Developing a Pedagogical Partnership Program" resource and the "Templates and Activities to Explore Hopes, Concerns, and Strategies for Developing Pedagogical Partnership Programs" resource. These documents provide discussion questions and structures for conversations, as well as concrete examples of what this work can accomplish and resources to delve into particular areas of partnership (e.g., Where can you learn more about other colleges' and universities' approaches to developing pedagogical partnership programs? What are some common areas of focus for pedagogical partnerships? What approaches can student and faculty partners take to curriculum-focused partnerships?). All of the following resources could inform such a conversation:
  » Checklist for Developing a Pedagogical Partnership Program
  » Templates and Activities to Explore Hopes, Concerns, and Strategies for Developing Pedagogical Partnership Programs
  » Threshold Concepts in Pedagogical Partnership
  » Student Partners' Particular Contributions to Pedagogical Partnership
  » Outcomes of Pedagogical Partnership Work
  » Selected Reading Lists
  » Partial List of Themed Issues of *Teaching and Learning Together in Higher Education*
- **To consider options and institutional structures for supporting pedagogical partnership, both when programs launch**

and in terms of sustainability, ask variously positioned people to read the following resources and then meet to compare notes:
- » Options for Incoming Faculty to Work in Partnership through the SaLT Program
- » Choosing Names for Partnership Programs and Participants
- » Creating Post-Bac Fellow Positions to Support the Development of Pedagogical Partnership Programs
- » Three Stages of Backward Design for Creating Post-Baccalaureate Pathways to Educational Development
- » Working toward Programmatic Sustainability

- **To compare how different kinds of institutions have launched pedagogical partnership programs**, spend some time reading through the history of the SaLT program and how a variety of institutions launched partnership programs on their campuses:
  - » History and Structure of the SaLT Program
  - » Five Stories of Developing Pedagogical Partnership Programs
  - » How the SaLT Program Got Started
  - » Steps in Launching Pedagogical Partnership Programs

- **To begin to craft detailed structures for participant engagement**—invitations to participants, plans for partner orientations and summer institutes for faculty, and guidelines for participants—look at:
  - » Advertising Student Partner Positions
  - » Inviting Faculty and Students to Participate in Pedagogical Partnership
  - » Sample Message to Student Partners from the SaLT Program Director
  - » SaLT Program Student Consultant Application Form
  - » Sample Student Partners Course Syllabus
  - » Summer Institute for Faculty Participants in Pedagogical Partnership
  - » Sample Outlines for Student Partner Orientations
  - » Plans to Orient New Faculty and Student Partners
  - » Guidelines for Student and Faculty Partners in Classroom-focused Pedagogical Partnerships

» General Guiding Principles for Weekly Reflective Meetings of Student Partners
» Sample Outline of Topics for Weekly Meetings of Student Partners
- **To dig into the various approaches student and faculty partners might take if they are focused on classroom practice**, go to the following resources:
   » Guidelines for Student and Faculty Partners in Classroom-focused Pedagogical Partnerships
   » Visiting Faculty Partners' Classrooms and Taking Observation Notes
   » Ways of Conceptualizing Feedback
   » Ways of Thinking about Listening
   » Questions that Facilitate Productive Talking and Listening
   » Mapping Classroom Interactions
   » Gathering Feedback
   » Representing What Student and Faculty Partners Have Explored

Why is such challenging work worthwhile?

Among us we have almost twenty-five years' worth of experiencing pedagogical partnership work. What makes such challenging work worthwhile? We do not wish to downplay the challenges of this work—the significant demands on everyone's time, the complexities of managing everyone's schedules, the sometimes taxing negotiations of power and responsibility, the intersections of the diversity of identities and roles partners bring, and the emotional labor involved in this work. And yet both the range of benefits and positive outcomes we can name, as well as the way it feels to do this work, far outweigh the challenges and potential drawbacks, to our minds.

Even if partnership work were to support faculty only some of the time in experiencing the benefits—acclimating more quickly to campus culture and unfamiliar students; developing a confidence and clarity about their pedagogical commitments; finding the courage to follow through on their pedagogical convictions and responsibilities; gaining a perspective that they cannot achieve on their own; receiving formative feedback on teaching; recognizing and making intentional good pedagogical practices; sharing power (and responsibility) with students; turning pedagogical learnings into publishing opportunities; developing greater empathy, understanding, and appreciation for students; and building resilience through navigating difficult and ambiguous institutional situations—the effort would be worthwhile.

Likewise, even if partnership work were to support students only some of the time in experiencing the benefits—gaining confidence in and capacity to articulate their perspectives; developing deeper understanding of learning and themselves as learners; developing deeper understanding of teaching; developing greater empathy for faculty and other students; sharing power (and responsibility) with faculty; experiencing more agency and taking more leadership; feeling stronger connections to departments and institutions; getting to "take" as well as observe a course they otherwise might never experience; turning pedagogical learnings into opportunities to host workshops, lead panels, publish, and more; developing creative and innovative ways to troubleshoot pedagogical challenges; and building resilience through navigating difficult and ambiguous institutional situations—the effort would be worthwhile.

And finally, even if partnership work contributed only some of the time to positive outcomes for institutions—nurturing faculty and students who feel a deeper sense of confidence, engagement, and belonging; supporting distribution and rhizomatic spread of understanding of teaching and learning; seeing how individual empowerment leads to new projects and initiatives that enhance the whole institution; and distinguishing the institution to prospective students and teachers and the wider world of higher education—the effort would be worthwhile.

This work is worthwhile because there is something intangible about the way of being that partnership requires and fosters: a perspective-giving, difference-valuing, both/and-promoting, life-affirming quality that makes everything better. When offered and embraced with good will, generosity of spirit, willingness to wrestle productively, and openness to change when needed, partnership confers the benefits of the positive psychology practices it enacts (see Cook-Sather et al. 2017). And while it is still and may always be countercultural work, it can be guided and sustained by principles such as the feminist ethic of risk: "an ethic that begins with the recognition that we cannot guarantee decisive changes in the near future or even in our lifetime" and that "responsible action does not mean the certain achievement of desired ends but the creation of a matrix in which further actions are possible, the creation of the conditions of possibility for desired changes" (Welch 1990, 20). Most peaceful change comes through such efforts to create such conditions and by taking one step at a time, making the road by walking, as Myles Horton and Paulo Freire (1990) call one set of their conversations (in turn borrowing from the Spanish poet Antonio Machado's words "se hace camino al andar"). We hope our recommendations will make your road and your walking as smooth as it can be but also prepare you for the inevitable and educative bumps.

AFTERWORD

Beth Marquis, McMaster University, Canada
Mick Healey, Healey HE Consultants and University of Gloucestershire, UK
Kelly E. Matthews, University of Queensland, Australia

As this volume makes eminently clear, pedagogical partnership has the potential to be both powerfully beneficial and intensely challenging. Working as partnership practitioners and researchers in our varied, international contexts (Australia, Canada, and the UK), and connecting with others interested in partnership around the world, we have heard and experienced the simultaneous enthusiasm and difficulty articulated in this book on numerous occasions. Partnership has the capacity to confer many different kinds of benefits on students, staff, and institutions. It offers an exciting antidote to the growing emphasis in postsecondary education on students as consumers and has the potential to push back against the neoliberal culture of individualism, competition, and performativity that is increasingly dominant in today's world. In its focus on building and valuing relationships, destabilizing traditional hierarchies, and recognizing a wider range of voices, knowledges, and perspectives, partnership has also been seen to contribute to making postsecondary institutions more human, equitable, and democratic spaces. At the same time, it is undeniably hard work, which can be rife with uncertainty and require considerable emotional labor, and it may well fall short of at least some of its goals on some occasions.

This complexity is an important piece of what makes this volume so timely and significant. By offering a clear and detailed view of one model of engaging students and staff as partners in classroom- and curriculum-focused pedagogical partnerships, and by drawing on extensive research and experience to name and explore some of the key challenges that attach to this work, Alison Cook-Sather, Melanie Bahti, and Anita Ntem have developed a highly practical resource that will support others interested in engaging in partnership, particularly those looking to establish and sustain institutional partnership programs. Indeed, those of us who have been involved in developing partnership programs on our own campuses can attest to how valuable this resource would have been as we went about that work. Significantly, the three authors, an experienced member of faculty and two recent graduates, "talk the talk and walk the walk" not only in working in partnership as co-authors but also in sharing their reflections on their own experiences of working together in pedagogical partnership. Moreover, by including examples and insights drawn from a number of different partnership programs and initiatives, and by posing a series of key questions designed to help readers articulate their own goals and commitments and tailor partnership opportunities to their own contexts, the volume makes clear that there is no "one size fits all" approach to partnership work. In this respect, we see the book not only as a valuable window into the day-to-day functioning and processes of one highly successful partnership program, but also as a call to develop a wide range of partnership practices that respond to and work within diverse institutional and cultural contexts.

Building on this call, we invite readers not only to engage in applying, translating, and assessing the ideas set out in this guide, but also to extend and add to its insights by taking up its invitation to consider the variety of ways in which partnership might unfold and be supported in different cases and spaces. Most essentially in this regard, we need further consideration of how partnership plays out in a range of countries and cultural contexts, particularly given the growing recognition that much of the existing partnership literature has focused on examples from "Western," predominantly English-speaking institutions. It would also be instructive to see similarly detailed considerations of how to establish, support, and sustain pedagogical partnerships that are not focused primarily or immediately on the classroom or curriculum, for example student-staff co-inquiry on discipline-based research or the scholarship of teaching and learning, or partnerships playing out within the realm of institutional governance. We would also benefit from additional resources taking up and documenting strategies for effectively supporting or recognizing student-student partnerships (e.g., through peer learning and mentorship), or partnership approaches that engage a wider variety of campus and community partners. Likewise, following from the research and recommendations Alison Cook-Sather, Melanie Bahti, and Anita Ntem provide about the possibilities for partnership to contribute to equity and inclusion in postsecondary education, we need further consideration and assessment of various models for working toward this essential goal.

As even these few examples make clear, then, this volume doesn't simply provide a singular roadmap for others to follow. Instead, it offers a helpful guide to one set of (research and experience-informed) partnership practices and objectives, an invitation to consider applying, adapting, and extending these, and permission to do things differently. We look forward to seeing how readers take up these possibilities in their own partnership practice and research.

Along with Alison and Anita we are all, with a few others, co-editors of the *International Journal for Students as Partners*.

REFERENCES

Abbot, Sophia, and Alison Cook-Sather. Under review. "The Generative Power of Pedagogical Disagreements in Classroom-Focused Student-Faculty Partnerships."

Abbot, Sophia, Alison Cook-Sather, and Carola Hein. 2014. "Mapping Classroom Interactions: A Spatial Approach to Analyzing Patterns of Student Participation." *To Improve the Academy: A Journal of Educational Development* 33(2): 131–52. https://doi.org/10.1002/tia2.20014.

Abbott, Clara, and Laura Been. 2017. "Strategies for Transforming a Classroom into a Brave and Trusting Learning Community: A Dialogic Approach." *Teaching and Learning Together in Higher Education* 22. https://repository.brynmawr.edu/tlthe/vol1/iss22/3.

Ahmad, Arshad, and Alison Cook-Sather. 2018. "Taking Roads Less Traveled: Embracing Risks and Responsibilities Along the Way to Leadership." *Teaching and Learning Together in Higher Education* 24. https://repository.brynmawr.edu/tlthe/vol1/iss24/7/.

Alter, Zanny. 2012. "Discerning Growth: Lessons from One TLI Partnership." *Teaching and Learning Together in Higher Education* 6. https://repository.brynmawr.edu/tlthe/vol1/iss6/3.

Anonymous. 2014. "Silence in the Classroom." *Teaching and Learning Together in Higher Education* 11. http://repository.brynmawr.edu/tlthe/vol1/iss11/10.

Arao, Brian, and Kristi Clemens. 2013. "From Safe Spaces to Brave Spaces: A New Way to Frame Dialogue Around Diversity and Social Justice." In *The Art of Effective Facilitation*, edited by Lisa M. Landreman, 135–50. Sterling, VA: Stylus.

Austin, Ann E., and Mary Deane Sorcinelli. 2013. "The Future of Faculty Development: Where Are We Going?" *New Directions for Teaching and Learning* 133: 85–97. https://doi.org/10.1002/tl.20048.

Bell, Amani, L. Carson, and L. Piggott. 2013. "Deliberative Democracy for Curriculum Renewal." In *The Student Engagement Handbook: Practice in Higher Education*, edited by Elisebth Dunne and Derfel Owen, 499–508. Bingley, UK: Emerald.

Bell, Amani, Tai Peseta, Stephanie Barahona, Suji Jeong, Longen Lan, Rosemary Menzies, Tracy Trieu, and Ann Wen. 2017. "In Conversation Together: Student Ambassadors for Cultural Competence." *Teaching and Learning Together in Higher Education* 21. https://repository.brynmawr.edu/tlthe/vol1/iss21/5.

Bergmark, Ulrika, and Susanne Westman. 2016. "Co-Creating Curriculum in Higher Education: Promoting Democratic Values and a Multidimensional View on Learning." *International Journal for Academic Development* 21(1): 28–40.

Bernstein, Basil B. 2000. *Pedagogy, Symbolic Control, and Identity: Theory, Research, Critique*. Lanham, MD: Rowman and Littlefield.

Berryman, Mere, Roseanna Bourke, and Alison Cook-Sather. In preparation. "Weaving Mana Ōrite, Ako and Pedagogical Partnership Principles: Understanding Partnership in Education Within and Beyond Aotearoa New Zealand."

Berryman, Mere, and Elizabeth Eley. 2017. "Succeeding as Māori: Māori Students' Views on Our Stepping Up to the Ka Hikitia Challenge." *New Zealand Journal of Educational Studies* 52(1): 93–107.

Boice, Robert. 1992. *The New Faculty Member: Supporting and Fostering Professional Development*. The Jossey-Bass Higher and Adult Education Series. San Francisco: Jossey-Bass.

Bok, Derek. 2013. "We Must Prepare Ph.D. Students for the Complicated Art of Teaching." *Chronicle of Higher Education*, November 11, 2013. http://chronicle.com/article/We-Must-Prepare-PhD-Students/142893/.

Bourke, Roseanna. 2018. "Playing with Partnership Approaches in Higher Education." *Teaching and Learning Together in Higher Education* 25. https://repository.brynmawr.edu/tlthe/vol1/iss25/1.

Bovill, Catherine. 2017a. "A Framework to Explore Roles Within Student-Staff Partnerships in Higher Education: Which Students Are Partners, When, and In What Ways?" *International Journal for Students as Partners* 1(1): 1–5. https://doi.org/10.15173/ijsap.v1i1.3062.

Bovill, Catherine. 2017b. "Breaking Down Student-Staff Barriers." In *Pedagogic Frailty and Resilience in the University*, edited by Ian M. Kinchin and Naomi E. Winstone, 151–61. Rotterdam: Sense Publishers.

Bovill, Catherine, Cathy J. Bulley, and Kate Morss. 2011. "Engaging and Empowering First-Year Students Through Curriculum Design: Perspectives from the Literature." *Teaching in Higher Education* 16(2): 197–209.

Bovill, Catherine, Alison Cook-Sather, and Peter Felten. 2011. "Students as Co-Creators of Teaching Approaches, Course Design and Curricula: Implications for Academic Developers." *International Journal for Academic Development* 16(2): 133–45.

Bovill, Catherine, Alison Cook-Sather, Peter Felten, Luke Millard, and Niamh Moore-Cherry. 2016. "Addressing Potential Challenges in Co-Creating Learning and Teaching: Overcoming Resistance, Navigating Institutional Norms and Ensuring Inclusivity in Student-Staff Partnerships." *Higher Education* 71(2): 195–208. https://doi.org/10.1007/s10734-015-9896-4.

Bovill, Catherine, and Cherie Woolmer. 2018. "How Conceptualisations of Curriculum in Higher Education Influence Student-Staff Co-Creation in and of the Curriculum." *Higher Education*: 1–16. https://doi.org/10.1007/s10734-018-0349-8.

Brew, Angela, David Boud, and Sang Un Namgung. 2011. "Influences on the Formation of Academics: The Role of the Doctorate and Structured Development Opportunities." *Studies in Continuing Education* 33(1): 51–66. https://doi.org/10.1080/0158037X.2010.515575.

Bron, Jeroen, Catherine Bovill, and Wiel Veugelers. 2016. "Students Experiencing and Developing Democratic Citizenship Through Curriculum Negotiation: The Relevance of Garth Boomer's Approach." *Curriculum Perspectives* 36(1): 15–27.

Bron, Jeroen, and Wiel Veugelers. 2014. "Why We Need to Involve Our Students in Curriculum Design." In *Curriculum and Teaching Dialogue*, edited by David J. Flinders, P. Bruce Uhrmacher, and Christy M. Moroye. Vol 16, 1 & 2, 125–39.

Brunson, Mary. 2018. "The Formation and Power of Trust: How It Was Created and Enacted Through Collaboration." *Teaching and Learning Together in Higher Education* 23. https://repository.brynmawr.edu/tlthe/vol1/iss23/2.

Bunnell, Sarah, and Daniel Bernstein. 2014. "Improving Engagement and Learning through Sharing Course Design with Students: A Multilevel Case." *Teaching and Learning Together in Higher Education* 13. https://repository.brynmawr.edu/tlthe/vol1/iss13/2.

Cates, Rhiannon M., Mariah R. Madigan, and Vicki L. Reitenauer. 2018. "'Locations of Possibility': Critical Perspectives on Partnership." *International Journal for Students as Partners* 2(1): 33–46. https://doi.org/10.15173/ijsap.v2i1.3341.

Cecchinato, Graziano, and Laura Carlotta Foschi. 2017. "Flipping the Roles: Analysis of a University Course Where Students Become Co-Creators of Curricula." *Teaching and Learning Together in Higher Education* 22. https://repository.brynmawr.edu/tlthe/vol1/iss22/5.

Charkoudian, Lou, Anna C. Bitners, Noah B. Bloch, and Saadia Nawal. 2015. "Dynamic Discussions and Informed Improvements: Student-Led Revision of First-Semester Organic Chemistry." *Teaching and Learning Together in Higher Education* 15. https://repository.brynmawr.edu/tlthe/vol1/iss15/5/.

Cheng, Xiaotang. 2000. "Asian Students' Reticence Revisited." *System* 28(3): 435–46.

Chin, Jean Lau, and Nancy Felipe Russo. 1997. "Feminist Curriculum Development: Principles and Resources." In *Shaping the Future of*

Feminist Psychology: Education, Research, and Practice, edited by Judith Worell and Norine G. Johnson, 93–120. Washington, DC: American Psychological Association. http://dx.doi.org/10.1037/10245-005.

Chng, Huang Hoon. 2019. "The Possibilities of Students as Partners–A Perspective from Singapore." *Teaching and Learning Together in Higher Education* 27. https://repository.brynmawr.edu/tlthe/vol1/iss27/3.

Chukwu, Amarachi, and Kim Jones. (Forthcoming). "Feminist Interventions in Engineering: Co-creating across Disciplines and Identities." In *Building Courage, Confidence, and Capacity in Learning and Teaching through Pedagogical Partnership: Stories from across Contexts and Arenas of Practice*, edited by Alison Cook-Sather and Chanelle Wilson. Lanham, MD: Lexington Books.

Colón García, Ana. 2017. "Building a Sense of Belonging Through Pedagogical Partnership." *Teaching and Learning Together in Higher Education* 22. http://repository.brynmawr.edu/tlthe/vol1/iss22/2.

Conner, Jerusha. 2012. "Steps in Walking the Talk: How Working with a Student Consultant Helped Me Integrate Student Voice More Fully into My Pedagogical Planning and Practice." *Teaching and Learning Together in Higher Education* 6. http://repository.brynmawr.edu/tlthe/vol1/iss6/6.

Cook-Sather, Alison. 2020, in press. "Student Engagement through Classroom-focused Pedagogical Partnership: A Model and Outcomes from the United States." In *Global Perspectives of Student Engagement in Higher Education: Models for Change*, edited by T. Lowe and Y. El Hakim. London: Routledge.

Cook-Sather, Alison. 2019a. "Increasing Inclusivity through Pedagogical Partnerships Between Students and Faculty." *Diversity & Democracy* 22(1). https://www.aacu.org/diversitydemocracy/2019/winter/cook-sather.

Cook-Sather, Alison. 2019b. "Respecting Voices: How the Co-creation of Teaching and Learning Can Support Academic Staff, Underrepresented Students, and Equitable Practices." *Higher Education*. https://doi.org/10.1007/s10734-019-00445-w.

Cook-Sather, Alison. 2018a. "Developing 'Students as Learners and Teachers': Lessons from Ten Years of Pedagogical Partnership That Strives to Foster Inclusive and Responsive Practice." *Journal of Educational Innovation, Partnership and Change* 4(1). https://journals.gre.ac.uk/index.php/studentchangeagents/article/view/746.

Cook-Sather, Alison. 2018b. "Listening to Equity-Seeking Perspectives: How Students' Experiences of Pedagogical Partnership Can Inform Wider Discussions of Student Success." *Higher Education Research and Development* 37(5): 923–36.

Cook-Sather, Alison. 2018c. "Perpetual Translation: Conveying the Languages and Practices of Student Voice and Pedagogical Partnership Across Differences of Identity, Culture, Position, and Power." *Transformative Dialogues* 11(3). http://www.kpu.ca/sites/default/files/Transformative%20Dialogues/TD.11.3_Cook-Sather_Perpetual_Translation.pdf.

Cook-Sather, Alison. 2017. "What Our Uses of Theory Tell Us About How We Conceptualize Student-Staff Partnership." RAISE Conference. Birmingham, England. http://www.raise-network.com/resources/partnership-colloquium-2017/.

Cook-Sather, Alison. 2016a. "Undergraduate Students as Partners in New Faculty Orientation and Academic Development." *International Journal of Academic Development* 21(2): 151–62.

Cook-Sather, Alison. 2016b. "Creating Brave Spaces Within and Through Student-Faculty Pedagogical Partnerships." *Teaching and Learning Together in Higher Education* 18. https://repository.brynmawr.edu/tlthe/vol1/iss18/1.

Cook-Sather, Alison. 2015. "Dialogue Across Differences of Position, Perspective, and Identity: Reflective Practice in/on a Student-Faculty Pedagogical Partnership Program." *Teachers College Record* 117(2).

Cook-Sather, Alison. 2014. "Student-Faculty Partnership in Explorations of Pedagogical Practice: A Threshold Concept in Academic Development." *International Journal for Academic Development* 19(3): 186–98.

Cook-Sather, Alison. 2011a. "Lessons in Higher Education: Five Pedagogical Practices that Promote Active Learning for Faculty and Students." *Journal of Faculty Development* 25(3): 33–39.

Cook-Sather, Alison. 2011b. "Layered Learning: Student Consultants Deepening Classroom and Life Lessons." *Educational Action Research* 19(1): 41–57.

Cook-Sather Alison. 2009. "From Traditional Accountability to Shared Responsibility: The Benefits and Challenges of Student Consultants Gathering Midcourse Feedback in College Classrooms." *Assessment & Evaluation in Higher Education* 34(2): 231–41.

Cook-Sather, Alison. 2008. "'What You Get Is Looking in a Mirror, Only Better': Inviting Students to Reflect (on) College Teaching." *Reflective Practice* 9(4): 473–83.

Cook-Sather, Alison. 2001. "Unrolling Roles in Techno-Pedagogy: Toward Collaboration in Traditional College Settings." *Innovative Higher Education* 26(2): 121–39.

Cook-Sather, Alison, and Sophia Abbot. 2016. "Translating Partnerships: How Faculty-Student Collaboration in Explorations of Teaching and Learning Can Transform Perceptions, Terms, and Selves." *Teaching and Learning Inquiry* 4(2). https://doi.org/10.20343/teachlearninqu.4.2.5.

Cook-Sather, Alison, and Praise Agu. 2013. "Students of Color and Faculty Members Working Together toward Culturally Sustaining Pedagogy." In *To Improve the Academy: Resources for Faculty, Instructional, and Organizational Development*, edited by James E. Groccia and Laura Cruz, 271–85. San Francisco: Jossey-Bass/Anker.

Cook-Sather, Alison, and Zanny Alter. 2011. "What Is and What Can Be: How a Liminal Position Can Change Learning and Teaching in Higher Education." *Anthropology & Education Quarterly* 42(1): 37–53.

Cook-Sather, Alison, Catherine Bovill, and Peter Felten. 2014. *Engaging Students as Partners in Learning and Teaching: A Guide for Faculty*. San Francisco: Jossey-Bass.

Cook-Sather, Alison, and Crystal Des-Ogugua. 2018. "Lessons We Still Need to Learn on Creating More Inclusive and Responsive Classrooms: Recommendations from One Student-Faculty Partnership Program." *International Journal of Inclusive Education* 23(6): 594-608. https://doi.org/10.1080/13603116.2018.1441912.

Cook-Sather, Alison, and Crystal Des-Ogugua. 2017. "Advocating Diversity: Co-Creating Structures for Listening, Learning, and Taking Action." Workshop, Lafayette College, Pennsylvania.

Cook-Sather, Alison, Crystal Des-Ogugua, and Melanie Bahti. 2018. "Articulating Identities and Analyzing Belonging: A Multistep Intervention that Affirms and Informs a Diversity of Students." *Teaching in Higher Education* 23(3): 374–89.

Cook-Sather, Alison, and Peter Felten. 2017a. "Ethics of Academic Leadership: Guiding Learning and Teaching." In *Cosmopolitan Perspectives on Academic Leadership in Higher Education*, edited by Frank Su and Margaret Wood, 175–91. London: Bloomsbury Academic.

Cook-Sather, Alison, and Peter Felten. 2017b. "Where Student Engagement Meets Faculty Development: How Student-Faculty Pedagogical Partnership Fosters a Sense of Belonging." *Student Engagement in Higher Education Journal* 1(2): 3–11. https://journals.gre.ac.uk/index.php/raise/article/view/cook.

Cook-Sather, Alison, and Alia Luz. 2015. "Greater Engagement in and Responsibility for Learning: What Happens When Students Cross the Threshold of Student-Faculty Partnership." *Higher Education Research & Development* 34(6): 1097–109.

Cook-Sather, Alison, Kelley E. Matthews, and Amani Bell. 2019, in press. "Transforming Curriculum Development through Co-Creation with Students." In *Reimagining Curriculum: Spaces for Disruption*, edited by Lynn Quinn.

Cook-Sather, Alison, Kelly E. Matthews, Anita Ntem, and Sandra Leathwick. 2018. "What We Talk about When We Talk about Students as Partners." *International Journal for Students as Partners* 2(2): 1–9. https://doi.org/10.15173/ijsap.v2i2.3790.

Cook-Sather, Alison, Anita Ntem, and Peter Felten. In preparation. "The Role of Emotion in Pedagogical Partnership."

Cook-Sather, Alison, and Olivia Porte. 2017. "Reviving Humanity: Grasping Within and Beyond Our Reach." *Journal of Educational Innovation, Partnership and Change* 3(1). http://dx.doi.org/10.21100/jeipc.v3i1.638.

Cook-Sather, Alison, Sri Krishna Prasad, Elizabeth Marquis, and Anita Ntem. 2019. "Mobilizing a Culture Shift on Campus: Underrepresented Students as Educational Developers." *New Directions for Teaching and Learning* 159: 21–30. https://doi.org/10.1002/tl.20345.

Cook-Sather, Alison, Joel Schlosser, Abigail Sweeney, Laurel Peterson, Kimberley Cassidy, and Ana Colón García. 2017. "The Pedagogical Benefits of Enacting Positive Psychology Practices through a Student-Faculty Partnership Approach to Academic Development." *International Journal for Academic Development* 23(2): 123–34. https://doi.org/10.1080/1360144X.2017.1401539.

Corbin, Kathryn A. 2014. "Get Out the Map: The Use of Participation Mapping in Planning and Assessment." *Teaching and Learning Together in Higher Education* 11. https://repository.brynmawr.edu/tlthe/vol1/iss11/8.

Curran, Rosin, and Luke Millard. 2016. "A Partnership Approach to Developing Student Capacity to Engage and Staff Capacity to Be Engaging: Opportunities for Academic Developers." *International Journal for Academic Development* 21(1): 67–78.

Curtis, Nicholas A., and Ashton Trice. 2013. "A Revision of the Academic Locus of Control Scale for College Students." *Perceptual and Motor Skills* 116(3): 817–29. https://doi.org/10.2466/08.03.PMS.116.3.817-829.

Daviduke, Natasha. 2018. "Growing into Pedagogical Partnerships Over Time and Across Disciplines: My Experience as a Non-STEM Student Consultant in STEM Courses." *International Journal for Students as Partners* 2(2): 151–56. https://doi.org/10.15173/ijsap.v2i2.3443.

Deaker, Lynley, Sarah J. Stein, and Dorothy Spiller. 2016. "You Can't Teach Me: Exploring Academic Resistance to Teaching Development."

International Journal for Academic Development 21(4): 299–311. https://doi.org/10.1080/1360144X.2015.1129967.

de Bie, Alise, Elizabeth Marquis, Alison Cook-Sather, and Leslie Luqueño. 2019. "Valuing Knowledge(s) and Cultivating Confidence: Contributing to Epistemic Justice via Student-Faculty Pedagogical Partnerships." In *Strategies for Fostering Inclusive Classrooms in Higher Education: International Perspectives on Equity and Inclusion*, edited by Jaimie Hoffman, Patrick Blessinger, and Mandla Makhanya, 35–48. Innovations in Higher Education Teaching and Learning, Volume 16. Emerald Publishing Limited. https://doi.org/10.1108/S2055-364120190000016004.

de Bie, Alise, and Rille Raaper. 2019. "Troubling the Idea of Partnership." International Institute on Students as Partners, Connect Blog, March 29, 2019. https://macblog.mcmaster.ca/summer-institute/2019/03/29/troubling-the-idea-of-partnership/.

Deeley, Susan J., and Catherine Bovill. 2017. "Staff Student Partnership in Assessment: Enhancing Assessment Literacy through Democratic Practices." *Assessment and Evaluation in Higher Education* 42(3): 463–77.

Deeley, Susan J., and Ruth A. Brown. 2014. "Learning through Partnership in Assessment." *Teaching and Learning Together in Higher Education* 13. http://repository.brynmawr.edu/tlthe/vol1/iss13/3.

Delgado-Bernal, Dolores 2002. "Critical Race Theory, Latino Critical Theory, and Critical Raced-Gendered Epistemologies: Recognizing Students of Color as Holders and Creators of Knowledge." *Qualitative Inquiry* 8(1): 105–26.

Delpish, Ayesha, Alexa Darby, Ashley Holmes, Mary Knight-McKenna, Richard Mihans, Catherine King, and Peter Felten. 2010. "Equalizing Voices: Student-Faculty Partnership in Course Design." In *Engaging Student Voices in the Study of Teaching and Learning*, edited by Carmen Werdeer and Megan Otis, 96–114. Sterling, VA: Stylus.

Devlin, Marcia. 2013. "Bridging Socio-cultural Incongruity: Conceptualising the Success of Students from Low Socio-economic Status

Backgrounds in Australian Higher Education." *Studies in Higher Education* 38(6): 939–49. http://dx.doi.org/10.1080/03075079.2011.613991.

Doktor, Stephanie DeLane, Dorothe Bach, Sophia Abbot, and Jacob Hardin. 2019. "At the Threshold: A Case Study of a Partnership Between a Student Organization and an Educational Development Center." *International Journal for Students as Partners* 3(1): 150–59. https://doi.org/10.15173/ijsap.v3i1.3511.

Duah, Francis, and Tony Croft. 2014. "Faculty-Student Partnership in Advanced Undergraduate Mathematics Course Design." *Teaching and Learning Together in Higher Education* 13. http://repository.brynmawr.edu/tlthe/vol1/iss13/5.

Duda, Gintaras Kazimieras, and Mary Ann Danielson. 2018. "Collaborative Curricular (Re)construction—Tracking Faculty and Student Learning Impacts and Outcomes Five Years Later." *International Journal for Students as Partners* 2(2): 39–52. https://doi.org/10.15173/ijsap.v2i2.3568.

Dunne, Elisabeth, Derfel Owen, Hannah Barr, Will Page, James Smith, and Sabina Szydlo. 2014. "The Story of Students as Change Agents at the University of Exeter: From Slow Beginnings to Institutional Initiative." *Teaching and Learning Together in Higher Education* 13. http://repository.brynmawr.edu/tlthe/vol1/iss13/9.

Dunne, Elisabeth, and Roos Zandstra. 2011. *Students as Change Agents. New Ways of Engaging with Learning and Teaching in Higher Education*. Bristol, UK: ESCalate Higher Education Academy Subject Centre for Education / University of Exeter. http://escalate.ac.uk/8064.

Egan, Kieran. 1978. "What Is Curriculum?" *Curriculum Inquiry* 8(1): 65–72. https://doi.org/10.1080/03626784.1978.11075558.

Eze, Amaka. 2019. "From Listening to Responding to Leading: Building Capacity through Four Pedagogical Partnerships." *Teaching and Learning Together in Higher Education* 26. https://repository.brynmawr.edu/tlthe/vol1/iss26/2.

Felten, Peter. 2011. "From the Advisory Board: Monet Moments and the Necessity of Productive Disruption." *Teaching and Learning Together in Higher Education* 2. https://repository.brynmawr.edu/tlthe/vol1/iss2/1.

Felten, Peter. 2017. "Emotion and Partnerships." *International Journal for Students as Partners* 1(2). https://doi.org/10.15173/ijsap.v1i2.3070.

Felten, Peter, Sophia Abbot, Jordan Kirkwood, Aaron Long, Tanya Lubicz-Nawrocka, Lucy Mercer-Mapstone, and Roselynn Verwoord. 2019. "Reimagining the Place of Students in Academic Development." *International Journal for Academic Development* 24(2): 192–203. https://doi.org/10.1080/1360144X.2019.1594235.

Ferrell, Ashley, and Amanda Peach. 2018. "Student-Faculty Partnerships in Library Instruction." *Kentucky Libraries* 82(3): 15–18.

Fink, L. Dee. 2013. *Creating Significant Learning Experiences: An Integrated Approach to Designing College Courses*, Expanded 2nd Edition. San Francisco, CA: Jossey-Bass.

Fink, L. Dee. 1984. "First Year of College Teaching." *New Directions for Teaching and Learning* 17: 11–119. San Francisco, CA: Jossey-Bass.

Fraser, Sharon, and Agnes Bosanquet. 2006. "The Curriculum? That's Just a Unit Outline, Isn't It?" *Studies in Higher Education* 31(3): 269–84.

Freire, Paulo. 2005. "The Banking Concept of Education." In *Ways of Reading* (7th ed.), edited by David Bartholomae, 255–67. New York: St. Martin Press.

Frison, Daniela, and Claudio Melacarne. 2017. "Introduction – Students-Faculty Partnership in Italy: Approaches, Practices, and Perspectives." *Teaching and Learning Together in Higher Education* 20. http://repository.brynmawr.edu/tlthe/vol1/iss20/1/.

Gale, Trevor, and Stephen Parker. 2014. "Navigating Change: A Typology of Student Transition in Higher Education." *Studies in Higher Education* 39(5): 734–53.

Gawande, Atul. 2011. "Personal Best: Top Athletes Have Coaches. Should You?" *New Yorker*, October 3, 2011. https://www.newyorker.com/magazine/2011/10/03/personal-best.

Gibson, Suanne, Delia Baskerville, Ann Berry, Alison Black, Kathleen Norris, and Simoni Symeonidou. 2017. "Including Students as Co-Enquirers: Matters of Identity, Agency, Language and Labelling in an International Participatory Research Study." *International Journal of Educational Research* 81: 108–18.

Gibson, Suanne, and Alison Cook-Sather. Forthcoming. "Politicised Compassion and Pedagogical Partnership: A Discourse and Practice for Social Justice in the Inclusive Academy." *International Journal for Students as Partners*.

Glasser, Howard, and Margaret Powers. 2011. "Disrupting Traditional Student-Faculty Roles, 140 Characters at a Time." *Teaching and Learning Together in Higher Education* 2. https://repository.brynmawr.edu/tlthe/vol1/iss2/5/.

Goff, Lori, and Kris Knorr. 2018. "Three Heads are Better than One: Students, Faculty, and Educational Developers as Co-Developers of Science Curriculum." *International Journal for Students as Partners* 2(1):112–20. https://doi.org/10.15173/ijsap.v2i1.3333.

Goldsmith, Meredith, and Nicole Gervasio. 2011. "Radical Equality: A Dialogue on Building a Partnership–and a Program–through a Cross-Campus Collaboration." *Teaching and Learning Together in Higher Education* 3. http://repository.brynmawr.edu/tlthe/vol1/iss3/4.

Goldsmith, Meredith, Megan Hanscom, Susanna A. Throop, and Codey Young. 2017. "Growing Student-Faculty Partnerships at Ursinus College: A Brief History in Dialogue." *International Journal for Students as Partners* 1(2). https://doi.org/10.15173/ijsap.v1i2.3075.

Griffiths, John. 2018. "Reconceptualising History Teaching and Assessment to Meet Student Expectation." *Teaching and Learning Together in Higher Education* 25. https://repository.brynmawr.edu/tlthe/vol1/iss25/9.

Gulley, Emma. 2014. "Letting Us All Be Learners." *Teaching and Learning Together in Higher Education* 11. http://repository.brynmawr.edu/tlthe/vol1/iss11/11.

Gunersel, Adalet Baris, Pamela Barnett, and Mary Etienne. 2013. "Promoting Self-Authorship of College Educators: Exploring the Impact of a Faculty Development Program." *Journal of Faculty Development* 27(1): 35–44.

Hafferty, Frederick W., Elizabeth H. Gaufberg, and E. DiCroce. 2015. "Hidden Curriculum." In *A Practical Guide for Medical Teachers*, edited by John Dent, Ronald Harden, and Dan Hunt, 35–41. New York: Elsevier.

Hayward, Lorna, Susan Ventura, Hilary Schuldt, and Pamela Donlan. 2018. "Student Pedagogical Teams: Students as Course Consultants Engaged in the Process of Teaching and Learning." *College Teaching* 66(1): 37–47. https://doi.org/10.1080/87567555.2017.1405904.

Healey, Mick, Abbi Flint, and Kathy Harrington. 2014. *Engagement through Partnership: Students as Partners in Learning and Teaching in Higher Education.* York, UK: Higher Education Academy. https://www.advance-he.ac.uk/knowledge-hub/engagement-through-partnership-students-partners-learning-and-teaching-higher.

Healey, Mick, and Ruth Healey. 2018. "'It Depends': Exploring the Context-Dependent Nature of Students as Partners' Practices and Policies." *International Journal for Students as Partners* 2(1): 1–10. https://doi.org/10.15173/ijsap.v2i1.3472.

Hermsen, Tara, Thomas Kuiper, Fritz Roelofs, and Joost van Wijchen. 2017. "Without Emotions, Never a Partnership!" *International Journal for Students as Partners* 1(2). https://doi.org/10.15173/ijsap.v1i2.3228.

Hockings, Christine. 2010. *Inclusive Learning and Teaching in Higher Education: A Synthesis of Research.* York, UK: The Higher Education Academy. https://www.advance-he.ac.uk/knowledge-hub/inclusive-learning-and-teaching-higher-education.

Horton, Miles, and Paulo Freire. 1990. *We Make the Road by Walking: Conversations on Education and Social Change.* Philadelphia: Temple University Press.

Hughes, Clair, and Simon Barrie. 2010. "Influences on the Assessment of Graduate Attributes in Higher Education." *Assessment & Evaluation in Higher Education* 35(3): 325–34.

Hurtado, Sylvia, and Deborah Faye Carter. 1997. "Effects of College Transition and Perceptions of the Campus Racial Climate on Latino College Students' Sense of Belonging." *Sociology of Education* 70(4): 324–45. https://doi.org/10.2307/2673270.

Jack, Anthony Abraham. 2019. *The Privileged Poor: How Elite Colleges Are Failing Disadvantaged Students*. Cambridge, MA: Harvard University Press.

Jackson, Philip W. 1968. *Life in Classrooms*. New York: Holt, Rinehart and Winston.

Kahler, Leah. 2014. "Learning from Respect: Multiple Iterations of Respect in the Classroom." *Teaching and Learning Together in Higher Education* 11. http://repository.brynmawr.edu/tlthe/vol1/iss11/7.

Kaur, Amrita, Rosna Awang-Hashim, and Manvender Kaur. 2018. "Students' Experiences of Co-Creating Classroom Instruction with Faculty: A Case Study in Eastern Context." *Teaching in Higher Education* 24(4): 461–77. https://doi.org/10.1080/13562517.2018.1487930.

Kaur, Amrita, and Toh Yong Big. (Forthcoming). "Untangling the Power Dynamics in Forging Student-Faculty Collaboration." In *Building Courage, Confidence, and Capacity in Learning and Teaching through Pedagogical Partnership: Stories from across Contexts and Arenas of Practice*, edited by Alison Cook-Sather and Chanelle Wilson. Lanham, MD: Lexington Books.

Keeney-Kennicutt, Wendy, Adalet Baris Gunersel, and Nancy Simpson. 2008. "Overcoming Student Resistance to a Teaching Innovation." *International Journal for the Scholarship of Teaching and Learning* 2(1), Article 5. https://doi.org/10.20429/ijsotl.2008.020105.

Kehler, Angela, Roselynn Verwoord, and Heather Smith. 2017. "We Are the Process: Reflections on the Underestimation of Power in Students as Partners in Practice." *International Journal for Students as Partners* 1(1). https://doi.org/10.15173/ijsap.v1i1.3176.

King, Catherine, and Peter Felten. 2012. "Threshold Concepts in Educational Development: An Introduction." *Journal of Faculty Development* 26: 5–7.

Kurimay, Anita. 2014. "From Tennis to Teaching: The Power of Mentoring." *Teaching and Learning Together in Higher Education* 11. https://repository.brynmawr.edu/tlthe/vol1/iss11/3/.

Land, Ray, Glynis Cousin, Jan H. F. Meyer, and Peter Davies. 2005. "Threshold Concepts and Troublesome Knowledge (3): Implications for Course Design and Evaluation." In *Improving Student Learning: Diversity and Inclusivity*, edited by Chris Rust, 53–64. Oxford: Oxford Centre for Staff and Learning Development.

Land, Ray, Jan H. F. Meyer, and Michael T. Flanigan. 2016. *Threshold Concepts in Practice*. Educational Futures: Rethinking Theory and Practice, volume 68. Rotterdam: Sense Publishers.

Lang, James. 2006. "The Promising Syllabus." *Chronicle of Higher Education*, August 28, 2006. https://www.chronicle.com/article/The-Promising-Syllabus/46748.

Lewis, Karron G. 1996. "Faculty Development in the United States: A Brief History." *International Journal for Academic Development* 1(2), 26–33. https://doi.org/10.1080/1360144960010204.

Lillehaugen, Brook Danielle, Gabriela Echavarría Moats, Daniel Gillen, Elizabeth Peters, and Rebecca Schwartz. 2014. "A Tactile IPA Magnetboard System: A Tool for Blind and Visually Impaired Students in Phonetics and Phonology Classrooms." *Language* 90(4): e274–e283. https://doi.org/10.1353/lan.2014.0074.

Lubicz-Nawrocka, Tanya Michelle. 2018. "Students as Partners in Learning and Teaching: The Benefits of Co-Creation of the Curriculum." *International Journal for Students as Partners* 2(1): 47–63. https://doi.org/10.15173/ijsap.v2i1.3207.

Lynch, Kathleen. 2010. "Carelessness: A Hidden Doxa of Higher Education." *Arts and Humanities in Higher Education* 9(1): 54–67. https://doi.org/10.1177/1474022209350104.

Marquis, Elizabeth, Christine Black, and Mick Healey. 2017. "Responding to the Challenges of Student-Staff Partnership: The Reflections of Participants at an International Summer Institute." *Teaching in Higher Education* 22(6): 720–35. https://doi.org/10.1080/13562517.2017.1289510.

Marquis, Elizabeth, Alise de Bie, Alison Cook-Sather, and Leslie Luqueño. (Under review). *Promoting Equity and Inclusion through Pedagogical Partnership.* Sterling, VA: Stylus.

Marquis, Elizabeth, Rachel Guitman, Christine Black, Mick Healey, Kelly E. Matthews, and Lucie Sam Dvorakova. 2018a. "Growing Partnership Communities: What Experiences of an International Institute Suggest about Developing Student-Staff Partnership in Higher Education." *Innovations in Education and Teaching International* 56(2): 184–94. https://doi.org/10.1080/14703297.2018.1424012.

Marquis, Elizabeth, Ajitha Jayaratnam, Anamika Mishra, and Ksenia Rybkina. 2018b. "'I Feel Like Some Students Are Better Connected': Students' Perspectives on Applying for Extracurricular Partnership Opportunities." *International Journal for Students as Partners* 2(1). https://doi.org/10.15173/ijsap.v2i1.3300.

Marquis, Elizabeth, Varun Puri, Stephanie Wan, Arshad Ahmad, Lori Goff, Kris Knorr, Ianitza Vassileva, and Jason Woo. 2016b. "Navigating the Threshold of Student-Staff Partnerships: A Case Study from an Ontario Teaching and Learning Institute." *International Journal for Academic Development* 21(1): 4–15. https://doi.org/10.1080/1360144X.2015.1113538.

Mathrani, Sasha. 2018. "Building Relationships, Navigating Discomfort and Uncertainty, and Translating My Voice in New Contexts." *Teaching and Learning Together in Higher Education* 23. https://repository.brynmawr.edu/tlthe/vol1/iss23/6.

Mathrani, Sasha, and Alison Cook-Sather. 2020. "Discerning Growth: Tracing Rhizomatic Development through Pedagogical Partnerships" in *The Power of Partnership: Students, Staff, and Faculty Revolutionizing Higher Education*, edited by Lucy Mercer-Mapstone and Sophia Abbot.

Elon, NC: Center for Engaged Learning. https://doi.org/10.36284/celelon.oa2.

Matthews, Kelly E. 2019. "Rethinking the Problem of Faculty Resistance to Engaging with Students as Partners in Learning and Teaching in Higher Education." *International Journal for the Scholarship of Teaching and Learning* 13(2): Article 2. https://doi.org/10.20429/ijsotl.2019.130202.

Matthews, Kelly E. 2017a. "Five Propositions for Genuine Students as Partners Practice." *International Journal of Students as Partners* 1(2). https://doi.org/10.15173/ijsap.v1i2.3315.

Matthews, Kelly E. 2017b. "Students and Staff as Partners in Australian Higher Education: Introducing Our Stories of Partnership." *Teaching and Learning Together in Higher Education* 21. https://repository.brynmawr.edu/tlthe/vol1/iss21/1.

Matthews, Kelly E. 2016. "Students as Partners as the Future of Student Engagement." *Student Engagement in Higher Education Journal* 1(1): 1–5. https://journals.gre.ac.uk/index.php/raise/article/view/380.

Matthews, Kelly E., Alison Cook-Sather, Anita Acai, Sam Lucie Dvorakova, Peter Felten, Elizabeth Marquis, and Lucy Mercer-Mapstone. 2018. "Toward Theories of Partnership Praxis: An Analysis of Interpretive Framing in Literature on Students as Partners in Teaching and Learning." *Higher Education Research & Development* 38(2): 280–93. https://doi.org/10.1080/07294360.2018.1530199.

Matthews, Kelly E., Alison Cook-Sather, and Mick Healey. 2018. "Connecting Learning, Teaching, and Research through Student-Staff Partnerships: Toward Universities as Egalitarian Learning Communities." In *Research Equals Teaching: Inspiring Research-based Education through Student-Staff Partnerships*, edited by Vincent C. H. Tong, Alex Standen, and Mina Sotiriou, 23–29. London: University College of London Press.

Mayo, J. B. Jr., and Vichet Chhuon. 2014. "Pathways to the Tenure Track: Reflections from Faculty of Color on their Recruitment to a Research University." *International Journal of Educational Reform* 23(3): 223–39.

McAlpine, Lynne, and Gerlese Åkerlind. 2012. "Becoming an Academic: International Perspectives." *Higher Education* 63(3): 391–92.

McAlpine, Lynne, and Gerlese Åkerlind. 2010. *Becoming an Academic: Universities into the 21st Century*. Basingstoke: Palgrave MacMillan.

McLaren, Peter. 1989. *Life in Schools: An Introduction to Critical Pedagogy in the Foundations of Education*. New York, NY: Longman.

Mejia, Yeidaly. 2019. "Carrying Partnership Skills Beyond Formal Partnerships: When Conflicts Grow into Connections." *Teaching and Learning Together in Higher Education* 26. https://repository.brynmawr.edu/tlthe/vol1/iss26/6.

Mercer-Mapstone, Lucy, Sam Lucie Dvorakova, Kelly E. Matthews, Sophia Abbot, Breagh Cheng, Peter Felten, Kris Knorr, Elizabeth Marquis, Rafaella Shammas, and Kelly Swaim. 2017. "A Systematic Literature Review of Students as Partners in Higher Education." *International Journal of Students as Partners* 1(1): 1–23. https://doi.org/10.15173/ijsap.v1i1.3119.

Mercer-Mapstone, Lucy, Elizabeth Marquis, and Catherine McConnell. 2018. "The 'Partnership Identity' in Higher Education: Moving from 'Us' and 'Them' to 'We' in Student-Staff Partnership." *Student Engagement in Higher Education Journal* 2(1): 12–29.

Meyer, Jan H. F., and Ray Land. 2006. *Overcoming Barriers to Student Understanding*. London: Routledge.

Mihans, Richard, Deborah Long, and Peter Felten. 2008. "Power and Expertise: Student-Faculty Collaboration in Course Design and the Scholarship of Teaching and Learning." *International Journal for the Scholarship of Teaching and Learning* 2(2): Article 16. https://doi.org/10.20429/ijsotl.2008.020216.

Monsen, Sue, Sarah Cook, and Lauren Hannant. 2017. "Students as Partners in Negotiated Assessment in a Teacher Education Course." *Teaching and Learning Together in Higher Education* 21. http://repository.brynmawr.edu/tlthe/vol1/iss21/2.

Moore, Jessie, Lindsey Altvater, Jillian Mattera, and Emily Regan. 2010. "Been There, Done That, Still Doing It: Involving Students in

Redesigning a Service-Learning Course." In *Engaging Student Voices in the Study of Teaching and Learning*, edited by Carmen Werder and Megan Otis, 115–29. Sterling, VA: Stylus.

Nave, Lillian, Alejandra Aguilar, Matthew Barnes, Aliesha Knauer, Erica-Grace Lubamba, Kendall Miller, Verolinka Slawson, and Taylor Taylor. 2018. "On Confederate Monuments, Racial Strife, & the Politics of Power on a Southern Campus." *Teaching and Learning Together in Higher Education* 24. https://repository.brynmawr.edu/tlthe/vol1/iss24/3.

Nguyen, Tuong Hung. 2005. "Cultural Background for ESL/EFL Teachers Cuyahoga Community College." Paper appeared in a multicultural project at Northeast ABLE Resource Center (Ohio).

Ntem, Anita. 2017. "Relating Resistance and Resilience in Student-Faculty Pedagogical Partnership." Poster presentation, McMaster Summer Institute on Students as Partners. Hamilton, Canada.

Ntem, Anita, and Alison Cook-Sather. 2018. "Resistances and Resiliencies in Pedagogical Partnership: Student Partners' Perspectives." *International Journal for Students as Partners* 2(1): 82–96. https://doi.org/10.15173/ijsap.v2i1.3372.

Nuhfer, Edward. 1995. *A Handbook for Student Management Teams*. Denver: University of Colorado.

Oh, Seung-Youn. 2014. "Learning to Navigate Quickly and Successfully: The Benefits of Working with a Student Consultant." *Teaching and Learning Together in Higher Education* 11. https://repository.brynmawr.edu/tlthe/vol1/iss11/5.

Oleson, Kathryn. 2016. "Introduction–Collaborating to Develop and Improve Classroom Teaching: Student-Consultant for Teaching and Learning Program at Reed College." *Teaching and Learning Together in Higher Education* 17. https://repository.brynmawr.edu/tlthe/vol1/iss17/1.

Ong, Maria, Janet M. Smith, and Lily T. Ko. 2017. "Counterspaces for Women of Color in STEM Higher Education: Marginal and Central

Spaces for Persistence and Success." *Journal of Research in Science Teaching* 55(2): 206–45.

O'Shea, Sarah, and Janine Delahunty. 2018. "Getting through the Day and Still Having a Smile on My Face! How Do Students Define Success in the University Learning Environment?" *Higher Education Research and Development* 37(5): 1062–75.

Pagram, Penporn, and Jeremy Pagram. 2006. "Issues in E-learning: A Thai Case Study." *Electronic Journal of Informations Systems in Developing Countries* 26(6): 1–8.

Pallant, Miriam. 2014. "The Dynamics of Expertise." *Teaching and Learning Together in Higher Education* 11. http://repository.brynmawr.edu/tlthe/vol1/iss11/2.

Paris, David. 2013. "The Last Artisans? Traditional and Future Faculty Roles." *Peer Review* 15(3): 17–20.

Perez, Kerstin. 2016. "Striving toward a Space for Equity and Inclusion in Physics Classrooms." *Teaching and Learning Together in Higher Education* 18. https://repository.brynmawr.edu/tlthe/vol1/iss18/3.

Perez-Putnam, Miriam. 2016. "Belonging and Brave Space as Hope for Personal and Institutional Inclusion." *Teaching and Learning Together in Higher Education* 18. http://repository.brynmawr.edu/tlthe/vol1/iss18/2.

Pinar, William. 2004. *What Is Curriculum Theory?* Mahwah, NJ: Lawrence Erlbaum Associates.

Quinn, Lynn. 2012. "Understanding Resistance: An Analysis of Discourses in Academic Staff Development." *Studies in Higher Education* 37(1): 69–83. https://doi.org/10.1080/03075079.2010.497837.

Ray, Julie, and Stephanie Marken. 2014. "Life in College Matters for Life after College." *GALLUP News*, May 6, 2014.

Reckson, Lindsay V. 2014. "The Weather in Hemingway." *Teaching and Learning Together in Higher Education* 11. http://repository.brynmawr.edu/tlthe/vol1/iss11/6.

Rose, Eli, and Cynthia Taylor. 2016. "Using a Student Consultant in a Computer Science Course: An Experience Report."

Proceedings of the 2016 ACM Conference on Innovation and Technology in Computer Science Education (ITiCSE 16). https://doi.org/10.1145/2899415.2899434.

Rudy, Sayres. 2014. "Consultancy, Disruption, and the Pulse of Pedagogy." *Teaching and Learning Together in Higher Education* 11. http://repository.brynmawr.edu/tlthe/vol1/iss11/12.

Schubert, William H. 1986. *Curriculum: Perspective, Paradigm, and Possibility*. New York: Pearson College Division.

Schlosser, Joel, and Abigail Sweeney. 2015. "One Year of Collaboration: Reflections on Student-Faculty Partnership." *Teaching and Learning Together in Higher Education* 15. https://repository.brynmawr.edu/tlthe/vol1/iss15/2/.

Schwarzer, Ralph, and Matthais Jerusalem. 1995. "Generalized Self-efficacy Scale." In *Measures in Health Psychology: A User's Portfolio. Causal and Control Beliefs*, edited by J. Weinman, S. Wright, and M. Johnston, 35–37. Windsor, UK: NFER-NELSON.

Seow, Yvette. 2019. "Taking a Small Step Towards Partnership." *Teaching and Learning Together in Higher Education* 27. https://repository.brynmawr.edu/tlthe/vol1/iss27/5.

Sheth, Jagdish N., and Walter H. Stellner. 1979. "Psychology of Innovation Resistance: The Less Developed Concept (LDC) in Diffusion Research." Faculty working papers, College of Commerce and Business Administration, University of Illinois at Urbana-Champaign.

Shore, Elliott. 2012. "'Changing Education': Helping to Conceptualize the First 360." *Teaching and Learning Together in Higher Education* 7. http://repository.brynmawr.edu/tlthe/vol1/iss7/3.

Shulman, Lee. 2004. *Teaching as Community Property: Essays on Higher Education*. San Francisco, CA: Jossey-Bass.

Sim, Jonathan Y. H. 2019. "The 'Face' Barriers to Partnership." *Teaching and Learning Together in Higher Education* 27. https://repository.brynmawr.edu/tlthe/vol1/iss27/4.

Smith, Karl A, and Alisha A. Waller. 1997. "Afterword: New Paradigms for College Teaching." In *New Paradigms for College Teaching*, edited by William E. Campbell and Karl A. Smith. Edina, MN: Interaction Book Company.

Smith College Student-Faculty Pedagogical Partnership Program. https://www.smith.edu/about-smith/sherrerd-center/pedagogical-partnership.

Solberg, V. Scott, Karen O'Brien, Pete Villareal, Richard Kennel, and Betsy Davis. 1993. "Self-efficacy and Hispanic College Students: Validation of the College Self-efficacy Instrument." *Hispanic Journal of Behavioral Sciences* 15(1): 80–95. https://doi.org/10.1177/07399863930151004.

Solórzano, Daniel, Miguel Ceja, and Tara Yosso. 2000. "Critical Race Theory, Racial Microaggressions, and Campus Racial Climate: The Experiences of African American College Students." *The Journal of Negro Education* 69 (1/2): 60–73.

Sorcinelli, Mary Deane. 1994. "Effective Approaches to New Faculty Development." *Journal of Counseling & Development* 72(5): 474–79.

Sorenson, D. Lynn. 2001. "College Teachers and Student Consultants: Collaborating about Teaching and Learning." In *Student-Assisted Teaching: A Guide to Faculty-Student Teamwork*, edited by Judith E. Miller, James E. Groccia and Marilyn S. Miller, 179–83. Bolton, MA: Anker.

Stone, Douglas, and Sheila Heen. 2014. *Thanks for the Feedback: The Science and Art of Receiving Feedback Well*. New York: Penguin.

Storrs, Debbie, and John Mihelich. 1998. "Beyond Essentialisms: Team Teaching Gender and Sexuality." *National Women's Studies Association Journal* 10(1): 98–118.

Sunderland, Mary. 2013. "Using Student Engagement to Relocate Ethics to the Core of the Engineering Curriculum." *Science and Engineering Ethics*. https://doi.org/10.1007/s11948-013-9444-5.

Sylla, Fatoumata. 2018. "The Power of Trust in Education: Lessons from My Courses and Pedagogical Partnerships." *Teaching and Learning Together in Higher Education* 23. https://repository.brynmawr.edu/tlthe/vol1/iss23/3.

Takayama, Kathy, Matthew Kaplan, and Alison Cook-Sather. 2017. "Advancing Diversity and Inclusion through Strategic Multi-level Leadership." *Liberal Education* 103(3/4). http://www.aacu.org/liberaleducation/2017/summer-fall/takayama_kaplan_cook-sather.

Taylor, Carol, and Catherine Bovill. 2018. "Towards an Ecology of Participation: Process Philosophy and Co-Creation of Higher Education Curricula." *European Educational Research Journal* 17(1): 112–28.

Torda, Lee, and Richardson, Karen. 2015. "Introduction: Developing Student-Faculty Partnerships at Bridgewater State University." *Teaching and Learning Together in Higher Education* 16. https://repository.brynmawr.edu/tlthe/vol1/iss16/1.

Trowler, Paul, and Ali Cooper. 2002. "Teaching and Learning Regimes: Implicit Theories and Recurrent Practices in the Enhancement of Teaching and Learning through Educational Development Programmes." *Higher Education Research and Development* 21(3): 221–40. https://doi.org/10.1080/0729436022000020742.

Trowler, Paul, and Peter T. Knight. 2000. "Coming to Know in Higher Education: Theorising Faculty Entry to New Work Contexts." *Higher Education Research and Development* 19(1): 27–42. https://doi.org/10.1080/07294360050020453.

Turner, Caroline S. 2015. *Mentoring as Transformative Practice: Supporting Student and Faculty Diversity.* New Directions for Higher Education, Number 171. New York: John Wiley & Sons.

US Department of Education, Office of Planning, Evaluation and Policy Development and Office of the Under Secretary. 2016. *Advancing Diversity and Inclusion in Higher Education.* Washington, DC. http://www2.ed.gov/rschstat/research/pubs/advancing-diversity-inclusion.pdf.

Van Manen, Man, Jerry McClelland, and Jane Plihal. 2007. "Naming Student Experiences and Experiencing Student Naming." In *International Handbook of Student Experience in Elementary and Secondary School*, edited by Dennis Thiessen and Alison Cook-Sather, 85–98. New York: Springer Publishing Company.

Vaquera, Elizabeth. 2009. "Friendship, Educational Engagement, and School Belonging: Comparing Hispanic and White Adolescents." *Hispanic Journal of Behavioral Sciences* 31(4): 492–514. https://doi.org/10.1177/0739986309346023.

Vidali, Amy. 2010. "Seeing What We Know: Disability and Theories of Metaphor." *Journal of Literary & Cultural Disability Studies* 4(1): 33–54.

Wang, Yi, and Yonglin Jiang. 2012. "An Equal Partnership: Preparing for Faculty-Student Team Teaching of 'Cultural History of Chinese Astronomy' through the TLI." *Teaching and Learning Together in Higher Education* 6. https://repository.brynmawr.edu/tlthe/vol1/iss6/9/.

Welch, Sharon A. 1990. *A Feminist Ethic of Risk*. Minneapolis, MN: Fortress Press.

Werder, Carmen, Shevell Thibou, and Blair Kaufer. 2012. "Students as Co-Inquirers: A Requisite Threshold Concept in Educational Development?" *Journal of Faculty Development* 26(3): 34–38.

Wiggins, Grant, and Jay McTighe. 2005. *Understanding by Design*, 2nd ed. Alexandria, VA: Pearson.

Wolkoff, Alexandra. 2014. "Teaching and Learning as Learning to Be: Finding My Place and Voice as a Leader." *Teaching and Learning Together in Higher Education* 11. http://repository.brynmawr.edu/tlthe/vol1/iss11/4.

Woolmer, Cherie, Peter Sneddon, Gordon Curry, Bob Hill, Szonja Fehertavi, Charlotte Longbone, and Katherine Wallace. 2016. "Student Staff Partnership to Create an Interdisciplinary Science Skills Course in a Research Intensive University." *International Journal for Academic Development* 21(1): 16–27.

Wynkoop, Paul. 2018. "My Transformation as a Partner and a Learner." *Teaching and Learning Together in Higher Education* 23. https://repository.brynmawr.edu/tlthe/vol1/iss23/4.

ABOUT THE AUTHORS

Alison Cook-Sather is a professor of education at Bryn Mawr College and director of Students as Learners and Teachers (SaLT), the signature program of the Teaching and Learning Institute (TLI) at Bryn Mawr and Haverford Colleges. In addition, she has served as a consultant at institutions across the United States and around the world as others develop pedagogical partnership programs. Finally, Alison has engaged in extensive research on pedagogical partnership and is founding editor and founding co-editor, respectively, of two journals focused on pedagogical partnership: *Teaching and Learning Together in Higher Education* and *International Journal for Students as Partners*.

Melanie Bahti is a former student partner in SaLT who graduated from Bryn Mawr College in 2016 with a degree in linguistics. In addition to co-authoring an article on partnership with Alison and another former student partner (Cook-Sather, Des-Ogugua, and Bahti 2018), she has presented at conferences and consulted on partnership, and she serves as a reviewer for *International Journal for Students as Partners*. She recently completed a Master's degree in higher education at the University of Pennsylvania and now works in the Center for Teaching & Learning at Thomas Jefferson University.

Anita Ntem graduated from Bryn Mawr College in 2018 with a degree in psychology. As a student partner in SaLT she worked in partnership with faculty in four different departments. In addition, she has engaged in research as a Fellow of the Teaching and Learning Institute. Anita has presented her research on partnership at conferences (Ntem 2017), co-authored articles on pedagogical partnership (Cook-Sather, Ntem, and Felten in preparation; Ntem and Cook-Sather 2018), served as a facilitator of the International Summer Institute for Students as Partners at McMaster University in Canada, and is co-editor for *International Journal for Students as Partners*.

INDEX

A

academic development 1, 34, 60
administrators as partners 55–56
advertising partnership programs 77, 116, 121–128
affirmation of partners 95–98, 112
aim of partnership 2–5, 15–17, 26–30
Ako in Action at Victoria University of Wellington 46–47
Arthur Vining Davis Foundations 56, 88
assessing (e.g., reflecting on for improvement) pedagogical partnership 253–271
  formative assessment questions for 266–269
assumptions about pedagogical partnership 30–33
attitudes and behaviors of partnership 40–41, 105–116

B

benefits of pedagogical partnership 2–3, 13, 16–17
  for faculty 3, 18
    new faculty 19–22
    underrepresented faculty 20
  for institutions 4–5, 24–26
  for program directors 4
  for students 3–4, 18
    underrepresented students 22–24
Berea College, United States 55, 66, 68, 70–72, 80, 83, 100, 103, 122, 137, 139, 222–224
Birmingham City University, England 18
Bowdoin College, United States 61
Bryn Mawr College, United States 9, 16, 19, 21, 47, 49, 51, 54, 55, 60, 69, 70, 86–88, 113, 122, 130, 148, 150, 152, 178, 186, 195, 212, 270

C

challenges to developing pedagogical partnership 217–250
classroom-focused pedagogical partnership 9–10, 157–178
  support from program directors 130–146
  techniques for 172–178
classroom observations 163–165, 172–173
  challenges to 30–32, 244–246
Co-create UVA at the University of Virginia 11, 38, 43–44, 65
co-creation approach 110–112
Collaborative for Learning and Teaching at Trinity University 51, 123, 125, 229
compensation
  for faculty 69–72
  for students 51, 66–69
conceptual framework for partnership 39
concluding partnerships 169–170
confidentiality 65, 107, 112–114, 115
context 27, 38–41, 41–47

Creighton University, United States 151
culture shift 24–25
curriculum co-creation at Victoria University of Wellington in Aotearoa New Zealand 46–47
curriculum-focused pedagogical partnership 10–11, 181–214
　co-creating a course in progress 189–196
　co-planning a course 185–188
　redesigning a course 197–200
　support from program directors 146–154

D

disability services staff as partners 55–56

E

Elon University, United States 150, 197
emotional labor of partnership 225, 231–242
expectations for pedagogical partnership 30–33

F

faculty development. *See* academic development
feedback
　conceptualizing 99–101
　for program assessment 129
focus areas for partnership 161–163, 205–209

G

guidelines for participants 135–137, 158

H

Haverford College, United States 9, 16, 19, 21, 47, 48, 49, 54, 55, 60, 67, 69, 70, 86, 87, 88, 113, 122, 151, 152, 178, 187, 198–199, 200, 206, 212, 270
hidden curriculum 151–153, 200–204

I

identity 226–228
institutional culture 24–26
institutional home/location 60–62
International Journal for Students as Partners 87, 265
International Summer Institute on Students as Partners 263

K

Kaye Academic College of Education, Be'er Sheva, Israel 45–46, 66

L

Lafayette College, United States 67
Lahore University, Pakistan 83
Learning and Teaching Fellowship in Australia 44–45
Lewis & Clark College, United States 67, 123
librarians as partners 54–55, 153, 205
Loughborough University, England 18

M

Massey University, Aotearoa New Zealand 18, 83
McMaster University, Canada 38, 42–43, 66, 67, 68, 133, 146, 148, 152, 185, 219, 225, 263
motivation to participate 47–54
　for faculty 47–50
　for students 50–54

N

naming partnership programs 72–75
National Australian Learning and Teaching Fellowship on Engaging Students as Partners 44–45
North Carolina A&T, United States 39

O

Oberlin College, United States 67, 85
orientations 137–139
   for students 137–139
outcomes of pedagogical partnership 17–26, 104–105

P

partnership, definition 39
Paul R. MacPherson Institute for Leadership, Innovation and Excellence in Teaching, McMaster University 42, 66, 85, 219
peer relationships 114, 125, 228–230
post-bac fellow position 66, 81–84, 146
power structures 24–26, 27–28, 52–54, 62–64, 133–134
preparing participants for partnership 135–139, 158–160
program directors 4, 121–154
promotion and tenure review 64–65
purposes for developing pedagogical partnership programs 26–30

Q

Queensland University, Australia 44–45, 84

R

rapport, establishing in partnership 159–161
reasons for participating in partnership 47–54
reciprocity 29, 35, 39, 73, 102, 170
recruiting participants 80, 121–128, 153–154, 227–228
Reed College, United States 28, 67, 77, 79, 123
ReinventED Lab, University of Virginia 43–44, 65
relationships, building 101–102, 115–116, 159–161, 170–172
reporting structures 60
resources
   Advertising Student Partner Positions 77, 275
   Checklist for Developing a Pedagogical Partnership Program 274
   Choosing Names for Partnership Programs and Participants 69, 75, 77, 275
   Creating Post-Bac Fellow Positions to Support the Development of Pedagogical Partnership Programs 66, 81, 82, 146, 275
   Five Stories of Developing Pedagogical Partnership Programs 11, 41, 56, 275
   Gathering Feedback 129, 174, 209, 215, 233, 276
   General Guiding Principles for Weekly Reflective Meetings of Student Partners 141, 142, 258, 276
   Guidelines for Student and Faculty Partners in Classroom-focused Pedagogical Partnerships 110, 135, 256
   History and Structure of the SaLT Program 9, 41, 56, 74, 79, 124, 275
   How the SaLT Program Got Started 56, 65, 74, 79, 91, 124, 275

resources, *continued*
  Inviting Faculty and Students to Participate in Pedagogical Partnership 123, 220, 227, 228, 275
  Mapping Classroom Interactions 168, 173, 209, 215, 276
  Options for Incoming Faculty to Work in Partnership through the SaLT Program 20, 275
  Outcomes of Pedagogical Partnership Work 5, 17, 19, 53, 75, 85, 105, 258, 274
  Partial List of Themed Issues of *Teaching and Learning Together in Higher Education* 116, 274
  Plans to Orient New Faculty and Student Partners 137, 139, 275
  Questions that Facilitate Productive Talking and Listening 104, 276
  Representing What Student and Faculty Partners Have Explored 169, 170, 176, 178, 209, 215, 260, 276
  SaLT Program Student Consultant Application Form 78, 127, 275
  Sample Message to Student Partners from the SaLT Program Director 114, 275
  Sample Outline of Topics for Weekly Meetings of Student Partners 145, 258, 276
  Sample Outlines for Student Partner Orientations 111, 115, 275
  Sample Student Partners Course Syllabus 68, 145
  Selected Reading Lists 56, 163, 214, 250, 274

resources, *continued*
  Steps in Launching Pedagogical Partnership Programs 61, 79, 81, 91, 275
  Student Partners' Particular Contributions to Pedagogical Partnership 112, 274
  Summer Institute for Faculty Participants in Pedagogical Partnership 81, 123, 275
  Templates and Activities to Explore Hopes, Concerns, and Strategies for Developing Pedagogical Partnership Programs 274
  Three Stages of Backward Design for Creating Post-Baccalaureate Pathways to Educational Development 81, 84, 275
  Threshold Concepts in Pedagogical Partnership 34, 99, 102, 274
  Visiting Faculty Partners' Classrooms and Taking Observation Notes 165, 173, 209, 215, 276
  Ways of Conceptualizing Feedback 100, 118, 222, 276
  Ways of Thinking about Listening 103, 222, 276
  Working toward Programmatic Sustainability 87, 275
responsibilities in partnership 101–105, 116–117
roles in partnership 101–105
  faculty roles 62–64
  program director roles 33, 257
  student roles 163–165

S

scale of partnership 38–39, 85–86
scheduling 131–132
selecting participants 80, 121–128, 153–154, 227–228
sense of belonging 1, 3, 4, 16, 18, 22

Smith College, United States 28, 33, 40, 67–68, 80, 95, 122, 126, 227, 243
Student Partners Program at McMaster University 11, 26, 38, 42–43, 65, 133, 225
Students as Change Agents program at the University of Exeter in England 39
Students as Learners and Teachers (SaLT) Program at Bryn Mawr and Haverford Colleges
  application process 77–78
  program options 47–50
  reasons faculty participate 47–50
  reasons students participate 50–54
  weekly meetings for student partners 141–144
summer syllabus development workshop at SaLT 19
supporting participants 128–152
surveillance, fear of 30–32, 107, 231–232
sustainability 84–90

T

T.A. Marryshow Community College, West Indies 83
Teaching and Learning Together in Higher Education 8, 87, 116, 209, 262, 274
teaching assistants versus student partners 222–225
threshold concepts to partnership 33–35
Tigers as Partners program at Trinity University 24, 76, 77, 125, 131, 137, 139, 259, 271
time frame of partnership 38–39
training. *See* preparing participants for partnership

Trinity University, United States 24, 51, 76, 77, 82, 83, 99, 123, 125, 131, 137, 139, 229, 259, 263
trust, building 107–110, 128

U

Universiti Utara, Malaysia 18, 192
University of California, Berkeley, United States 149, 196
University of Glasgow, Scotland 149
University of Kansas, United States 150, 190
University of Missouri, United States 83
University of Queensland, Australia 26, 44–45, 84, 279
University of Virginia, United States 43–44, 65, 103
Ursinus College, United States 55, 59, 64, 66, 97, 123, 138, 146

V

Victoria University of Wellington, Aotearoa New Zealand 46–47, 68

W

Wabash-Provost Scholars Program at North Carolina A&T 39
weekly meetings 114–116
  of faculty and student partners 164, 166–168, 212–213, 255–256
  of student partners 139–146, 257–259

Printed in Great Britain
by Amazon